D0555945

PLATO'S
PARMENIDES

MITCHELL H. MILLER, JR.

Plato's
Parmenides

The Conversion
of the Soul

THE PENNSYLVANIA STATE UNIVERSITY PRESS
University Park, Pennsylvania

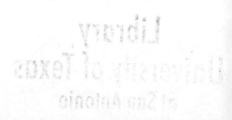

To the memory of my father,
MITCHELL MILLER,
and to my mother,
HELEN KNOX MILLER

But far more excellent, in my opinion, is the serious treatment of these things, the treatment given when one practices the art of dialectic. Discerning a kindred soul, the dialectician plants and sows speeches infused with insight, speeches that are capable of defending themselves and the one who plants them, and that are not barren but have a seed from which there grow up different speeches in different characters. Thus the seed is made immortal and he who has it is granted well-being in the fullest measure possible for mankind.

Phaedrus 276e–277a

ANALYTICAL TABLE OF CONTENTS

PART TWO
"A HOST OF VERY REMOTE
ARGUMENTS"

ACKNOWLEDGMENTS

I AM very grateful to a number of friends and colleagues for the help they have given me at various stages of this project—to members of the Philosophy Department at Vassar College, especially Jesse Kalin, Michael McCarthy, Michael Murray, and, formerly, David Lachterman for the benefit of their learning, support, and critical voices; to Kenneth Sayre and Charles Griswold, for challenging substantive comments; to Richard Bernstein, for timely encouragement. Most of all, I am indebted to Edward Lee, whose generous criticism has helped me see more clearly the proper place of this study within a web of further tasks, and to Michael Anderson, whose sympathetic insight has been a steady occasion for self-remembrance.

M.H.M., Jr.
January 1985

PLATO'S
PARMENIDES

Interpreting the
Parmenides

THE *Parmenides* has surely proven itself the most enigmatic of all of Plato's dialogues. In spite of a sustained and extensive history of discussion,[1] there is no positive consensus about the basic issues central to its interpretation. Above all, there is no agreement on the meaning of the subject of the hypotheses, τὸ ἕν ("the One"),[2] or about how (if at all)[3] the two main sections of the dialogue—Parmenides' criticisms of Socrates' theory of forms and the hypotheses—fit together. These issues are of course interdependent: to clear up, or at least fix the range of, an obscure term requires establishing its context, and this, in turn, requires understanding the way the parts of the dialogue make a whole. This, however, presupposes a more basic question: what sort of whole ought we to look for? On this issue there is a remarkable and unfortunate negative consensus. Almost universally, interpreters have neglected the *specifically dramatic* wholeness of the *Parmenides*.[4] The habit has been to look to the hypotheses as a response to the problems Parmenides has raised with his criticisms of the theory of forms. This in itself makes good sense. The difficulty is that interpreters have focused almost exclusively on the explicit argumentative content of the dialogue to find the specific problem/response connection. To be sure, most of the *Parmenides* is extraordinarily dense with argument.[5] Nonetheless, Plato takes care to frame and stage it as a drama; he preserves all of the conventions of characterization and (as we shall gradually see) structure proper to dialogue form. In this way he establishes the particular context within which the argumentation first has its specific function. To ignore the dramatic form of the *Parmen-*

ides is, therefore, to deny oneself access to this function; it is to risk seeing only the overt content of the arguments, to the neglect of the specific work that Plato intends them to perform.

Put simply, the project of the present study is to read the *Parmenides* with unwavering attention to its dramatic wholeness. Close attention to the dialogical features of the *Parmenides* will make possible a determinate interpretation of its otherwise indeterminate and riddling content. In particular, it will reveal both the definite range of Parmenides' obscure One and the precise function of his hypotheses, and this, in turn, will permit the intended philosophical significance of the dialogue as a whole to emerge.[6]

A. Dialogue Form: Mimetic Irony and Structure

To prepare the way for this project, however, we should begin with some preliminary reflections. First, what are the essential features of dialogue? Or, to ask this less ambitiously: to see a dialogue in its dramatic wholeness, to what, in particular, must the interpreter attend? To bring my way of reading into focus, some general observations on two principles and their interplay, as evidenced throughout the Platonic corpus, are in order.

1. Mimetic Irony

One sees this in various forms within the action in many of the dialogues. By one device or another the philosophical protagonist mimes his interlocutor's situation and the way beyond it. Consider, for example, Socrates' play with the slave-boy for Meno[7] and his supposedly autobiographical recollections of his own youthful ignorance for Agathon and for Cebes.[8] Significantly for the *Parmenides*, moreover, this maneuver is not peculiar to Socrates; there is also, for instance, the Eleatic stranger's repeated ironic imitation of Young Socrates' impulsive leap to the familiar in the *Statesman*.[9] In each case the philosopher holds back from giving explicit, authoritative criticism and instead puts the interlocutor on stage before himself. This reticence and indirectness preserves for the latter the possibility of *self*-confrontation, of coming *by his own action* to recognize his ignorance and his need for philosophy. Once, in turn, we identify such mimetic irony within the dialogues, it is only a short step to recognize its more fundamental presence at the heart of dialogue form itself. Here we must shift attention from the dramatized interplay between the philosophical and nonphilosophical *personae* to the function this interplay serves in Plato's indirect relation to his intended audience.[10] Analogously as Socrates mirrors an antagonist, so Plato, through the presentation of the encounter itself, mirrors his audience back to itself. The key elements are casting and the elenchtic force of the dramatic action. By focusing his nonphilosophical *personae* in specific ways, Plato effectively represents different aspects of contemporary culture; thus a Euthyphro, a Critias, and a Cebes bring pointedly different claims and aspirations to the fore.[11] In each case, however, the tacit challenge to the audience is basically the same; the hearer is invited to recognize himself, actually or potentially, in the figure on stage. If the hearer can do so, then the elenchtic action of the dialogue will have an internal significance for him; Socrates' examination of the interlocutor will be, for the hearer, an opportunity for *self*-examination. Finally, the way the two levels of mimetic irony work together should be noted. Strikingly, Plato's protagonists almost never succeed; in a variety of ways the interlocutors manage to resist (consider Meno[12] and Agathon[13]) or simply miss the opportunity for (consider Young Socrates[14] and even Cebes[15]) self-recognition. The interlocutor's failure *within* the drama, however, serves to intensify and compound the challenge Plato makes *by means of* the drama. Plato not only exposes certain forms of ignorance; he also exposes various ways in which, at a further level, one tends to preserve oneself from facing one's ignorance. The hearer is thus doubly confronted: both the limitations of his insight (again, actual or potential) and the subtle self-evasion that keeps them in force are put before him, and he is invited to attempt to know and transcend himself on both levels at once.[16]

2. Dialogue Structure

Although, remarkably, this has been largely ignored in the secondary literature,[17] the same fundamental structure recurs in dialogue after dialogue. The core motif of the dialogues, of course, is the encounter of philosopher and nonphilosopher; four key moments mark the process of this encounter in almost every dialogue.[18] The philosopher begins by eliciting the basic position of the nonphilosopher. This often takes the form of a series of challenges that force the nonphilosopher to express himself more and more clearly or fundamentally, as, for instance, in the *Euthyphro* (5c, 6b, 7a) or *Meno* (71b, 72a ff., 73d ff.); sometimes, in the more complex dramatics of, e.g., the *Gorgias* or *Republic* I, the philosopher may provoke one speaker to give way to another's more radical representation of his own position;[19] and sometimes, too, in an ironic variation the elicitation takes the form of the philosopher's provocation of the nonphilosophers to deeper and deeper challenges of him, as, e.g., in the *Phaedo*[20] and the main body of the *Republic*.[21] In any case, the goal is the strongest and the most transparent formulation of the nonphilosopher's position. This sets the stage for the second structural moment, a basic refutation by the philosopher. Within the dramatic action, this refutation characteristically brings the nonphilosopher into aporia and appears to bring dialogue itself to a decisive impasse. "I'm afraid, Socrates," Agathon confesses, "that I didn't know what I was talking about" (*Symposium* 201c). Or as Phaedo reports,

> we all felt very much depressed. . . . We had been quite convinced by the earlier part of the discussion; and now we felt that [the refutations Socrates provokes Simmias and Cebes to give] had upset our convictions and destroyed our confidence . . . (*Phaedo* 88c).

"Don't you see," the Eleatic stranger warns Theaetetus at the decisive juncture in the *Sophist*, "that really we are wholly in the dark about [being] . . . ?" (249c). This "darkness," however, is really an achievement; it marks the release from the false light of presumption and opinion and, as such, the necessary preparation for genuine thinking. This is why it is at just this point—and this is the third structural moment—that the philosopher makes his most basic contribution, a reorienting insight that shows a path through the aporia. This insight is characteristically the most profound and original of the dialogue; one thinks, for example, of the introductions of the concepts of justice in the *Euthyphro* (11e ff.) and the intermediate in the *Symposium* (202a ff.), of the method of hypothesis in the *Phaedo* (99c ff.) and the figure of the philosopher in *Republic* V, and of the notions of communion and difference in the *Sophist* (251a ff., 257d ff.) and paradigm and the mean in the *Statesman* (277d ff., 283b ff.). The new insight renews inquiry on a higher plane; it would seem that philosophy has prevailed. For this reason, it is striking that no dialogue ever ends at this point. Rather, there is invariably, as the fourth and final moment, a return to the issues or difficulties or, even, the plane of discourse prior to the basic refutation. This return takes very different forms. Sometimes the nonphilosopher lapses back into his initial prejudices, as in the *Euthyphro*; in other dialogues the philosopher may himself turn back to apparently nonphilosophical modes of discourse (e.g., the myths at the ends of the *Gorgias*, *Phaedo*, and *Republic*) or themes (consider Socrates' turn back to the philosopher's opposite, the tyrant, in *Republic* IX, and compare this with the way Alcibiades' presence in the last part of the *Symposium* puts on vivid display the failure to transform *eros* into *philosophia*). There is even a lapse in apparently successful dialogues like the *Sophist* (in which the closing distinctions fail to differentiate Socrates' ironic elenchtic, based on the knowledge of ignorance, from sophistry)[22] and the *Statesman* (in which the philosophical interior of statesmanship is left pointedly undisclosed).[23]

3. Failure and Provocation

Seen together, the first three moments of dialogue structure make good sense. As a full "elicitation" is prerequisite for a genuine and significant "refutation," so the latter is the necessary educative preparation for philosophical "insight." What, however, is the place and function of the moment of "return"? If we take our cue from the typical pattern exemplified by the *Euthyphro*, one compelling possibility is that the philosopher seeks to test the nonphilosopher: having provided Euthyphro with a substantive starting point in the concept of justice, Socrates gives him the initiative, testing, in effect, to see how well he has understood the new level of inquiry it affords. Such a maneuver would be characteristically Socratic; insight is nothing if it remains external, another's opinion and not one's own act, and so the philosopher must step back to permit the nonphilosopher to attempt to appropriate what he has been given. Really, however, this line of interpretation only raises the question of the moment of return in a deeper way. If we grant that it is Socratic to test, why does *Plato* choose so often to have the test end in *failure*? Why do so many interlocutors—including some of the brightest, like Simmias and Cebes[24] or even Theaetetus and Young Socrates in the *Sophist* and the *Statesman*[25]—misappropriate philosophical insight? The question points to the way mimetic irony and dialogue structure work together. Obviously, Plato's real interest lies not with his *dramatis persona* but with the audience that the *persona* mimes. The failure of an interlocutor to meet the philosopher's test within the drama is, in its basic function, Plato's test and provocation of his hearer. Having put the hearer on stage before himself (the elicitation), exposed his limitations (the basic refutation) and provided the basis for a philosophical overcoming of these limitations (the reorienting insight), now, by having the interlocutor—and, with him, the Socratically reticent philosopher—fall short of the insight, Plato challenges the hearer *to recover it for himself*. Just insofar as the hearer recognizes the failure, he will be moved to overcome it: critically distancing himself from the interlocutor, he will go back to the reorienting insight and try to develop it properly. Since, as we noted, the interlocutor is a dramatic representation of the hearer's own actual or potential limitations, by this act the hearer will transcend himself. In this way the final moment in dialogue

structure—the return—serves to open the sole genuine path
into "philosophy" in the Socratic/Platonic sense,[26] the path of
self-movement, of one's own activity of critical inquiry.

B. The *Parmenides* as a Dialogue:
Prognosis and Program

If we cast a first glance at the *Parmenides* in the light of these
reflections, it should begin to become clear both that and how
the notion of dialogue form may be a key to its interpretation.
Both essential features are conspicuously present. First, the
Parmenides' mimetic irony is pronounced. As we shall see, not
only does Parmenides mirror back to Socrates the latter's own
misunderstanding of forms in a number of passages, but also,
more fundamentally, there are good internal and external reasons to regard the *persona* Socrates as a re-presentation, to the
young students of the Academy, of themselves and their difficulties with the theory of forms. Second, the two main parts
of the *Parmenides* fit together to constitute a typical dramatic
whole, seen in the light of the dialogue structure just outlined.
By his eristic treatise, Zeno elicits Socrates' presentation of his
theory of forms. Parmenides, in turn, offers a series of basic,
apparently unanswerable refutations, bringing Socrates into
aporia and then, in response to the latter's request, proposes
his method of hypothesis as the needed means of reorientation
and reestablishment of the theory of forms. The one major
point that must remain open until we begin detailed analysis is
the sense in which Parmenides' execution of his method, the
hypotheses themselves, constitutes the moment of return.
Even on this matter, however, the signs are promising. In a
twofold sense, just the features of the hypotheses that have
most perplexed interpreters of the *Parmenides* now seem to
have their proper place and function. On the one hand, both
the form and the logical deficiencies of the hypotheses suggest
a lapse back to the sort of Zenonian discourse with which the
conversation began; in their contradictory consequences, in
the ambiguity in the sense of the One, and in the fallacy that,
as we shall see, laces their argumentation, the hypotheses re-

turn us to the level of Zeno's treatise. On the other hand, these features also serve to provoke the hearer; just as Socrates did on his first hearing of Zeno (127d ff.), so the hearer will want to go back to the beginning for a critical rethinking of the puzzles Parmenides has put before him. This desire is only heightened, moreover, by the curiously passive acceptance of the hypotheses by young Aristotle, companion of Socrates and also a mimetic re-presentation of the would-be philosophers in the Academy. Here we can already recognize in the *Parmenides* precisely the co-functioning of mimetic irony and dialogue structure: by having the *persona* Aristotle fail to penetrate the contradictions, Plato tests his hearers, the Academicians, and in good Socratic fashion invites and provokes them to make this penetration for themselves.

The primary concern of this study will be to work out, critically and in detail, such a reading of the dialogue. My orienting question will be: what is the test and provocation Plato intends in devising his hypotheses, and what is the response he seeks to occasion in his hearers? Part One justifies and prepares the question itself. Chapter I discusses the narrative framing, dramatic context, and *dramatis personae* of the *Parmenides*, and Chapter II analyzes the elicitative and refutative arguments with which Zeno and Parmenides confront Socrates. A main project in these reflections will be to identify the sort of hearer Plato aims, most of all, to reach[27] and to specify what Plato sees as this hearer's predicament and task. If these reflections succeed, we will have set the stage for the central project of Part Two: the reconstruction of the subsurface significance that Plato intends such a hearer, provoked to a critical rethinking, to find in the hypotheses.

C. A Note on the Problem of Subjective Reading

Quite apart from the obvious density of argument in the *Parmenides*, there is a second, much more general reason why scholars have paid so little attention to the features that distinguish the work as a dramatic or poetic whole. This is the fear that interpretation may become incorrigibly subjective. The exploration of dramatic context and *personae*, the attempt to revivify, so to speak, Plato's intended hearer, and the interpretation of the content of arguments in light of their projected function—all of this must surely stir up the worry that we will be reading meaning into, not out of, the text.

I share this concern; indeed, it energizes and disciplines my own work from within, serving as a goad to argument and accountability. I hope that this will be concretely evident throughout the course of this study. For the moment, let me just make two observations in behalf of my way of reading. First, that there are hazards in any search for meaning beyond the surface of a text is not, in itself, sufficient reason to hold back from the search. The crucial factor is, of course, the nature of the text and the sort of demand it makes on its readers. If my preceding remarks about the nature of Plato's dialogues are well oriented, we have little choice. In particular, if it is true that mimetic irony and the distinctive structure just outlined are essential features of dialogue form, then, since these function to provoke the hearer beyond the surface, one must make the attempt; to refrain in an effort to avoid misreading is, instead, to fail to honor the text's own form and hence to misread in another way. Second, the sort of exegesis I propose need not be in any way capricious or fanciful. In this regard, some of the major features of my analysis that may at first glance appear dangerously subjective are, quite the contrary, attempts to protect against this. By my sustained reflections on the mimetic or re-presentative function of the *dramatis personae*, for instance, I intend to curb the natural and for the most part unwitting tendency on the part of every reader—myself included—to presume that he himself, with all the interests and concepts that govern his immediate reactions, is Plato's intended hearer; to *not* make such analysis, to *not* hold oneself accountable for one's judgment about the specificity of the intended hearer, is to run the greatest risk of making this presumption. By my concern for structure, in turn, I require myself to approach each part of the dialogue with an eye to its relationship to the others, hence with an eye to its place in the whole; this serves as a check against the danger—always present when one is examining small stretches of text at a time—of reading out of context and under the spell of inappropriate concerns. Finally, in working out the subsurface argument of the hypotheses, I have made a point of asking, again and again, whether and how the presence of this argument helps to explain the many puzzling details of the surface of the text. The hypotheses are at once so massive and so perplexing that there is an almost irresistible temptation to concentrate instead on the internal coherence of one's interpretation of them. Yielding to this temptation, however, brings the danger that the interpretation may become schematic and self-serving, substituting itself for the text rather than exploring it; the best safeguard is a repeated critical return to the surface details of the text.[28]

Of course, methodological declarations of this sort are only of prefatory value. For any interpretive stance, what counts is the actual richness of sense and range of coherence that it allows to come to light in the text. With this in mind, let these methodological remarks stand as an hypothesis. If the exegesis to come is, in one respect, the 'application' of a 'method,' it shall also be, more deeply, a test of both. The means of the test shall be the *Parmenides* itself in all its riddling complexity.

PART ONE
PREPARING TO
RETHINK THE THEORY
OF FORMS

CHAPTER I

The Dramatic Context

PLATO's stage-setting in the *Parmenides* is remarkably intricate and detailed. This is especially so in the opening pages, in which Plato provides a series of intermediary *personae* to introduce the conversation proper between Socrates, Zeno, and Parmenides; the structure of this series serves both to warn and to prepare us for the difficult, intensely conceptual, and critical labor of thinking through Parmenides' hypotheses. In addition, the setting of the conversation proper is carefully established, and there is some deft, pointed characterization of Parmenides and Zeno. These aspects of the dialogue's staging also serve to prepare us: the first evokes the *Republic* as specific background for the *Parmenides*, while the second signals Plato's peculiar, nontraditional appropriation of Eleatic thought. These three aspects are closely related, and we will explore each of them in turn. The whole of the dramatic context will then emerge gradually, step by step.

A. The Motif of Welcoming Reception and the Levels of Penetration and Attunement

It is widely noted that the main body of the *Parmenides* is narrated as a report at third-hand. A certain "Cephalus" from Clazomenae recounts what Antiphon, half-brother of Adimantus and Glaucon, says that a companion of his youth, Pythodorus, has long ago recounted to him of the famous conversation. Largely unnoticed by the commentators, however, is that this narrative structure is only an aspect of a more complex structure of mediations.[1] By an analogical series of movements we are led (with Cephalus) back to Parmenides and his hypotheses on the One. Plato establishes the series by the pointed repetition of a motif borrowed, appropriately enough, from the poem of the historical Parmenides. In his opening proem, Parmenides tells of a demonic journey in which he is brought to the home of an all-knowing goddess. On his arrival she receives him graciously,

> taking [his] right hand in hers and speaking this speech to [him], ". . . welcome!"[2]

She then informs him of the inquiry or, in Parmenides' metaphor, the further journey[3] that has been specially granted to him.[4] In Plato's appropriation of this motif of welcoming reception, the inspirational elements, of course, are set aside: the journeyer knows his purpose in advance and makes a "request" ($\delta\acute{\epsilon}\eta\sigma\iota\varsigma$) of his welcoming host.[5] But otherwise Plato stays close to the original imagery, repeating it three times. In the opening sentence Cephalus tells how, on his arrival in the Athenian agora, he is immediately recognized and welcomed by Adimantus and Glaucon. "Taking my hand," reports Cephalus in words which echo Parmenides, "Adimantus said, 'Welcome!' "[6] Cephalus then "requests" that he be taken to Antiphon to hear the conversation between Socrates, Zeno, and Parmenides. Declaring this "not difficult" ($o\mathring{v}\ \chi\alpha\lambda\epsilon\pi\acute{o}v$, 126c6), Adimantus agrees, and they all leave the agora for Antiphon's home in Melite. The motif appears a second time when, not immediately but only after his half-brothers have begun to explain, Antiphon "recognizes . . . and welcomes" ($\mathring{\alpha}\nu\epsilon\gamma\nu\acute{\omega}\rho\iota\sigma\acute{\epsilon}\nu\ \tau\epsilon\ \ldots\ \kappa\alpha\grave{\iota}\ \mathring{\eta}\sigma\pi\acute{\alpha}\zeta\epsilon\tau o$, 127a4-5) Cephalus.[7] But when they make their "request"—now for a "going-through" or journey that is intellectual, not physical (cf. $\delta\iota\epsilon\lambda\theta\epsilon\hat{\iota}v\ \tau o\grave{v}\varsigma\ \lambda\acute{o}\gamma ovs$, 127a5-6)—Antiphon at first resists. The mnemonic work that Cephalus has requested is "a huge task" ($\pi o\lambda\grave{v}\ \ldots\ \acute{\epsilon}\rho\gamma ov$, 127a6). In the end Antiphon agrees, however, and begins to recount what he learned from Pythodorus. Plato's final use of the motif occurs within Pythodorus' report. Now it is Socrates, brought to aporia by Parmenides' refutations, who makes the "request" (136d5, d7, e3, e6), asking Parmenides for a demonstration of his method of hypothesis. Likening this to "swimming across a vast sea of thoughts" ($\delta\iota\alpha\nu\epsilon\hat{v}\sigma\alpha\iota$

τοιοῦτόν τε καὶ τοσοῦτον πέλαγος λόγων, 137a6),[8] Parmenides
hesitates at first; it would be "a huge task" (πολὺ ἔργον,
136d1), he says, precisely Antiphon's words. But he, too, finally agrees, on the basis of his recognition, urged by Zeno, of
the philosophical quality of the group (137a6-7). This recognition is directed especially at Socrates, who has been the only
Athenian to speak and who has distinguished himself in Zeno's and Parmenides' eyes for his sharp grasp of Zeno's treatise
(see 128b8-c2) and his distinction between things and forms
(see 130a5-7, 135d1-2).

What is the point of this complexity? While the motif itself
recalls the historical Parmenides (see C.2, below), its repetition establishes the spiritual frame of reference for the hearing
of the Platonic Parmenides' hypotheses. The general effect of
such a repetition is to set up parallels that will make points of
contrast conspicuous. One is struck, to begin with, by the
contrast between the immediate good will and cooperation of
Glaucon and Adimantus and the hesitations of Antiphon and
of Parmenides; this reflects the deeper contrast between the relatively easy, external task the former perform—physical guidance and social introduction—and the "huge" and difficult, intellectual tasks of Antiphon (in conjunction with Pythodorus)
and of Parmenides. Yet the contrasts between these latter tasks
are also striking: Antiphon's (and Pythodorus') prodigious labor is solely mnemonic, while Parmenides performs a tremen-
dous work of sheer creative intellect.[9] Thus we are led pro-
gressively into the heart of philosophy: we proceed from the
mere good will of Glaucon and Adimantus through the external aspect of intellectual interiority, the power of rote memory,[10] to the innermost activity of mind, systematic and conceptual inquiry.

This series of movements has a pedagogical point. It is no
accident that Parmenides yields to *Socrates'* request. Plato distinguishes and moves through levels of attunement and in this
way prepares his hearers for the highly philosophical project
he will give them. In spite of their slight condescension toward
their nonphilosophical half-brother (see 126c), Glaucon and
Adimantus have not themselves learned the conversation be-

tween Socrates, Zeno, and Parmenides; they are therefore replaced as mediators as soon as they have introduced Cephalus to Antiphon. The latter's memory, in turn, is quite extraordinary, yet it has not made him a philosopher; indeed, he has turned back from philosophy to the traditional aristocratic life and its equestrian pleasures.[11] Evidently, neither good-willed interest nor dogmatic retention—indeed, nothing less than the critical keenness that Zeno and Parmenides recognize in Socrates—will suffice. The audience is alerted that the task, while it presupposes both openness to philosophy and a prodigious capacity to absorb and retain argument, also transcends these: we must be prepared to listen with the keenness of Socrates, hence to inquire critically into the significance of the hypotheses.

B. The Setting: The Evocation of the *Republic*, for the Academy

In addition to the allusion to Parmenides' poem, the opening lines of the dialogue establish an unmistakable connection with the *Republic*. The first persons named are Adimantus and Glaucon, then the Cephalus from Clazomenae, who narrates; though the latter is no kin to Socrates' host in the Piraeus, the complex of names recalls the *personae* of the *Republic* immediately.[12] Equally striking, there is a direct analogy of dramatic situations. When Pythodorus tells how the well-known philosopher (Parmenides), accompanied by a favored younger friend (Zeno), comes to Athens for a festival (the Panathenian Games) but instead spends his time outside the city proper in a private household, engaged in philosophical talk with the young men of Athens, the hearer can hardly miss the parallels with the *Republic*.[13]

It is not surprising that Plato wants the hearer of the *Parmenides* to keep the *Republic* in mind. Both works are centrally concerned with his teaching of forms and participation. But reflection on the dramatic details of the *Parmenides* suggests that he intends something much more specific and precise than this. Once again, the parallels make points of contrast conspicuous, while the latter suggest a complex movement.

Consider, first of all, the points of contrast; they set the two dialogues apart as, relatively speaking, exoteric and esoteric presentations of philosophy. There is, first, the difference between the host Cephalus in the *Republic* and the narrator Cephalus in the *Parmenides*. The former is a commercial magnate who, after lamenting that his old age has kept him from visiting Socrates in town, takes the first opportunity to exit and escape a developing dialectical encounter when Socrates is in his own home. [14] By contrast, the Cephalus of the *Parmenides* leads a group "deeply interested in philosophy" (126b) on a journey far from home just to hear a report of Socrates; moreover, as narrator he has mastered, at the least mnemonically, the very difficult discussions of the forms and of the One. In addition, there is a pointed contrast between the philosopher's interlocutors in the situations of the two dialogues. In the *Republic* Socrates is with ambitious and undiscriminating[15] young men. Interested in politics and business, they are just as open to Thrasymachus' teaching of rhetoric—he is a welcome guest in Cephalus' house and has his youthful defenders in the showdown with Socrates (see *Republic* 340a-c)—as to Socrates' teaching of philosophy. Glaucon and Adimantus stand out from the group in intellectual tenacity (357a)[16] and power (368ab), of course; but in two aspects they serve to limit Socrates sharply. Both in making their basic challenge to Socrates (see especially 358a, 358c ff., 362e ff.) and at many particular junctures (e.g. 372d, 419a, 473e ff., 487b ff.) they take up the basic point of view of the nonphilosophical many and require him to defend philosophy against it. Again, being uneducated in philosophy themselves, they force Socrates, in his effort to be intelligible to them, to set aside conceptual discourse for imagery and simile at a number of key points, especially in presenting his theory of forms (see 506e and 508a ff., 509d ff., 514a ff.). In the *Parmenides*, by contrast, the philosopher Parmenides is blessed with Socrates himself as his interlocutor. (We will discuss the role of young Aristotle in ch. III.) Outside walls of the city (127b) in the home of Pythodorus, Parmenides is pointedly removed from the demands of the many (136d). If there is a need to defend or save philosophy, the assailant is now, in conspicuous contrast with the *Republic*, philosophy itself; the theory of forms, fundamental to the very possibility of philosophical discourse, must be saved from the philosopher's (Parmenides') own critical objections (135bc). Note that all this tends to reinforce our earlier interpretation of the replacement of Glaucon and Adimantus in the staging of the dialogue. Plato appears to promise, in the *Parmenides*, an undilutedly philosophical inquiry into the teachings that, in the *Republic*, he limited himself to presenting and defending in nonphilosophical terms.

But this picture is too simple; it neglects two other significant dramatic details. First, Plato makes Adimantus and Glaucon *themselves the agents* of their own replacement in the *Parmenides*. After meeting Cephalus in the agora, they themselves gladly guide him out of the city to Melite, where, furthermore, they join him in listening to Antiphon's recount. This deft touch suggests a certain continuity between the *Republic* and the *Parmenides*: Socrates' exposition to Adimantus and Glaucon is placed, in effect, as a proper preparation for Parmenides' to Socrates. At the same time, this is complemented by the implications of the age and level of development that Plato gives Socrates in the *Parmenides*.[17] As we shall see, though he has the first elements of his theory of forms, the youthful Socrates' responses to Parmenides' objections show that he is not yet in command of his own conception. As Parmenides says, "philosophy has not yet taken hold of [him] as fully as it eventually will" (130e). It is precisely to aid Socrates in reaching this command, moreover, that Parmenides prescribes the "gymnastic exercise" (135d) of the hypotheses. In these ways, the action of the *Parmenides* points toward and anticipates the philosophical maturity that Socrates has achieved and displays in the *Republic*. Thus Plato appears to subordinate the *Parmenides* to the *Republic* and to establish a continuity that is precisely the reverse of that just discussed: the elder Socrates' philosophical command of the theory of forms in the *Republic* is the goal, albeit retrospectively posed, toward which the conceptual labor prescribed in the *Parmenides* is a needed means.[18]

If we bring these several reflections together, Plato appears to present the two dialogues as complementary, mutually necessary beginnings for the philosopher-to-be. The *Republic* represents the first beginning, in which the philosopher addresses himself to nonphilosophers, giving them only images for what is, nonetheless, the ultimate truth. Of course, he also prescribes a long and difficult educational procedure, centered in mathematics, which is designed to prepare the nonphilosopher to free himself from the imagistic form of this initial understanding. The *Parmenides*, in turn, offers a second beginning for those who have taken up the first. The youthful Socrates' task is to appropriate fully, by critical and conceptual inquiry, what was given to Glaucon and Adimantus more in the manner of authoritative pronouncement and in the modes of image and analogy. The dramatically projected goal of this process of appropriation is, somewhat paradoxically, for Socrates to become himself, that is, to realize his philosophical potential and achieve the standpoint from which he speaks, albeit obliquely, as the accomplished philosopher in the *Republic*. Thus the point of Plato's careful allusions is to provoke a complex sense of the task ahead. Even while, in its conceptual mode of understanding, the *Parmenides* will transcend the *Republic*, this very transcending presupposes both the imagery of the *Republic* as its point of departure, and the philosophical insight which that imagery expresses as its final and orienting goal. The aim of the *Parmenides*, Plato seems to suggest, will be to reflect upon that imagery and to reappropriate its content at a higher, more adequate level of understanding.

THESE remarks on the dramatically projected relation between the *Parmenides* and the *Republic* bear directly on several further questions. The first is the question of the audience that Plato intends for the *Parmenides*. It is not (or, at least, should no longer be)[19] controversial that the dialogue is aimed especially at members of the Academy.[20] The dramatic touches removing the conversation from the agora and the many, the direct conceptual reflection on forms, and the forbidding logical density of the hypotheses all support this assumption. But there is more to be said.

To begin with, the character and topic of the *Parmenides* would seem to imply that it has a particularly crucial role to play in the educational life of the Academy. This will be true especially, but not only, if we accept the twofold thesis that the positive curriculum of the Academy was centered in the mathematical disciplines discussed in *Republic* VII and that Plato did not make any—or any very sustained and detailed—independent oral presentation of the theory of forms.[21] Whereas the *Republic* gives an imagistic discussion of the relation of participant thing and form and the *Sophist* and *Statesman* give a conceptual discussion of the interrelations of the forms, the *Parmenides* alone gives a conceptual discussion of the relation of participant thing and form.[22] For the Academician aiming to rethink his pre-mathematical understanding of the forms in light of his subsequent mathematical studies, the *Parmenides* is therefore *the* pivotal text. More than any other, it raises the issues and provokes the reflections proper to this rethinking.

Plato clearly regarded this, the second beginning, as an extremely difficult, even a treacherous task for the philosopher-to-be. In particular, just what makes mathematical studies a good propaideutic for philosophy, this reference to nonspatio-temporal, nonperspectival structures and relations (see *Republic* 510d-e, with 479a-b), may also make them equally alien to the mathematician himself. Thus in the *Republic* Socrates makes a point of singling out nonphilosophical aspects of mathematical practice, above all, the reliance on sensible images or models (510d-e, 529a-530b, 531b-c) and the uncritical acceptance of basic axioms as "obvious to everybody" (ὡς παντὶ φανερῶν, 510d).[23] If unchecked, such practices jeopardize the propaideutic value of mathematics; the student is not introduced to the super-sensible so much as taught to reduce it to familiar, sensible terms. In the trilogy of *Theaetetus-Sophist-Statesman*, Plato provides his hearers with a constant reminder of this danger in the form of the split character of Theodorus.[24] Although acknowledged as "one of our greatest mathematicians" (*Statesman* 257a), Theodorus also proves to be a Protagorean by disposition, inclined toward geometry in part from an antipathy to "abstract discussions" (*Theaetetus* 165a). In the action of the *Theaetetus*, in particular, he shows himself both unwilling[25] and seemingly unable[26] to transcend the ontological "trust," the immediate acceptance of the concrete particulars of experience as ontologically basic, which characterizes ordinary, nonphilosophical consciousness. It may be that as a *dramatis persona* Theodorus is meant to reflect Eudoxus, the great mathematician who brought his students to the Academy in about 368. In any case, the sort of materialization of the forms that Aristotle credits to Eudoxus[27]—and, strikingly, which appears to be portrayed in the *Parmenides* at 130e ff.—is the sort of lapse from the eidetic to the sensible that Plato warns against by his depiction of Theodorus.

With this in mind, we should not be surprised to find a double edge in the function of the *persona* Socrates in the *Parmenides*. Bearing in himself the potential of genuine philosophical insight, he represents the aspiring Academician's innermost goal and task. On the other hand, this insight is still just potential. As a youthful beginner, he also mirrors the limitations that must be identified and overcome if the movement beyond naïveté to a fully philosophical grasp of the forms is to be made. This dramatized mix of promise and limitation is pedagogically crucial. The youthful hearer who can recognize in himself the limitations of "Socrates" takes the first step. If, in addition, he can make use of the criticisms and the exercises prescribed by Parmenides to think beyond those limitations, then—fulfilling the projection Parmenides approvingly makes for the youthful Socrates (130e, quoted above)—he may become philosophically mature.[28]

There is also, secondly, the controversial question of the status Plato intends for Parmenides' arguments against the forms and, more generally, of the position he takes in the *Parmenides* toward the theory of forms in the "middle" dialogues. Of course, it would be premature to offer a judgment here.[29] Nevertheless, Plato's stage-setting maneuvers do suggest a preliminary orientation toward these questions. Scholarly debate generally takes the form of two related disjunctions. Some scholars hold that Plato intends Parmenides' arguments as a critical probing of the earlier theory of forms,[30] while others maintain that he considers them flawed and fully answerable within that theory and puts them in the dialogue as a means of eliciting such answers from his hearers.[31] Again, some hold these arguments to signal major substantive revisions in Plato's metaphysics,[32] while others regard them as essentially rhetorical in function, as Plato's way of preparing a context for a fresh evocation—but not a material revision—of his "middle" teachings.[33] In a subtle way, however, Plato's own stage-setting has the effect of resisting each of these lines of interpretation by undercutting the disjunctive way they are posed; Plato seems, instead, to be preparing us to think through an interplay between these different possibilities.[34] Thus he does, on the one hand, appear to set the mature Socrates' philosophical grasp of the forms as the goal for which Parmenides' conceptual dialectic is the means; in this regard, the project of critical inquiry that distinguishes the approach to the forms in the *Parmenides* is subordinated to the task of reappropriation of the mature insight represented by Socrates in the *Republic*. On the other hand, by his subtle acknowledgment of the relatively exoteric character of what Socrates says in the *Republic*, he also makes clear that the true content to be reappropriated is not simply the express teachings of the *Republic*; indeed, just insofar as many of the hallmark features of those teachings belong to the simile and analogy to which Socrates, straining to be intelligible to nonphilosophical interlocutors, must resort, the task of philosophical reappropriation will have to be thoroughly critical and revisionary. Plato warns us of this at a number of points in the opening part of the dialogue. By having the youthful Socrates rely on certain turns of phrase, metaphors, and analogies that, in the (dramatically projected) "later" time of the *Republic*, the mature Socrates will invoke in his presentations of the forms, Plato does more than just dramatize the brilliant anticipations of a young thinker; he also indirectly points out elements in those "later" presentations that belong to—or, at least, arise out of—the earliest, least mature stage in the development of the theory of forms. And by having Parmenides respond to these "anticipations" by sharply focused refutations, Plato indicates that these various motifs and theses, however appropriate in the context of the elder Socrates' pedagogical efforts with the not yet philosophical young, now require critical scrutiny. In these ways Plato sets the motifs of philosophical reappropriation and critical revision into close interplay. He does project the *Parmenides* as a recovery of the *Republic*—but as a radical one; thinking back beneath its surface will also mean thinking beyond its familiar teachings.[35]

C. Plato's Appropriation of Eleatic Thought

We turn now to a second nexus of *personae* and dramatic detail: Zeno, Parmenides, and the mention of Cephalus' home town of Clazomenae. These establish one of the central issues in pre-Socratic thought as a second background—intimately bound up with the *Republic*, as we shall see—for the *Parmenides*.

1. Clazomenae and the Anaxagorean Interest

Plato makes Clazomenae conspicuous as the home of Cephalus and his "philosophical" (126b8) companions in the opening phrase of the dialogue: "When we arrived in Athens from [our] home in Clazomenae" (126a1). To the contemporary Greek hearer, the Ionian town was distinguished only as the birthplace of Anaxagoras.[36] Yet the philosopher himself is not directly mentioned. Thus Plato establishes a loose, tacit association: Cephalus and his philosophical friends presumably share the basic interests and directions, but not necessarily the particular doctrines, of Anaxagoras.

That in itself is striking and raises a question. As a matter of intellectual history, we know that Anaxagoras accepted Parmenides' denial of nonbeing but rejected the consequence that

Parmenides—and his eristic defender Zeno—drew from it, that "what is" is "one."[37] (Plato recalls this history by having Socrates credit Parmenides' poem with the thesis that "the all is one," $\tilde{\varepsilon}\nu$ . . . $\varepsilon\tilde{\iota}\nu\alpha\iota\ \tau\grave{o}\ \pi\tilde{\alpha}\nu$, 128a8-b1, and by having Zeno accept the interpretation of his treatise as the converse denial of the existence of a plurality, 128d.) We also know from the *Phaedo* that Socrates rejected Anaxagoras' alternative proposal; initially hopeful at his declaration of the causal priority of mind, Socrates was disappointed to find that Anaxagoras actually addressed himself only to the material conditions of causality, and so he worked out his own theory of forms instead (see *Phaedo* 97c ff.). With an eye to these points, we cannot help but wonder at Cephalus' and his friends' motivation for making the journey to Athens: why should a group of Anaxagoreans make such an effort to hear a thinker (Socrates) who has rejected Anaxagoras submit his theory to others (Parmenides and Zeno) whom Anaxagoras in his own turn has rejected?

The answer emerges, in part, from a reflection on the relation between Anaxagoras' proposal, his doctrine of mixture, and Socrates' theory of forms. There is a striking resemblance. Like Anaxagoras, Socrates (or Plato) aims to accommodate Parmenides' denial of nonbeing[38] while preserving heterogeneity, plurality, and change; and to a point the Socratic way of doing this is close to the Anaxagorean. Anaxagoras had distinguished a plurality of heterogeneous "beings," which he called "seeds," from the ordinary things of sense experience, which he interpreted as mixtures of the "seeds"; and he restricted change to the mixtures. Thus the nonbeing that change entails was kept clear of "beings," and so Parmenides' denial was preserved. Analogously, Socrates distinguishes a heterogeneous plurality of ungenerated and indestructible "beings," the forms, from the physical things that participate in them; and he too relegates change to the latter. Thus the forms and their participants, respectively, are analogous to the "seeds" and the mixtures that are composed of them. This comparison, however, points up an important problem in the Anaxagorean doctrine, which the Socratic theory attempts, at least, to over-come. To preserve Parmenides' denial of nonbeing requires that the distinction between the levels of unchanging "beings" and their derivatives be absolute. The Anaxagorean distinc-tion, however, is only relative. In fragment 1 Anaxagoras de-clares that "all things were together, infinite in respect of both number and smallness."[39] And in fragment 3 he asserts explic-itly what this implies, that "neither is there a smallest part of what is small, but there is always a smaller." Thus the "seeds," having some size[40] and some number, are material things in just the same sense as the mixtures they make up. And this being so, there is no real justification for restricting change, and with it nonbeing, to the mixtures. If there is no difference in kind between "seed" and mixture, then the restriction be-comes arbitrary, and the denial of nonbeing collapses. It is just this defect, in turn, which Socrates seeks to remedy by his the-ory of forms. By making the forms incorporeal (*Symposium* 211a), he keeps them *essentially* distinct from the concrete things of sense that partake of them. More specifically, he tells us in key passages of the middle dialogues that each form is in-composite (*Phaedo* 78c-d)—and so must lack size, as such—and unique (*Republic* 597c)—and so must lack number, as such.[41]

These reflections suggest why Cephalus and his friends are so interested in hearing the conversation of the *Parmenides*. Socrates' theory of forms is an effort, in effect, to meet Anax-agoras' own basic goals; by making the distinction between form and thing absolute, a fundamental difference in kind, Socrates' theory aims to succeed just where Anaxagoras' failed. What is more, it is precisely this point that Parmen-ides—responding to the Anaxagorean-Socratic line of re-sponse to him—examines and tests in his questioning of Soc-rates. Whereas the explicit issues are the extent of the forms, the notion of participation, and the knowability of the forms, in each case Parmenides makes the distinction between form and thing his own critical focus. Thus the opening motif of the journey from Clazomenae to Athens is strikingly appropriate:

the Anaxagoreans have come to witness the radicalization and—should it survive Parmenides' critical examination—the fulfillment of their own basic philosophical project.

2. Plato's Claim to Parmenides' Line

This brings us directly to a second issue: why does Plato cast Parmenides in the role of Socrates' examiner? Since Socrates' theory (like that of Anaxagoras) asserts a real plurality, it would seem natural for Parmenides, once he has heard Socrates out, to oppose and refute him. Plato obviously knows this image of the historical relationship between Parmenidean thought and the theory of forms, for he both reproduces and plays upon it in the early dramatic action of the dialogue. We have just noted how Socrates interprets Parmenides' poem as arguing that "the all is one," $\dot{\varepsilon}\nu$ . . . $\varepsilon\dot{i}\nu\alpha\iota$ $\tau\dot{o}$ $\pi\tilde{\alpha}\nu$ (128a8-b1). If there could be any doubt about the strict monism of this, it seems to be cleared away by Socrates' interpretation of Zeno's treatise (128b), confirmed in substance by Zeno himself (128c-d): the treatise supports Parmenides' thesis by establishing the complementary denial of the existence of a plurality. Thus, when Socrates introduces the theory of forms as a way to undercut Zeno's argumentation, he is also opposing Parmenides, and we quite reasonably expect a counterattack from Parmenides. By saving Zeno's arguments against plurality, he would also be restoring his own monism. Plato reinforces this substantive expectation by some deft dramatic details. Socrates is rude[42] to Zeno and Parmenides. After all, they are his elders by approximately twenty and forty years, respectively, and they are distinguished guests in Athens. This makes his already rather forward allusion to Zeno's earlier intimacy with Parmenides—"that other [i.e. not intellectual] affection," $\tau\tilde{\eta}$ $\check{\alpha}\lambda\lambda\eta$ . . . $\phi\iota\lambda\dot{\iota}\alpha$ (128a5)[43]—all the more indelicate. And his objection that Zeno tries to "delude," $\dot{\varepsilon}\xi\alpha\pi\alpha\tau\tilde{\alpha}\nu$ (128a7), the audience into thinking he has something original to say verges on insult. It would be altogether natural, therefore, for Parmenides to want to put Socrates in his place.

In fact, Plato appears to generate these expectations in order to undercut them. The key passages are 130a and 135b-c. In the first, Plato uses the device of a personal self-observation by Pythodorus to guide the hearer's expectation and surprise.

> While Socrates was speaking, said Pythodorus, he himself kept thinking that Parmenides and Zeno would become irritated, but instead they listened very attentively and exchanged glances and smiles in admiration of Socrates.

Thus Parmenides and Zeno simply rise above Socrates' rudeness. Instead they pay close attention to what he says and even take genuine pleasure in his philosophical acuity. Nonetheless, when he enters the conversation, Parmenides does present Socrates with his seemingly invincible objections to the theory of forms. Do we thus get the expected Parmenidean defense of Zeno and restoration of monism, after all? The second key passage undercuts this interpretation decisively. Directly after concluding the last of his objections, Parmenides turns against their apparent thrust and speaks of the fundamental need to accept the forms.

> But on the other hand, Parmenides said, if someone, considering these and other [objections] of the same sort, should refuse to admit that there are forms of things (εἴδη τῶν ὄντων εἶναι) and not distinguish a certain form for each one (τι . . . εἶδος ἑνὸς ἑκάστου), then, since he rejects a character (ἰδέαν) which is ever the same (τὴν αὐτὴν ἀεὶ εἶναι) for each particular, he will have nothing on which to fix his thought, and thus he will destroy totally the possibility and power of dialectic (τὴν τοῦ διαλέγεσθαι δύναμιν).[44]

It is in order to help Socrates save himself from this disaster that Parmenides then prescribes the "exercise" and demonstrates it with his hypotheses on the One.

By this manipulation of the hearer's expectations, Plato signals a new interpretation—or, at least, appropriation[45]—of Parmenides' thought. By pointedly *not* coming to the defense of Zeno's antipluralism, Plato's Parmenides in effect disavows strict monism as the true construal of his thought. Zeno is disinherited, as it were. (We shall see that Plato's Zeno himself collaborates in this, in C.3, below.) And by his remarks at 135b-c, together with his prescription of the "exercise," Parmenides indicates his true heir. Evidently he wants to save the forms from his own objections. If this is so, then (as we suggested on different grounds earlier, in B) the objections must be intended to expose limitations not in the theory of forms as such but rather in Socrates' present understanding of it; and the "exercise," in turn, must be intended as a means for overcoming these limitations. This implies that it is the *mature* Socrates, saved from his own limitations by the "exercise," who is the true heir to Parmenides. Or, to step out of the dramatically projected context: Plato, through this projection itself, makes the striking claim that it is not the strict monism that the historical Zeno defended but, rather, his own theory of forms, properly understood, which captures the true point of Parmenides' thought.

THIS WAY of interpreting Plato's use of the *persona* Parmenides in the dialogue dovetails perfectly with our preceding interpretation of the relation of the *Parmenides* to the *Republic*. Plato, we found, establishes the *Republic* both as point of departure, in its imagistic way of thinking the forms, and as orienting goal, in the insights that he, as it were, veiledly, expressed by that imagistic thinking, for the journey of understanding that is to be made by the Academic hearer of the *Parmenides*. If, as I have just argued, Parmenides is to be understood as inviting the youthful Socrates to become heir to his thought, then we should expect the elder Socrates' theory of forms, as contained in the *Republic*, to be thoroughly Parmenidean. And indeed it is. In Book V of the *Republic* Socrates gives his first substantive explication of the forms by asserting Parmenides' fundamental contrast between "being" ($\check{o}\nu$) and "not being" ($\mu\grave{\eta}$ $\check{o}\nu$) (*Republic* 477a-b and ff., see Parmenides' B 2, 6.1-2, 8.16, etc.). "Not being" he declares "altogether unknowable" (recall Parmenides' B 2.6-8), while the forms, understood as "being," are the referents of knowledge (recall Parmenides' B 8.34-36). And he stresses the distinction between forms, which prescind altogether from "not being," and the things which are objects of "opinion" (δόξα, recall Parmenides' B 1.28-32, 8.51-52, 19.1) and undergo "becoming" (see *Republic* 509e-510a), for which he appropriates the Parmenidean conjunction of "to be and not to be" (*Republic* 477a, 478 d-e, recall Parmenides' B 6.8, 8.40).[46] Finally, he takes over for the forms the key predicate for "being" in Parmenides, namely, "one" (ἕν, see B 8.6, also 8.54)—*each* form, he asserts, stands in sharp contrast to its participants as "one" over against "many" (476a, 479a, also see 597c-d).[47]

At the same time, there is a striking opacity to Socrates' expositions of these Parmenidean notions. This reflects, at the least, the basic pedagogical limitation of the *Republic*. As we have already observed, within the dramatically projected context, Socrates is addressing polis-oriented young men who are not accustomed to make the philosophical distinction between forms and their participant things. Thus he speaks under a twofold constraint. He must introduce forms by simile and analogy; that is, he must begin with what is familiar to Glaucon and Adimantus, the perceptible particulars everywhere at hand in prereflective experience, and he must present the forms in terms of these, proceeding by contrastive comparisons. What is more, he lacks the philosophical context to step back and reflect explicitly on this; since the terms proper to particular things are the only terms his interlocutors know, these latter are hardly in position to recognize the difficulties and dangers involved. Thus some key ambiguities are left unexplored. The most striking pertain to the senses of being and unity in Socrates' contrasts of form and thing at the end of Book V. With regard to being, the coherence of the contrast of form as "what is"with thing as "what is and is not" would seem to require, on the one hand, that "is" have one selfsame sense; it is only the lack and presence, respectively, of the negative ("not") that specifically differentiates form from thing.[48] On the other hand, the ontological point of the contrast suggests that there must be essentially different senses of "is" in play: form and thing are fundamentally distinct sorts or levels of being. This tension is never brought up, much less worked through. The ambiguity with regard to unity is analogous. The coherence of the contrast of form with its participants as "one" and "many," respectively, would seem to require that the form be "one" in the sense of 'singular,' for 'singular' is the proper contrary to "many" (in the sense of 'plural'). On the other hand, this would leave the form characterized as the same kind of 'one' as each of the participants. It therefore comes partly as a relief when, in *Republic* X, Socrates describes the form as "one by nature" (or "in its nature," φύσει, 597d3), that is, presumably, as not merely 'singular' but 'unique.' Since, however, Socrates never pauses to connect the two passages nor, therefore, to clarify the implication of his second characterization for the initial "one"/"many" contrast, the second passage also compounds the original confusion.

These problems *are* explored, however, in the *Parmenides*. Here we come to the sense in which the *Parmenides*, because of its critical and conceptual character, enables a philosophical rethinking of the content of the *Republic*. As we shall see, Parmenides' root project is to elicit and work through a conceptual analysis of his own key notions, being and unity, as these pertain to the youthful Socrates' distinction of form and thing. Within the dramatically projected continuity of his life, this is what enables the elder Socrates to present his theory of forms in Parmenidean terms. But more fundamentally, Parmenides' analysis permits the conceptual clarification *of* these terms. In one selfsame step, therefore, the youthful Socrates is enabled to become the elder, and the full meaning of the elder's words is freed, as it were, from the constraints imposed by the limitations of his nonphilosophical audience. Or, to shift our attention to the actual audience of both dramas—the young Academicians—Plato enables them to rethink the theory of forms with the non-imagistic, conceptual clarity that its very content demands.

3. The Two Zenos: Youthful Eris and Pedagogical Dialectic

If we turn, finally, to Zeno, we find much to confirm—yet also to restrict and specify—the thesis that Plato replaces him with

Socrates as the heir to Parmenides.[49] Not only does Parmenides choose not to defend Zeno's antipluralism against Socrates, he does not even attend the reading of Zeno's treatise but instead remains outside, talking with Pythodorus and Aristotle (127d).[50] Moreover, Zeno himself chooses not to defend the substance of the treatise. In his reply at 128d-e, he differs from Socrates only on the issue of his motivation for having written it. And even these remarks are negative in balance. Zeno wrote the treatise, he explains, "out of the contentious spirit of [his] youth," attempting to "pay back the same and more" to those who tried to reduce Parmenidean monism to absurdities. Moreover, even in his youth he apparently had reservations about the treatise's content, for he never actually decided to publish it; rather, he recounts, someone "stole" it and released it without his permission.[51] All of this tends to belittle and discredit the treatise; the implication is that Zeno has long ago outgrown its project, the eristic defense of Parmenides as a monist.

The basic point of this manipulation of the *persona* Zeno seems clear.[52] Plato no more wants to re-present Zeno's supposed antipluralism than he does Parmenides' supposed monism. By having him "listen attentively" and "smile in admiration of Socrates" (130a), Plato makes Zeno too, together with Parmenides, receptive and approving of the youthful Socrates' theory of forms. Whereas, however, he retains the *substantive* notions of being and unity from Parmenides, it is the *method* of generating antithetical consequences from the same premise that Plato retains from Zeno. The "exercise" Parmenides prescribes for Socrates, Parmenides says at 135d-e, should take "the form which you have just heard [in the treatise] from Zeno." Parmenides makes just two qualifications. First, Socrates should continue to focus not only on "visible" things but also on objects "of thought" (λόγῳ), that is, the sorts of entities that "one would take to be forms";[53] and second, he should work out the consequences of the not-being (μὴ ἔστι) as well as of the being of the subject under investigation.

Zeno himself, of course, approves this appropriation of the method of his treatise; indeed, it is his exhortation at 136d-e that is decisive in persuading Parmenides to give the demonstration of the prescribed "exercise," the hypotheses on the One. There is a nice irony in all this, roughly analogous to that of the way in which Glaucon and Adimantus are themselves the agents of their own replacement by Antiphon (and Pythodorus). Since it is by means, somehow, of the hypotheses that the youthful Socrates will learn to think the true "being" and "unity" of the forms, and since it is just this thinking that makes him, rather than Zeno, the true heir to Parmenides, Plato in effect makes Zeno a willing agent of his own disinheritance.

ANALOGOUSLY with our interpretation of the *persona* Parmenides, this way of interpreting Plato's use of the *persona* Zeno in the dialogue dovetails with our remarks on the relation of the *Parmenides* to the *Republic*. In *Republic* VII the elder Socrates gives the famous curriculum of mathematical studies propaideutic to genuine dialectical thinking. The point of these studies is to facilitate the "conversion" of the soul from sense perception of the things of becoming to "the [intellectual] vision of being," that is, of the forms (525a). Strikingly, Socrates begins by introducing "the study *of the one*" (ἡ περὶ τὸ ἓν μάθησις, 525a2). Moreover, the key to the pedagogical value of this study is the presence of *contradiction*. As Socrates explains, when the senses report contradictory characters for a thing, the soul becomes aporetic and calls on the intellect to inquire. Thus, for example, the sight of the middle finger, at once bigger than the little finger but smaller than the index, provokes confusion; and, says Socrates at 524c,

> to clear this up, thinking is required to intuit (ἰδεῖν) great and small, not mixed together but distinguished, just the opposite from [the way they are perceived by] sight. . . . And isn't it from this that it first occurs to us to ask what the great and the small are?

In this way the soul is turned from sense perception to thoughtful inquiry into forms. But the ideal case of such provocation arises when the character of the contraries is interme-

diate between the sensible and the eidetic. Thus the ideal subject is "the one," understood as the unit basic to numbers and
to "calculation" (λογιστική) as the study of numbers. As Glaucon notes at 525a,

> Surely . . . sight, with respect to the one, has this char-
> acteristic [of presenting the soul with contradiction] to a
> very high degree. For we see the same thing at the same
> time as both one and as an unlimited multitude (ἄπειρα τὸ
> πλῆθος).

To resolve this contradiction, the soul must distinguish the
sense (or senses) in which the thing really is one from the sense
(or senses) in which it is many; and this distinction brings it to
study these, "the one" and "the many," in their natures. Thus,
again, the soul is turned from becoming to being.

There are complex echoes of all this in the *Parmenides*. On
the one hand, to put the matter once again in terms of the dramatically projected sequence of events, the mature Socrates of
the *Republic* seems to show how much he has learned from the
practice of Zenonian method in his "earlier" experience of the
Parmenides. What he proposes to Glaucon describes very
closely, even to the point of verbal repetition, the basic content
of the longest, in some respects most important, of the hypotheses, the second (142b–157b), in which Parmenides argues
that if a one is, it will be both one and "an unlimited multitude" (ἄπειρον τὸ πλῆθος, 143a2, and ἄπειρα τὸ πλῆθος,
144e4–5). On the other hand, the elder Socrates is limited by
Glaucon in a way in which Parmenides is not limited by the
young Socrates. Not only has the latter already posited forms
for unity and plurality (see 129b ff., also 130b), but he even displays an incipient sense of the difference between unity as integrity or wholeness and unity as singularity. At 129c ff., in the
course of refuting Zeno, he argues that he himself, as an exemplary thing, is both many in the sense of having many parts
(right and left, front and back, upper and lower) and one in the
sense of being a one among many others (the present group of
seven persons). Thus the young Socrates shows that he has already suffered and begun to respond to the provocation that,

as an elder, he proposes to Glaucon. To put the point more explicitly than young Socrates yet could, he has a working grasp of the senses of unity and plurality to which geometrical and arithmetical studies of things, respectively, should naturally lead. Thus he is more than ready for the expansion of thought that Parmenides proposes in his Zenonian exercises. In requiring that inquiry range from visible things to the sorts of entities "one would take to be forms" (135e), Parmenides tacitly generalizes from specifically mathematical forms to forms as such. The conceptual thinking in the hypotheses belongs not to mathematics but to general ontology. By his sets of contradictory hypotheses, Parmenides appropriates Zenonian method in order to show how unity pertains to what *is*, to what *is and is not*, and to what simply *is not*, and, conversely, how being pertains to what is *one*, to what is *one and not one*, and to what is simply *not one*.

Precisely how Parmenides' Zenonian knots of contradiction succeed in this display—and how this, in turn, enables a philosophically mature and adequate way of thinking the forms— can be shown only by detailed, analytic exegesis of the hypotheses themselves. We shall attempt this in due course. Already, however, it should be clear how the two projected backgrounds—the *Republic* and the pre-Socratic heritage for the theory of forms—fit together integrally in Plato's stage-setting for the *Parmenides*. To the young Academician who has made the first beginning offered in the *Republic*, the *Parmenides* presents the task of raising the ontology of forms to conceptual articulation. The key concepts for this, the very heart of the "conversion" that the *Republic* itself urges, are those by which the historical Parmenides first disclosed the super-sensible reference of thought: being and unity. And the method is a philosophical appropriation and tempering—that is, a provocative and exhibitive, rather than merely destructive use—of Zeno's originally eristic dialectic.[54]

CHAPTER II

Parmenides' Challenge
to Socrates

PLATO begins the argument proper with a nice play upon his hearer's natural expectations: as so often in the sophistic dialogues,[1] Socrates follows a performance by a distinguished visitor by requesting clarification and then making an elenchus; but then the tables are turned, and Socrates suffers a major elenchus at the hands of the visitors. Thus the first half of the dialogue follows Plato's typical structural pattern perfectly— but with the usual roles reversed. Socrates' elicitation (focally, 127d6-128a1) and elenchus (128e6-130a2) of Zeno's position together constitute the Eleatic visitors' *elicitation* of his position on the forms. Then Parmenides makes his *elenchus* of this position (130b1-134e8). Socrates is thus brought into inner contradiction, affirming both his theory of forms and the objections against it, and the stage is set for a mediating reorientation by Parmenides.[2] In this chapter our immediate concern will be the first two of these phases—the elicitation and elenchus of Socrates; at the same time, we will be generating the basic context for the following analyses of Parmenides' hypotheses.

A. The Elicitation: Socrates'
Twofold Distinction

Socrates first presents his theory of forms as a twofold distinction aimed at dissolving Zeno's antipluralist paradoxes. Key passages are 127e1-4, where Socrates rehearses a paradigm case of Zeno's *reductio* argument, and 128e6-129a6, where Socrates offers his distinction. The first reads as follows:

> if beings (τὰ ὄντα) are many, then . . . they necessarily
> are both like and unlike; but this is impossible, for neither
> can the unlike be like nor can the like be unlike.

Consequently, goes Zeno's argument, one must retract the pluralist premise. To Socrates, however, the "impossibility" is merely apparent. Once one accepts his theory of forms, the contradictions Zeno presents dissolve. "Tell me this," he begins,

> do you not believe that there is, itself by itself, a certain
> form of likeness, and likewise, as something other than
> this, its opposite, that which *is* unlike (ὃ ἔστιν ἀν-
> όμοιον)?[3] and that I and you and the other things we call
> many partake of these two? and that the things which par-
> take of likeness become like in that respect and to the de-
> gree they do partake, while the things [partaking] in un-
> likeness [become] unlike and the things [partaking] in
> both [become] both?

Socrates' distinction is complex in that it isolates the form on two sides at once. On the one hand, Socrates' phrase "itself by itself" (αὐτὸ καθ᾽ αὐτό) divides the form from the things that partake of it, its instances.[4] On the other hand, he also cuts off the form from the "opposite"(ἐναντίον), the form of unlikeness. For the distinction to be effective in dissolving Zeno's paradox, both sides are crucial. Only by sharply distinguishing the form from the thing, first of all, can Socrates free the thing for participation in an opposite form. To put it in Zeno's own terms, only if the complex entity called "the like" (τὰ ὅμοια) is analyzed into its aspects as *the thing that has* likeness, on the one hand, and *the character, likeness*, which the thing has, on the other, does it become thinkable that this same thing might also have the opposite character, unlikeness, as well. But at the same time, it is equally necessary that these two characters be disconnected from one another. The "opposition" between them must be interpreted as the separateness and independence of each from the other, not as an internal relation. For if each is thought as internally or essentially exclusive of the other, then a thing's participation in the one would preclude its participation in the other, and it is precisely the compatibility of the two participations that Socrates here seeks to establish.[5]

With his twofold distinction, then, Socrates undermines Zeno's position. A thing—or "the many" things—may be both like and unlike simply by participating separately in the separate forms, likeness and unlikeness. Purely as refutation, Socrates' conception seems to strike home; Zeno himself, by his silence and his "smiles in admiration of Socrates" (130a), appears to accept it. How far, however, can Socrates' distinction stand on its own, as positive doctrine? Plato's formulations in Socrates' opening speeches are of course made with an eye to the dialogue to come. With this in mind, it is worthwhile noting several potentially troubling features of Socrates' explication of his position.

Socrates' several exemplary references to particular forms attest the novelty, to the youthful thinker himself, of his distinction of forms from things. His own applications of the new principle are less precise and controlled than his general statements, and his terminology is equivocal. Thus, for example, in his general formulation at 128e6ff. (just quoted), he refers to the forms of likeness and unlikeness by the general noun (ὁμοιό-της, like-ness, 129a1) and the identifying phrase (ὃ ἔστιν ἀνόμοιον, that which *is* unlike, 129a2), while participant things are characterized by the plural adjective (ὅμοια, ἀνόμοια, 129a4, 6, 8). When he puts his distinction to work against Zeno's contradiction, however, his language becomes surprisingly ambiguous: in differentiating between like *things* being unlike and the *likeness itself* being unlike, he names the latter by the hybrid expression, αὐτὰ τὰ ὅμοια (literally, "the likes themselves," 129b1). This mixing of the intensive substantive, αὐτὸ τὸ . . . ("the . . . itself"), with the plural adjective seems to reflect a residual confusion in Socrates' thinking. He both distinguishes the form from its instances and yet still treats it as if, like the instances, it were subject to plurality.[6] In unwitting contradiction of his explicit intent, he fails to think the form as different in kind from its participant things. There is the same sort of equivocation in his references to the form plurality. Once again, when he explicitly introduces the form at 129b6, he distinguishes it from its instances by contraposing the general noun, [τὸ] πλῆθος ("plurality"), and the plural adjective, πολλά ("many"). In his subsequent arguments, however, he uses the plural substantive, τὰ πολλά (literally, "the many," 129b7, d5), interchangeably with [τὸ] πλῆθος (c8, d8) to name the form. This is striking, for τὰ πολλά can hardly help but function equivocally, suggesting the many *things*, the participants in plurality, even while explicitly referring to plurality as such. In this case, moreover, Plato shows both the power and the danger of the equivocation by letting it mislead Socrates into a potentially damaging error. To challenge Zeno, Socrates makes the polemical observation that, whereas it is not paradoxical for things to be like and unlike, one and many, it would be "amazing" if one could show "that which *is* one, this itself, [to be] many, and again, the many [to be] one" (129b7-c1, see also d5). But "the many" in the sense of the form plurality, 'that which *is* many,' *is indeed one*: it is a unique form. This is why Socrates could quite properly introduce it by the singular noun τό πλῆθος. It is only the participant things, not the form, which are not one but many. Thus Socrates fails to carry through on his own principle, lapsing into the same failure to distinguish form from things that he criticizes in Zeno.[7]

Socrates therefore needs to deepen his grasp of the very difference he declares, the difference of forms as such, in their nature, from the things that partake of them. If forms are really distinct from things, he must learn not to treat them as a sort of subclass of things, subject to the same categories. This, in turn, presupposes a prior understanding of these categories. Unless one grasps what it is, specifically, which forms are not, it will be next to impossible to grasp them for what they are. Thus the task of thinking forms *as forms* presupposes that of thinking things *as things*. Socrates, however, shows little or no awareness of this. In focusing on forms, he seems almost to take things for granted. To refer to them, he relies on ostension (note how he points to his own person as an exemplary physical thing with visible aspects, 129c. ff.), on examples ("sticks and stones and so on," 129d3-4), and on consensus (see καλοῦμεν, "we call," 129a3, φήσομεν, "we say," 129d4, πάντες ὁμολογοῖμεν, "we would all agree," 129d6). All these ways of referring presume understanding, and this preempts just what Socrates needs, an explicitly conceptual, categorial account of the participant thing.

Finally, Socrates seems to have given little thought to the basic issue of interrelations among the forms. Indeed, just as it seems obvious to him that things can have opposite characters, it seems obvious that forms cannot. Referring to the pairs likeness/unlikeness and unity/plurality, he declares,

> if the kinds and forms themselves (αὐτὰ τὰ γένη τε καὶ εἴδη) were shown to suffer, in themselves, these opposite conditions, that would be truly amazing (129c2-3).

And in closing the refutation, he says,

> My admiration would be much greater if someone were to show that this same difficulty is involved in all sorts of ways in the forms themselves—that is, if one could show it, just as you have exposed it in visible things (ὁρωμένοις), so also in those entities which are grasped by reasoning (τοῖς λογισμῷ λαμβανομένοις, 129e6-130a2).

What Socrates does not realize, however, is that his own argument implies the utmost "opposite conditions" for the forms. We have already seen why, if his distinction is to undercut Zeno's contradiction, each form must be considered essentially isolate and separate from the others. But at the same time, some of Socrates' formulations also suggest the contrary, what we will "later"—in the dramatically projected time both of the *Republic* (see 476a) and of the Eleatic dialogues— hear titled the "communion" or "blending" of forms. If plurality, for instance, is a form, it will be one; thus one form, plurality, will "commune with" or partake of its opposite, unity. This relation, of course, immediately suggests others. Each form will be one; but then each will be, as one, like the other forms and, so, will partake of likeness. On the other hand, as a distinctive one each will also be unlike the other forms and so will partake of unlikeness. This has a special bite, moreover, in the cases of the forms likeness and unlikeness, for likeness, as a distinctive one, will be unlike the other forms while unlikeness, as a one like all the others, will partake of likeness. In short, Socrates' new doctrine appears to introduce, on the level of forms, just the contradiction that he intends, refuting Zeno, to dissolve on the level of things. The forms, it seems, will be both unrelated and related; through their relations each will take on pairs of "opposite conditions"; and in some cases, a form will take on a condition, that is, another form, opposite to itself.[8]

At present, Socrates has not discovered any of these difficulties in his own new thought. Rather, he has only just begun to make the decisive "conversion" (περιαγωγή, *Republic* 518c ff.) of the soul from becoming to being. Indeed, to locate his stage of development on the pedagogical route projected in the *Republic*, he appears to stand at just the point to which, according to his "later" account, the mathematical "study of the one" can help bring the young dialectician-to-be. Zeno in his treatise has given him a collective "one" in which contrary qualities are mixed; and

> in order to clear this up, [his] intellect [has been] compelled to see [the various contraries, e.g. likeness/unlikeness, unity/plurality] not mixed up together but distinguished, doing the opposite of what the sight did (524c).

That is, he has distinguished, in principle, the forms both from the visible things that partake of them and from one another. But like any thinker who has just begun, he has not worked out the implications of his principle; nor has he freed his thought of the very habits that the principle means to overcome. It is this early stage of appropriation of the theory of forms that Plato puts before his hearer in the shape of Socrates' refutation of Zeno.[9]

B. The Refutation: Parmenides' Examination of Socrates

We must appreciate Socrates' philosophical youthfulness if we are to understand Parmenides' otherwise seemingly inconsistent response to him. On the one hand, we have already noticed how Parmenides begins and ends his examination of Socrates with shows of approval both for his acuity and for his specific assertion of the forms; the forms, he says at 135c, are the necessary and sole basis for the stability of thought and the "possibility and power of dialectic." On the other hand, in the body proper of his examination he raises a series of problems that, in defeating Socrates' responses and leaving him perplexed, function as objections and undercut the assertion of forms. Socrates himself, however, restricts[10] his perplexity to "the present moment" (ἐν γε τῷ παρόντι, 135c7), and this is the key to Parmenides' two-sidedness. Parmenides objects not to the theory of forms as such but to Socrates' present understanding of it. As we just put it, Socrates has not yet sufficiently grasped the inner implications of the form-thing distinction for his own thinking; in his own intellectual practice he remains involved in the very habits of mind his theory is directed against. This is the point, we shall see, of a number of Parmenides' objections. But Parmenides himself announces it indirectly by his opening question to Socrates:

> Tell me, Socrates, do you yourself (αὐτὸς σὺ) make this distinction which you speak of, between certain forms, on the one hand, and the [things] participant in them, on the other? (130b1-3)

The effect of all this on the hearer of the dialogue—and in particular on the young Academician who finds himself mirrored by Socrates—is well calculated. Because Parmenides affirms Socrates' assertion of forms, the hearer will not reject the theory of forms; yet because the youthful Socrates is genuinely perplexed by Parmenides' questions, the hearer cannot accept the theory as Socrates presently affirms it. Thus the hearer is given, between these extremes, a twofold task: he must recognize and purge from his own understanding that which, in Socrates' formulations, makes the latter vulnerable to Parmenides' objections; and he must take what remains—the basic impetus, so to speak, that the stripping away of these insufficient formulations leaves freshly exposed—and give it new life by more radically adequate articulation.

1. The Question of the Extent of the Forms

Though very brief, the opening exchange on the extent of the forms (130b3-e4) gives a remarkably clear indication of the sort of approach Parmenides will take toward the youthful Socrates—and through this, the approach Plato takes toward the young Academician—throughout the dialogue. Parmenides is an exemplary Socratic teacher. He poses his question, whether Socrates grants forms for all the sorts of things, concretely yet indirectly, by setting a series of four sorts before Socrates. Through the choice and order of the four he leads Socrates by measured steps from the familiar to the unfamiliar and puzzling; and having precipitated aporia in Socrates by the third sort, he resorts to a typically Socratic hyperbole in the fourth in order to expose clearly the underlying difficulty. Throughout, however, his basic posture is interrogatory, leaving Socrates himself—that is, the Academic hearer—to formulate and face the difficulty for himself.

What is this difficulty?[11] There is no question for Socrates— nor, again, for the Academician whom Socrates represents— that there are forms for the first two sorts Parmenides asks about. The Academician has been thoroughly introduced to formal relational and mathematical properties (likeness, unity, and plurality are the examples, 130b) in his mathematical training, and this training, in turn, is prescribed in *Republic* VII as preparation for a dialectical understanding of the value forms of "just and beautiful and good" (130b).[12] Socrates is perplexed, however, when Parmenides asks about "man . . . or fire or even water" (130c), and the reason surfaces in his denial of forms, in response to Parmenides' fourth sort, to things "utterly worthless and rank" like "hair, mud, and dirt" (130c). These, says Socrates, are "just the things which we see" (130d). By this he shows that he confuses his distinction of visible thing and invisible form with a value ranking, associating the visible with the valueless and the forms with the valuable. Thus man, fire, and water present special problems: they are *both* visible *and* of great value. In itself, however, this is only the surface of the difficulty. Parmenides objects not to Socrates' association of value, as such, with having a form but rather to his failure to grant value to what ordinary human opinion belittles. In his closing remark to Socrates at 130e, he credits the latter's error to his philosophical youth, saying,

> You are still young, and philosophy has not yet taken hold of you as fully as it eventually will, in my estimation—then you will deem none of these things worthless. But now you still defer, because of your age, to the opinions (δόξας) of men.

This remark sheds a retrospective light on Parmenides' choice of examples for his third sort. From the standpoint of ordinary, nonphilosophical anthropocentrism, man is the highest being and his welfare is the central value; the sophistic movement, moreover, raised this to an explicit teaching. Fire and water, on the other hand, recall the pre-sophistic efforts of Ionian thinkers—Heraclitus[13] and Thales, in particular—to relativize the things of the cosmos to some one of the elements within it, as the basis or ground for everything else. Both sorts of outlook, humanistic and cosmological, reflect a failure to transcend the sorts of distinctions proper to "opinion" (δόξα) and the world experienced through it. In the history of Greek thought, Parmenides was the first who clearly managed this; his notion of being, since it transcends contrariety and comprehends all things uniformly, as beings,[14] overcomes all partiality. By making his *persona* Parmenides guide Socrates in this direction, Plato claims his own kinship with Parmenides. And in the *Republic*, the mature Socrates shows that the *persona*

Parmenides' prophecy has been fulfilled. Describing what is distinctive about the philosophical nature, he tells Glaucon that true philosophers are

> lovers of all of [being] and don't willingly let any part go, whether smaller or greater, more valuable (τιμιωτέρου) or less (485b).

But how is the youthful Socrates of the *Parmenides* to gain this mature perspective? At 130d, Plato indicates that he is already under way; immediately after his self-certain denial of forms to "mud, hair, and dirt," Socrates confesses that, all the same, he is "sometimes troubled lest it [i.e. the presence of forms for particulars] be the same in all cases." Thus he is torn between his inclination to differentiate among sorts of things according to criteria of δόξα and a nascent sense for the universality of the being of forms. So far, he goes on, he has been unable to resolve the tension; when he has tried to think through what that universality would mean, and so to posit forms for "the things which we see," he has come to the edge of "an abyss of nonsense" (τινα βυθὸν φλυαρίας, 130d7) and has been forced to retreat to the familiar groups of mathematical and value forms. What is this "abyss"? Socrates' error, we have seen, is to mix into his thought of forms elements that belong properly to δόξα. If—quite in accord with the fourth sort of things, "the things which we see"—we shift the weight in the notion δόξα from its aspect of valuation to that of sense perception, then it appears likely that Socrates, when he posits forms for the fourth sort, thinks of them in *quasi*-perceptual terms. That is, to put the difficulty at its baldest, the form for mud, for example, would in a sense, as a *quasi*-visible and physical thing, itself be something muddy—a consequence Socrates himself would surely judge "nonsense." If we have made correct identifications of the "abyss," first, and of the youthful Socrates' basic difficulty, second, in the present passage as a whole, then the way to his later maturity will involve several key steps. First, he must be led back to the edge of the "abyss" and enabled to study it without flinching, in order to see why it presents itself in the first place. Beyond this, and more generally, he must be given a way, in the sense of a properly structured context, to learn to think forms *as forms*. In somewhat overly Aristotelian terms, Socrates needs to be led to a formal consideration of forms that, because it abstracts from their specific contents, will not be subverted by the special interests in the latter that characterize δόξα. The analyses to come will show how the youthful Socrates does in fact get both of these needed helps from Parmenides.

2. The Contradictions Between Participation and the Unity of the Form

Parmenides turns next to the question of the nature of "participation" (μετάληψις), and it is this issue that centers and integrates the second phase of his elenchus at 130e-133b. In contrast to his string of questions in the opening discussion, here Parmenides presents Socrates with carefully constructed counterarguments; the explicit point of these arguments is that participation, as Socrates understands it, is not compatible with the unity of the form. The whole passage divides into two distinct subphases, however, in accordance with a shift in the sense or sort of unity under consideration.[15] At 130e-131e Parmenides appears to have in mind the notion of integrity. Hence he gives as the contradictory to unity not the notion of plurality as such but rather those of being "separate from itself" (αὐτοῦ χωρὶς, 131b1-2) and of being "divisible into parts" (μεριστὰ, 131c5).[16] Thus, Parmenides' point in the first subphase is that Socrates' notion of participation undermines his assertion of the integrity of the form. In the second, 131e-133a, the sense of unity shifts to singularity. Here Parmenides presents his much discussed regress arguments, and his explicit conclusion is that, given Socrates' understanding of participation, there will be not one but "infinitely many" (ἄπειρα τὸ πλῆθος, 132b2) forms for each class of things.

As we enter into detailed discussion of 130e-131e and 131e-133b, we must pay close attention to the theme of the unity of the form. Not only does Parmenides make it central and emphatic—in fact, he asserts or refers to it more than a dozen times[17]—in the two sets of arguments here, but it is also *the* critical element, as we shall see, in the inner connection between the two halves of the dialogue.[18]

a. The Form as an Integral Whole?

Parmenides' formal argument in 130e-131e has the same basic structure as the *reductio* arguments in Zeno's treatise. He first establishes the seemingly uncontroversial premise that

> each participant thing (ἕκαστον τὸ μεταλαμβάνον) partakes either of the whole form or of part of it (131a4-5).

He then shows how, on the assumption that a thing's partaking of a form means the form's "being in" (εἶναι ἐν . . .) the thing, both of these alternatives contradict the unity of the form. If, on the one hand, the whole form is in each of its participant things, then, since these latter are "separate" (χωρὶς, 131b1) from each other, the form must be "separate from itself." If, on the other hand, not the whole but only a part of the form is in each participant, then the form will be a non-integral aggregate and no longer "one" in the first place (131c10).

Parmenides' argument serves to test the clarity and depth of Socrates' grasp of the nature of forms. The general force of the Zenonian reductive argument, we have already noted, is to drive the interlocutor back to a reconsideration of the premises. For Socrates, of course, the notions of participation and of the unity of the form are essential to his theory; thus the only feature of Parmenides' premises that is properly subject to question is his disjunctive characterization of the way the thing partakes of the form, "either of the whole form or of part of it." *Prima facie*, the characterization has a solid look about it. As polar terms, "as a whole" and "in part" have no mean nor third term; and the polarity itself seems universal. Any relation, it seems, that does bear on a thing but not on the whole of it, will bear on a part of it; and vice versa. Socrates appears to be thinking something like this when he gives Parmenides his initial approval at 131a7; to Parmenides' point-blank question whether "there might be any other way of partaking than these," Socrates answers rhetorically, "How could there be?"[19]

But Socrates' question should not be rhetorical. Since he has proposed a basic distinction of forms from things, there can be no presumption that concepts proper to things—even if applicable universally to all things—can be applied to forms as well. And there is no doubt that whole and part, in the present context, are just such concepts. To be a whole is to be a whole of parts, and divisibility into parts suggests a complex spatio-temporal individual.[20] Hence to approve Parmenides' disjunctive characterization is to treat the form as though it were a physical thing. As if to bring this to the surface for Socrates, Parmenides develops his characterization in pointedly spatial terms: "is the whole form *in* (ἐν) each of the many things, though it is one?" he asks at 131a8-9; and "as the many things are *separate* from one another, *just so* will [the form] itself be *separate* from itself," he concludes at 131b1-2.[21]

Socrates' response has just the poignant ambiguity that, given our analysis of his status as a beginner with great potential, we should expect. He attempts to block Parmenides' conclusion, and with it the argument as a whole, by introducing the simile of "day" (ἡμέρα, 131b3). "Day" is "in many places at the same time," yet it remains integrally "one and self-same"; if the form is like day, Socrates suggests, then it *can* be "in all [of the many things]" (131b5-6), yet still be one. In its conceptual content the simile is inspired. Though in a sense the daylight is spatially limited[22] and so a physical whole, it is arbitrary, if not nonsensical, to distinguish it into its parts; day suggests the notion of a partless whole—or rather, since a whole must have parts, of a simple unity. This is just what Socrates needs in order to meet Parmenides' test and articulate the distinction of form from thing; precisely because simple unity cannot be understood in terms of whole and part, to conceive the form this way frees it, together with the notion of participation,[23] from the reduction to thinghood that the application of whole and part implies.

There is a question, however, how fully Socrates really grasps this. Though his simile does have this conceptual content, it is nonetheless a simile. Does Socrates *require* the sense image—and thus the reference to physical things—in order to grasp the properly super-sensible nature it suggests? It is surely his interest in probing this that motivates Parmenides' response. He proposes to examine Socrates' suggestion by substituting, as equivalent to the image of day, the image of a "sail" (ἱστίον, 131b8) spread out overhead, as a sort of awning. On the level of immediate experience, there is a certain equivalence. The taut, pale surface of the sail resembles a day sky; indeed, it serves as a kind of substitute, creating an indoor space of its own and so, like day, functioning more as a whole environment than as a thing located at some place within an environment. Nonetheless, in its actual being, it is precisely such a thing, and as such it lacks precisely the key feature of day: since it is easily and naturally divisible, it is present "in" or "over" many places not indivisibly or simply, like day, but through its many parts. Parmenides knows this full well, as his following speech at 131c2-3 attests. He makes his proposal of the sail, however, for Socrates' sake; he is challenging Socrates to free himself of simile altogether by articulating conceptually what makes day a superior expression for the unity of the form. Socrates, however, is not yet able to do this: he accepts Parmenides' proposal with an ambivalent, inarticulately troubled "Perhaps" (Ἴσως, 131c1). He is in the same tenuous condition of half-knowledge that, as an elder in the *Republic*, he will "later" ascribe to the mathematician in his use of sensible figures and models. His mode of cognition is inadequate to his true object;[24] he grasps the ontologically prior in terms of what is posterior to it.

Parmenides' pedagogical interest in Socrates' difficulty accounts for the otherwise perplexing turn at the close of his argument. Once Socrates fails to reject the sail, the formal argumentation is all but complete. If the form is like the sail, then not the whole of it but only a part is in, or over, each participant; but if the form is thus divisible into many parts, then, as we noted above, it will no longer be "one" in the first place. This should be the end of the argument, with Socrates trapped in the contradiction, unable to accept the divisibility of the form but unable, too, to explicate participation without it.

Parmenides, however, scarcely pauses: "For look," he begins, and he proceeds to set forth a series of three conundrums that support Socrates' rejection of the divisibility of the form. These are not at all gratuitous. All three involve forms of quantity and turn on the fact that the part is smaller than the whole. Thus, briefly, (1) what partakes of largeness will, if partaking is having a part, be large by virtue of something smaller than largeness; (2) what partakes of the equal will be equal by virtue of something lesser than the equal; and (3) the small will be larger than that part of itself by virtue of which its participant is small, yet the participant, even though it thus partakes of what is larger, is nonetheless itself smaller, not larger, through the participation (131c12-e1). These absurdities presumably represent precisely the sort of "abyss of nonsense" to which Socrates earlier referred when he described why he denies forms to "the things which we see." Now, however, it is timely for Parmenides to lead Socrates to the edge. The argument regarding participation plays on Socrates' thinking of forms in terms proper to their participant things; but it has not succeeded in *showing to* Socrates that this is in fact the source of his difficulties. The conundrums, however, make this obvious. Largeness, equality, and smallness are treated as large or equal or small things, respectively, composed of smaller things as their parts. In each case, the form is blatantly misconceived as a physical whole of parts and, so, as having just the same nature as the things that participate in it. Thus the conundrums serve to connect Socrates' present perplexity with his past experiences of the "abyss of nonsense" and to give him a pointed indication of its source.[25]

The basic upshot of 130e-131e is thus a task. Socrates must rethink his notion of participation in light of his distinction of forms and things. The first step in this rethinking will be to work out a proper conceptual articulation for the sort of "one" the form is, rather than treating it in terms—here, whole and part—proper instead to its participant things. This is the implicit thrust of the not at all rhetorical question with which Parmenides closes this passage:

In what way, Socrates, shall the things other (τὰ ἄλλα) than the forms partake of them, if they can partake of them neither as wholes nor as parts? (131e3-5)

b. The Form as a One Among Many?[26]

Parmenides now turns to the experience that motivates Socrates to regard each form as "one" (ἕν) in the first place.[27] But as we noted, he varies the sense of "one." Whereas he first contested the integrity of the form, now by his several regress arguments he contests the singularity of the form. The whole exchange (131e-133b) follows the same rhetorical-pedagogical pattern we saw in 130e-131e. Parmenides' argument, ostensibly countering Socrates' theory of forms at its heart, is really phrased and ordered in a pointed way, aimed to test Socrates' self-understanding and provoke fundamental articulation. But Socrates' two major responses, characteristically, are unwittingly ambiguous; he is not in full possession of his own insight. Hence Parmenides, just as in his earlier substitution of the sail for day, presses his pointed, elicitative criticism all the harder. Given this pattern, it is easiest to examine the opening argument and each of the two responses in turn.

Parmenides' statement of his opening argument (132a1-b2) is strikingly simple.[28] He begins by winning Socrates' unhesitating approval of this description of the experience that has motivated him to posit each of his forms as "one";

whenever many things (πόλλ' ἄττα) seem to you to be large, then, perhaps, a certain one character (μία τις . . . ἰδέα) seems to you, as you look (ἰδόντι) at them all,[29] to be the same—for which reason you deem the large (τὸ μέγα)[30] to be one[31] (132a2-4).

He then goes on to set the form among its participants and to make this new group the object of an experience precisely analogous to the first.

But, then, what about the large itself and the others (τἆλλα), the large things, if, with the soul (τῇ ψυχῇ), you look (ἴδῃς) at them all in just the same way? Will not large appear, once again, as a certain one (ἕν τι), through which all of these appear large (132a6-8)?[32]

Insofar as there is such an object field, including form and participants together, an infinite regress is inescapable. If in the first experience there is a one character common to all the visible objects, then so will there be in the second. And, first, since the form emergent from the first experience is there with "the others" as one of many objects in the second experience, and, second, since the common character emergent in the second experience cannot, as *common to all* these many objects, itself be one of them,[33] then there will be two forms, not one. Finally—and this restates Parmenides' own concluding observation at 132a10-b2—if the first common character, or form, stands as an object in the second experience, so the second will stand as an object in a third, precisely analogous experience; and so on *ad infinitum*. The result, of course, is that there must be not just two but "infinitely many" (ἄπειρα τὸ πλῆθος, 132b2) forms for each class of participant things.[34]

As with the preceding argument, this disastrous conclusion is meant to force a search for the assumptions that lead to it. And also as before, the key is a reduction of the form to the status of a thing; here, however, the aspect of thinghood unwittingly applied to the form is not its material whole-part structure but its epistemic status as a singular object of perceptual or *quasi*-perceptual "looking."[35] That is, the regress requires that the form, though it first emerges as a "character" (ἰδέα) *of* the many visible particulars, stand together *with* these to constitute a collective object for a "looking" or "seeing" (ἴδῃς, 132a7). (It is true that Parmenides qualifies this "looking" by the instrumental phrase, τῇ ψυχῇ, "with the soul"; but by his expression, ὡσαύτως, "in just the same way," 132a6, he also makes this "looking" precisely analogous to the strictly perceptual "looking" or "seeing," confined to sensible particulars, which he describes at 132a2-4.) But can a form be set together with its participants as part of such a collective object of perception without losing its distinctive status as a form? When Parmenides first describes the unity of the form by setting it in contrast, as "the same," with the many different particulars, he seems to suggest that the form is different in kind from them and unique; it differs from the many essentially, not merely as they differ from one another, and it therefore stands essentially alone, unique in the sense that the particulars that instantiate it are not on par with it. But all this is undermined by the object-character he then asserts: to make the form stand together with visible particulars reduces it from a one-over-many to a one *among* them. Essentially comparable to its participants, it must be of the same fundamental nature as they. Thus it will be not unique so much as merely singular, a one which—as attested by the subsequent emergence of a new form to express its community with its participants—is but one of many similar ones.

Socrates rightly sees that he can block the regress only by undercutting this assimilation of form to thing. In this respect, both of his responses are well oriented. But the first goes too far, the second not far enough. In the first, at 132b3-6, Socrates picks up Parmenides' suggestive qualification—$\tau\tilde{\eta}\ \psi\upsilon\chi\tilde{\eta}$, "with the soul"—and expands it into a basic distinction. Perhaps, he suggests,

> each of the forms is a thought ($\nu\acute{o}\eta\mu\alpha$) and properly comes into existence nowhere but in souls; then each could be one and no longer suffer the problems just asserted.

That is, the form as a "thought" would exist *only* in the soul (or mind). As such, it would differ essentially from things as physical entities existing apart from the mind in nature. This difference, Socrates evidently thinks, would make it impossible to set the two side by side as objects of the same "looking."

Insofar as his suggestion distinguishes form and thing as "intelligible" ($\nu o\eta\tau\acute{o}\nu$) and "perceptible" ($\alpha\grave{\iota}\sigma\theta\eta\tau\acute{o}\nu$) or "visible" ($\acute{o}\rho\alpha\tau\acute{o}\nu$), respectively, Socrates is on the right track. As basically distinct kinds of cognition, intellection ($\nu\acute{o}\eta\sigma\iota s$) and sense-perception have basically distinct kinds of referent; thus what Parmenides' argument suggests—that the same sort of "looking" can take in both kinds of referent as its objects—is nonsensical. Still, to be on the right track is not enough. Once again, the youthful Socrates shows himself to be in the grip of just those habits of mind he struggles to overcome, and, as Parmenides' refutation shows, this subverts his proposal. Note, to begin with, his language. To speak of forms as "com[ing] into existence (ἐγγίγνεσθαι) nowhere (οὐδαμοῦ) but in (ἐν) souls" is, even in the very act of setting forms apart from the physical-sensible, to think forms and souls on the model of things and places. As before, Socrates unwittingly thinks forms as if they were things, subject to genesis and location. What is even worse in the present context, however: by making the location for this genesis "souls" (ψυχαῖς), he makes the forms depend for their very being on the particular souls, or minds, that think them. This devastates the theory of forms in two obvious ways, and Parmenides brings these out in quick succession. First, if the form is taken in this way[36] as a "thought," then the theory will be reduced from the status of an ontological account of the genuine and universal intelligibility of the world to a psychologistic account of how each mind generates meaning for itself. What Socrates needs to ponder—and this is the focus of Parmenides' opening line of reply at 132b8-c8—is the difference between being a thought (νόημα) and being the referent of a thought (νοούμενον, c6). Though he leaves this for Socrates to work out, Parmenides' distinction effectively saves Socrates from himself: as the referent of νόησις, the form remains specifically "intelligible" (νοητόν), not "perceptible," as an object of cognition, yet its existence is not relativized to the mind. Second—and this is the thrust of Parmenides' closing objection at 132c9-11—if the form were only a "thought," its constitutive relation to its participants would be, if not absurd, quite mysterious. Earlier Socrates treated participation as a material relation; now he has characterized the form as a mental entity. In a piece of dry irony, Parmenides brings the two points together: if forms are thoughts, then, he asks, will particulars "be made out of thoughts" (ἐκ νοημάτων . . . εἶναι, 132c10-11)? And if so, then will "they all think" (πάντα νοεῖν) or—if that is too absurd—"being thoughts, will they be thoughtless" (νοήματα ὄντα ἀνόητα εἶναι, 132c11)? Of course, Parmenides is pushing Socrates to begin again. He must rearticulate his distinction without relativizing the forms to particular minds and with attention to their constitutive relation to things.[37]

Socrates' second response, at 132c12-d4, meets these conditions with another shrewd simile:

> It appears to me, rather, that matters are like this: these forms stand in nature just as models (ὥσπερ παραδείγματα) while the others resemble and are likenesses of them (τὰ δὲ ἄλλα τούτοις ἐοικέναι καὶ εἶναι ὁμοιώματα), and this participation which the others (τοῖς ἄλλοις) have in the forms is nothing else than their being made in the image of them.

On three counts at once, Socrates' simile provides a promising answer to Parmenides' objections. First, by situating the forms "in nature" (ἐν τῇ φύσει), Socrates overcomes his confinement of them "in souls." Second, by introducing the relation of model to likeness he offers an important alternative to his earlier materializing notion of participation as a physical being-in. (Though Socrates and Parmenides do not pause to make this explicit, it should be noted that the model-likeness simile frees the forms from being subject, so far as they are participated in, to divisibility; it would be nonsensical to speak of a model being divided up and distributed to its many likenesses.)[38] Third, and most important, the model-likeness simile seems to counter Parmenides' regress at the key point. Likeness to a model is an asymmetrical relation of beings that have, within the context of the relation, fundamentally different standing. What is used as a model must exist from the outset and in its own right, but a likeness can exist only through and by reference to its model. This is why the elder Socrates will "later," again in *Republic* VI, invoke the similar contrast of physical things with their reflections and shadows as an analogue for the ontological and causal priority of the forms relative to their participant things.[39] In the present context, the simile directly undercuts Parmenides' initial reduction of the form to an object on par and of a kind with—that is, to a one among—its many participants.

Once again, however, Socrates is not able to realize the promise of his own thought; he is not yet fully in command of his insight. The very fact that he again turns to simile is troubling; does he require the reference to sensible things as a means of thinking what is, properly understood, super-sensible? More specifically, there is a crucial ambiguity in the simile of forms as models. Whereas models are like forms in their causal priority to their likenesses, they are unlike forms in that, in their actual being, they are singular, visible things. And in this latter respect, they are, after all, on par and of a kind with their likenesses. We can sharpen the ambiguity by comparing the genetic process and the end result of the production of likenesses. It is true that the artist works *from* (or "looks *from*," ἀπο-βλέπειν) the model in fashioning its likeness; here the priority Socrates intends is clear. But it is also true that the artist's end result will be a second visible thing—thus something of the same general ontological standing as the model—which will share a relation of reciprocal or symmetrical likeness (ὁμοιότης), of "like to like" (ὅμοιον ὁμοίῳ), with the model. It is therefore crucial that Socrates know the general limitation and the precise point of his simile: he must be able, even while invoking the model-likeness *relation* as a structure of ontological difference in kind, to distinguish the *actual mode of being* of models from that of forms, in order to avoid a collapse of the difference in kind into just the similarity he means to oppose. And this requires, more basically, that he be able to transcend sensible simile and give a conceptual characterization of the distinctive being of forms.

Parmenides puts Socrates to the test on just these points with his counterargument at 132d5-133a6. He takes the same basic tack as in his earlier response to Socrates' simile of day, when he offered the seemingly equivalent figure of the sail: ostensibly accepting Socrates' suggestion, he in fact reinterprets it to mean just what Socrates does not intend and shows how it fails. This challenges Socrates to articulate just what he does intend—and, so, to free himself from sensible simile. Parmenides focuses the challenge in his immediate response, a two-part question, at 132d5-7.

Tell me, if something is in the image (ἔοικεν)[40] of the form, is it possible for that form to be not like (μὴ ὅμοιον) the thing made in its image (τῷ εἰκασθέντι), to the extent that that thing is fashioned as its likeness (ἀφωμοιώθη)? Or is there some way for the like to be like what is not like it (τὸ ὅμοιον μὴ ὁμοίῳ ὅμοιον εἶναι)?

There are two keys to Parmenides' strategy here. First, he opens by directly identifying things as images (or likenesses) and forms as their originals (or models); thus he takes Socrates' simile literally, as a directly definitional characterization of the form as a model. Second, he reinterprets the asymmetrical relation of model to likeness as a symmetrical or reciprocal relation of "like to like" (ὅμοιον ὁμοίῳ). Were it not for the first point, the second would be only an eristic, sophistic maneuver, the unwarranted application to the form of just the sort of similarity of terms on par that Socrates seeks to undercut.[41] However, insofar as the simile is taken literally and the form is interpreted as being—not merely being like—a model, the application is justified.[42] As we have just noted, as a singular, visible thing, a model does indeed stand on par and in reciprocal likeness with what is made in its image.

Once again, Socrates is unable to meet the test Parmenides poses. To Parmenides' double question (just quoted), he responds with a minimal Οὐκ ἔστι ("There is not," 132d8). Thus he addresses only the second part, affirming its articulation of the principle of reciprocal likeness. To the first part, whether "it is possible for the form to be not like" what is made in its image, he says nothing. This silence is telling. On the one hand, he has been struggling all along to assert this possibility, that is, to deny the "likeness" of form with its participants; this is the precise point of his introduction of the asymmetrical relation of model to what is fashioned after it. On the other hand, to argue for this requires that he deny the literal meaning of his simile and explicitly distinguish the actual mode of being proper to forms from that proper to models. Socrates' silence shows that he is not yet able to do this. Evidently, he has no other means than sensible simile to consider the nature of the form. In this sense, sensible simile is not *merely* simile for him:

he still thinks the form as if it were a singular, visible object, and so he has no way to resist the application of reciprocal likeness to form and its participants.

Once this likeness is established, of course, Parmenides has no trouble restoring the regress argument. Since it is "like" its participants, the form stands together with them as a one among many, and the likeness that unites this many requires, as its basis, a new "one and the same [form]" (132d9-31). This new form, in turn, will again be "like" its participants, requiring, beyond the many that it and they together make up, yet another new form, and so on *ad infinitum* (132e-133a).

As before, the upshot of this exchange is a task. Socrates must learn to give a conceptual account of the nature of the form if he is to preserve the point of his simile. That is, he must transcend simile itself, in order to be able to establish the uniqueness and difference in kind of the form, as participated, from its participants.[43] As if to underscore this, Parmenides closes this phase of argument by focusing on the central difficulty which Socrates, so long as he depends on imagery, will not be able to overcome, the basic likeness of form and thing:

Not, then, by likeness (ὁμοιότητι) do the others (τἆλλα) partake of the forms—rather we must search for some other way by which they partake (133a5-6).

3. The Absurdities Regarding Unknowability

Parmenides brings his elenchus to a close with two arguments (133b-134e) that challenge the knowability, respectively, of the forms for human minds and of particulars for the gods. At first sight, his presentation of these arguments is a puzzle. Their intermediate steps contain some flagrant[44] omissions and distortions of the theory of forms. Moreover, in introducing the first argument Parmenides indicates indirectly but clearly that he disagrees with its conclusion, for he tells Socrates that a man

of wide experience and natural ability, [who would be] willing to follow one through a host of very remote arguments . . . (133b7-9), would come to judge against the unknowability of the forms. This implies that in the final analysis the argument's persuasiveness derives not from its substantive merit but, rather, from a lack of education and ability and patience on the part of the hearer.[45] Why, then, should Parmenides be interested in presenting it in the first place?

The puzzle begins to dissolve if we take seriously the exchange between Parmenides and Socrates that serves as the transition from the second into the third phase of elenchus.

> —Do you see, Socrates, Parmenides said, how great the difficulty (ἡ ἀπορία) is when one asserts that forms have a being in and for themselves (ὡς εἴδη ὄντα αὐτὰ καθ᾽ αὑτά)?
>
> —Quite so, yes.
>
> —Well, he said, be apprised that really you have only just touched on the immensity of the difficulty (ἡ ἀπορία) involved, if you posit a unitary form (ἓν εἶδος) for each being you distinguish (133a8–b2).

Plato dramatizes one of the most poignantly difficult moments in the process of Socratic education. Refuted, the student admits his perplexity. But in a way that only the teacher is in position to see, the admission is a false one: precisely because he is ignorant, the student cannot know precisely what it is of which he is ignorant, nor can he see precisely how his thought deforms it. What is the teacher—and, above all, the Socratic teacher—to do in this situation? Twice before, we have witnessed Parmenides in this delicate moment, once at 130c5, when he had precipitated an aporia in Socrates over the existence of forms for "man or fire or even water," and the other time at 131c12, after he had caught Socrates in contradiction by his proposal of the sail. In both cases Socrates appears to know *that* but not really *why* he has been checked, and both times Parmenides tries to show him by recourse to illustrative absurdities. "Mud, hair, and dirt" force into view Socrates' association of the visible and the worthless, while the conundrums involved in treating the forms of size as sizable things make vivid Socrates' materialization of the forms. These passages, however, marked the close of phases within Parmenides' elenchus. In an analogous way but as a close for the elenchus as a whole, Parmenides now gives a set of arguments that—precisely by the flagrancy of its omissions and distortions—focuses and reflects the general mis-orientation of which Socrates' earlier errors are specific results. By this miming, he offers Socrates the opportunity for a basic self-knowledge, that is, for a recognition of those fundamental habits of nonphilosophical thinking that still intrude upon his new conception of forms and must be overcome if that conception is to come into its own.

Consider first the basic course of each of the two arguments. (1) The first argument, at 133c-134c, purports to show why the forms are unknowable to men. It proceeds through five basic steps. (i) The forms, since they are each "in and for itself" or "by itself," καθ' αὑτό, are not themselves immanent or "in our domain," ἐν ἡμῖν (133c-7). (ii) In accordance with (i), (a) those forms which are what they are in relation to one another stand in such relations exclusively to other forms, not to the particulars "of our domain," παρ' ἡμῖν; (b) conversely, those particulars which are homonymous with such forms (ὁμώνυμα ὄντα ἐκείνοις) are themselves related exclusively to other particulars, not to forms (133c8-d6). (iii) As a key example of (ii)(b) and (a), respectively, a particular human slave is slave not of the form mastery but of a human master, and *mutatis mutandis* for a particular human master, while

mastery itself is what it is of slavery itself, and slavery itself is likewise slavery of mastery itself,

exclusively and not, in either case, in relation to a particular slave or master (133d7-134a1). (iv) In accord with (ii) as illustrated by (iii), "knowledge itself," the form, will be knowledge of the truth itself (i.e. of the forms),[46] while the sort of knowledge that is "in our domain" will be knowledge of particulars (134a3-b1). (v) But since, according to (iv), the forms "are known by the form of knowledge" (γιγνώσκεται . . . ὑπ' αὐτοῦ τοῦ εἴδους τοῦ τῆς ἐπιστήμης)[47] and, according to (i), the latter form is not "in our domain," we cannot know any of the forms (134b3-c3). (2) The second argument, at 134c4-e6, purports to show that by the same token the gods cannot know (or even be masters of) particulars. It proceeds in three steps: (i) Since the form of knowledge is, as a form, "much more perfect" or "precise" (πολὺ ... ἀκριβέστερον) than the knowledge "in our domain," no one could be more justly said to "have" (ἔχειν) it than "a god" (θεὸν) (134c6-12). (ii) But it has been agreed earlier, in (1)(ii) as exemplified in (1)(iii) and (iv), that forms which, in their being, relate to others can have such relations only to other forms (134d4-8). (iii) Thus the gods, who have the forms of knowledge and (by analogy) of mastery, cannot, through these forms, "know us or anything else of what is in our domain" or "master anything of ours" (134d9-31). Rather there is perfect symmetry:

> Alike (ὁμοίως), both we with our rule do not rule them and with our knowledge do not know the divine at all, and they in turn, by the same argument, are neither masters of us nor know human affairs, being gods (θεοὶ ὄν-τες) (134e2-6).

These arguments mime Socrates' two key errors. First, Parmenides conceives the forms of mastery and slavery and of knowledge directly on the model of their respective particular participant things; thus he parodies the split between Socrates' theory, which has declared forms as "models" for particulars, and practice, in which he has treated forms as material wholes and visible singulars. In (1) (iii) Parmenides, reversing the order of (ii)(a) and (b), first establishes the relation of particular master and slave by introducing the genitive case, which expresses both possession and an agent-patient correlation; he *then* applies this genitive to the relation between the forms of mastery and of slavery. But to make mastery itself relate to slavery itself as master does to slave is to think the forms in the image of particulars. Likewise, in the movement from (1)(iv) to (1)(v), the internal reference of knowledge itself to the truth itself, initially expressed by a genitive, is spelled out explicitly as an agent-patient relation in the context of an action: truth or the forms "*are known by* the form itself of knowledge" (134b6-

7). But again, for the form to be an agent in an action is for it to be a particular—and for the internal reference between forms to be thought as the sort of particular action that holds only between particulars.[48] If this point is not already striking in the first argument, Parmenides makes it blatant in the second; there he gives the lie to the first argument by simply replacing the form knowledge as the agent of knowing by "a god" and finally—as if to make the aspect of particularity fully conspicuous—by "gods."

Second, the first argument is built on the assumption, in (1)(ii) especially, that forms and particulars are mutually distinct but parallel systems of entities: *just as* forms relate only among themselves, *so too* do things. Once again, the second argument carries this misrepresentation to an extreme: immediately after establishing the relative and superlative "perfection" (ἀκριβέστερον, 134c7, ἀκριβεστάτην, c11) of the form of knowledge and restricting access to it to "a god," Parmenides sets men free of the gods ("they . . . are not masters of us," 134e4-5) and ranks the two as equal in their respective ignorance of the others' objects. His language makes the reference pointed: by his emphatic "alike," ὁμοίως, at 134e2, he mimes Socrates' unwitting treatment of form and thing as "likes," beings equal and on par.

In this miming of Socrates' errors, Parmenides' argumentation must necessarily omit what it at the same time shows to be needed most of all: a substantive account of the constitutive role that the form, precisely as different in kind from things, has for them. In this regard, Parmenides' opening thesis, (1)(i), bears enormous irony. Socrates finds it obvious that the form's status as "in and for itself" prevents it from being "in our domain"; he affirms Parmenides' thesis unhesitatingly. But the notion καθ᾿ αὑτό, "in and for itself," has strikingly different implications. That the form is, in its essential being, related to itself alone implies that it has no essential relatedness to things.[49] But this is to say that the being of the form does not presuppose the separate—much less, parallel—existence of things. Strikingly, just this nonrelatedness permits the form to stand as a true foundation for things. As the consequence of the form's independence, it is also the precondition for the form's priority to things; only if the form is essentially independent from its participants, can these be essentially dependent upon it. Furthermore, since form does not stand to its participant things as to commensurate others, there is nothing to keep it apart from them; since they are not terms in a real relation, the separation that such a relation implies does not apply. Hence there is nothing to prevent the form from being in things in the metaphysical sense of serving as the basis for their being.[50] What Socrates finds obvious is therefore just the reverse of the truth he really means to defend. He ought to object to Parmenides' thesis by pointing out that it is only *because* the form is "in and for itself" that it *can* be "in our domain." In putting Socrates' errors on display, Parmenides' arguments show, however, why this cannot yet occur to him. Since he unwittingly thinks the form after the model of a thing, Socrates cannot help thinking that its status as "in and for itself" requires that it be situated in a separate domain. Again, since he treats form and thing as "likes," he cannot avoid thinking that, like two things, they must be separate from each other, each located in its own place. Of course, this is quite incompatible with his earlier insistence on participation. Interestingly, however, Parmenides' arguments expose the underlying—and devastating—consistency in his habits of thought: just as he earlier spatialized the notion of "being in" or immanence, so now he spatializes the notion of transcendence, consigning the forms to a separate world.[51]

Thus Parmenides closes his elenchus with synoptic parody. In terms of the dramatic interplay within the dialogue, Parmenides shows the youthful Socrates just how he does *not*—to recall the opening question at 130b2—"[him]self make this distinction [he] speaks of" between form and thing. Though he means to have thought beyond the dimension of things to their foundation, Socrates has in fact set up a new class of entities on par with things and made them thinkable by invoking the basic structures of thinghood itself. This is quite understandable. The point of view of δόξα knows no other point of view—and so has its own specificity hidden from itself. But it is also a fundamental defect in the philosophical advocacy of forms, for this implies the claim to know this specificity and to have somehow transcended it. Socrates therefore has an enormous task of further reflection and analysis before him.

C. Transition: Socrates and the Academic Hearer

Earlier we argued that mimetic irony pervades the Platonic dialogues. We are now in position to see the *Parmenides* as a case in point: just as Parmenides, *within* the dialogue, mirrors Socrates back to himself, so Plato, *by* the dialogue and especially by his portrayal of Socrates, mirrors his youthful Academic hearers back to themselves.

In his portrayal of Socrates, Plato is serving notice that an indirect, analogical understanding of the doctrine of forms is not enough. The youthful Socrates is right to insist—as he will "again" in his projected maturity in the *Republic*—that the form is a noetic "one" that, in its causal priority, stands "over" the many things of sense. In his recourse to simile and analogy, however, he understands the form in terms proper to things. Here it becomes relevant to recall our earlier reflections on the subtle interplay between the youthful Socrates' "anticipations" of some of the central motifs that, as an elder, he will "later" use with Glaucon and Adimantus and the pointed implication of the replacement of Glaucon and Adimantus in the *Republic* by the youthful Socrates in the *Parmenides*. On the one hand, there is an element of genius in the youthful Socrates' invocations of the similes of daylight and of model and likeness. As the thoughts of one straining to get free of the limitation of a nonphilosophical "trust" in the physical-sensible as the primary reality, they represent striking glimpses of the strange— in particular, the notions of the partless unity and constitutive priority of the form—through the familiar. And for just the same reason, they are fully appropriate to the elder Socrates' efforts to awaken such presentiments in the nonphilosophical Glaucon and Adimantus. On the other hand, the *personae* Glaucon and Adimantus represent fundamentally different as-

pirations than the *persona* young Socrates. For Glaucon and
Adimantus, men of the polis who finally defer to philosophy
rather than becoming philosophers themselves, the partial understanding that the elder Socrates affords them is an achievement; for the young Socrates, however, who does seek to give
himself to philosophy, it is insufficient. As his helplessness before Parmenides shows, so long as he relies on[52] simile, the
mode of his thinking will deform its own content and frustrate
its own intention. Since simile and analogy start from the familiar, they must assimilate form to things even while expressing the difference between them. In relying on them, therefore, Socrates shows that, in terms of Parmenides' opening
question at 130b, "[he him]self does *not* make the distinction
[he] speaks of" in refuting Zeno; that is, to turn to the language of the *Republic*, he has not yet made the "conversion" of
soul from becoming to being. What he must do, therefore, is
break away from his own genial similes in order to rethink the
intuitions they express in a more adequate way. Or, now to
step back from the action of the drama to its intended audience, what the young Academician must do is to become critical of the formulations and procedures of the *Republic* in order
to think through their content and its implications in a deeper,
philosophically more radical way.[53] If Parmenides' refutations
are to be met, it will require a mode of thinking that is adequate to the forms in their own nature and priority, a mode
that, in its conceptual character, keys from forms rather than
things and so reflects the true ontological relativity.[54]

While the young Academician is in a good position to recognize the youthful Socrates' limitations, however, he is also
likely to share the latter's perplexity about how to try to overcome them. On the one hand, his extensive mathematical
studies give him "much experience" (133b7) with nonsensi-
ble, noetic objects. Specifically, his arithmetical work with
numbers gives him familiarity with an essentially nonspatial
object, and this should make him sensitive to the pointedly
spatializing character of Parmenides' comparison of the form
to the sail. Further, he has a practical acquaintance with geometrical forms that, through their definitions, relate to partic-

ulars "*just as* models" without thereby *being* models—in the precise sense of serving as guides for the construction of particular figures. In this work, the Academician will have had no problem generating many particulars from each one form. And since, in this function of guide, the form is present only noetically, not visibly, he will have a strong working sense for the difference in kind between form and thing. Thus when Socrates finds himself unable to resist the divisibility and plurality of the form, the Academician should recognize that he has collapsed the noetic into the physical-visible dimension.

But it is one thing to cultivate a familiarity and a working sense of something, and quite another to raise this sense to reflective, explicit self-consciousness.[55] In part, an inner tension in mathematical practice may be responsible; as Plato has the mature Socrates point out in *Republic* VI, though the mathematician's insight is noetic and directed toward forms, he is accustomed to rely on sensible models. At best, this merely facilitates his intuitions. At worst, it enables him to postpone and even evade[56] the difficult philosophical work of developing an alternative, genuinely conceptual mode of articulation. And without this, the Academician will be caught in precisely the youthful Socrates' predicament: though his intuitions, strengthened by his mathematical studies, may be good, his way of explicitly understanding and formulating them will be sense- and thing-bound and, so, inadequate. As a result, he may well have a good critical sense of the difficulties the youthful Socrates encounters, but he will lack any positive solution to them. Of course, the awareness of such lack is precisely the precondition for genuine learning. Once the Academic hearer's critical—indeed, self-critical—energies are aroused, he should be eager for the needed "conversion" and open to whatever help Parmenides can offer toward it.

PART TWO
"A HOST OF VERY REMOTE ARGUMENTS"

CHAPTER III

Parmenides' Help

The central problem for the interpreter of the *Parmenides* is the relation of its two halves.[1] It is therefore almost disconcerting to note that the transitional middle section at 135a-137c seems to bind the two halves together in a clear and—against the background of the dramatic structure of other dialogues— quite typical way. Consider these main features of the action at this stage: the philosopher's elenchus has reduced the interlocutor to aporia (see Socrates' admissions at 135b3-4, c4, c7), and to get help through the difficulty the latter must, for the first time, defer to the philosopher (see Socrates' questions at 135d7 and 136a3 and his "request" for a display of the method of hypothesis at 136c6-8); moreover, the audience shares the aporia and joins in urging the philosopher for help (thus Zeno at 136d4-e4 and "[Pythodorus] himself and Aristotle and the others" at 136e6-7); the philosopher therefore takes the initiative and offers a positive response of his own to the problems he has stirred up (Parmenides' suggestion of "exercise" at 136d ff. and his display of the proper method at 137c ff.).[2] This typical, seemingly nonproblematic connection between the two halves serves to focus what *is* problematic into three key questions: Just what sort of help are Parmenides' hypotheses for Socrates? What, if anything, are they about, and do they respond in any material way to the problems Parmenides has raised? Finally, why, given that it is Socrates who is in aporia and needing help, does Parmenides drop him from the conversation and engage the young Aristotle instead?

Parmenides himself stresses that the hypotheses are to serve as "exercise" for Socrates. Four times he speaks of "gymnastic training" (γυμνάζειν and variants, 135c8, d4, 136a2, c5). The sense of this emerges especially in his admonition at 135c8–d6. There Parmenides credits Socrates' difficulties to the fact that

> you are attempting to define *beautiful* and *just* and *good* and each one of the forms too soon, before you have had a pre-liminary training in what seems useless (δοκούσης ἀχρή-στου εἶναι) and is called idle talk by the many.

In part Parmenides is reiterating his earlier criticism, that Socrates' philosophizing is not yet free of the parochial values of ordinary opinion (δόξα). Socrates focuses on what is ob-viously important and "useful," at the expense of a formal training in dialectical thinking as such. Of course, these are not in principle exclusive; one *could* treat the good and the just and the beautiful merely as exemplary forms and concentrate rather on learning the conceptual thinking proper to forms as such.[3] But this points to the deeper thrust of Parmenides' crit-icism. Socrates has lost himself in the peculiar features of the good and the just and the beautiful, and so he has not learned to think of them *as forms*. This is why, in spite of his eager talk of forms, he still thinks in terms proper to their participants.

In several related respects, Parmenides' hypotheses serve well as a specimen of formal training. First, by insisting that one consider the consequences of positing not only the being of the chosen subject but also its not being, Parmenides under-mines the partisanship of the advocate in favor of the uncom-mitted—or even, more positively, the playful—spirit neces-sary for formal thinking. To entertain the possible not being of X is to put a check on any unquestioning presumption that X is; thus Parmenides' insistence should have the effect of liber-ating one's thought about X from the grip of a dogmatic com-mitment to it as it first presents itself, and of enabling the more spacious, open-minded attitude that is prerequisite to general reflection.[4] Second, Parmenides generates the hypotheses by means of purely formal methodological principles: as just noted, one must infer the consequences of positing both the being and the not being of the subject chosen; moreover, one must infer these first for the subject in its relations to itself and to what is other than itself, then for what is other than the subject, both in its relations to itself and to the subject. As a result, there are two major phases of the inquiry, each of which is divided in turn into two subphases. All this is laid down without regard for what, specifically, the chosen subject is; thus the procedures by which reflection is organized are completely indifferent to the particular nature of the subject matter. Finally, and perhaps most importantly, the actual discourse of the hypotheses is carried out with extraordinary sustained abstractness. No value terms are introduced, and when the physical-sensible aspect of things is discussed, it is always treated generally, with no reference to any particular thing or things. To cite some instances of this, in the second hypothesis the One is said to

> have some shape, either straight or round or a mixture of both (145b3-5),

and also to

> partake of time and of becoming older and younger [and, therefore,] of past and present and future. . . . (155c8-d2)

Never in the discussion of these and hosts of other features is the One given a definite shape or time, nor is it ever said just what particular thing the One might be, in order to have shape and time, nor are any particular things ever cited as concretizing instances of the One.[5] As a result, it is necessary at every step to think indefinite generalities, without fixing on determinate particulars. Thus, following both the methodological motivation of the hypotheses and their every particular step requires one to think universally and abstractly. And this means, in turn, that one must proceed by means of concepts rather than percepts, dianoetically rather than imagistically.[6] Hence the student who immerses himself in the hypotheses will find himself that much further advanced in the "conversion" from particulars to forms.

That the hypotheses do serve this general educational function is not to say, however, that this exhausts their significance. Our analysis of the first half of the dialogue has already disclosed the multileveled character of Platonic expression: on the surface we are given criticisms of the coherence of the theory of forms—but for the hearer capable of grasping the specific character of Socrates' understanding, as this is brought out by the criticisms, the subsurface meaning is the complex but precisely delineated task of rethinking the theory. There is the same copresence of surface and subsurface meaning in the second half of the dialogue. To disclose the subsurface, it is necessary to take seriously two features of the hypotheses not required by their function as exercises: Parmenides' introduction of contradictions and his choice of τὸ ἕν, the One, as the subject of inquiry.

The only contradiction specifically anticipated in his programmatic remarks at 135e-136c is that between the being and the nonbeing of the subject chosen; the consequences of both must be deduced, Parmenides insists. Yet, as we shall see, the hypotheses are riddled with contradictions. Here it is sufficient to observe that each of the projected four deductions is immediately countered by its contradictory. As a result, the four subphases just noted really break down further into eight hypotheses, four pairs of mutually contradictory deductions. This is obviously no accident; at every turn—in particular, in the synoptic statements[7] that Parmenides makes throughout the first two hypotheses, at the break after completing the first four hypotheses (see 160b2-3), and at the conclusion of the whole series (see 166c2-5)—he makes a point of collecting and reiterating the various contradictory characters he has deduced.

Why does Parmenides go to such Zenonian lengths?[8] On the surface, the contradictions serve to strengthen the function of the hypotheses as exercise. Insofar as each characterization of the One or, in hypotheses III-IV and VII-VIII, of "the others" is put in check by its contradictory, it becomes impossible to apply these notions or to interpret them as referring to any definite things; forced to regard the conceptualizations simply as conceptualizations without reference, the hearer is kept from lapsing back to δόξα, to the thinking of characters solely in terms of the concrete things that have them. But the contradictions also serve a further purpose, twofold in nature. First of all, the sheer intellectual exasperation they generate puts the hearer to a test. Precisely because they help to deny the familiar reference to particulars that δόξα involves, they bring the hearer to a moment of decision: in the face of his own impatience, he must choose whether to suffer the loss of reference for the sake of his philosophical development or to give up philosophy and, in particular, the study of the hypotheses in order to recover his familiar context.[9] Second, for the one who survives his own impatience and holds to the work of conceptual exercise, the contradictions will have a provocative power. This is most easily explicated by reference to three highly relevant passages in the dialogues. In the *Republic*, the text that the *Parmenides* calls to mind as its proper background, the mature Socrates describes the pedagogical value of confronting the aspiring philosopher with contradictions when he outlines "the study of the one";[10] the recognition of contradictory characters mixed together in the self-same object of perception provokes the mind to dianoetic analysis and reflection.[11] In the *Sophist*—a text for which, as we shall see later (pp. 152ff.), the *Paramenides* pointedly prepares the way—the Eleatic stranger makes a point of contradicting the merely "quibbling" and "showy" generation of contradictions for their own sake with the properly educational use of "apparent contradictions" (259b). "What is hard and at the same time worth the pains," he explains:

> [is] to be able to follow our [apparently contradictory] statements step by step and, in criticizing the assertion that a different thing is the same or the same thing is different in a certain sense, to take account of the precise sense and the precise respect in which they are said to be one or the other (259c-d).[12]

Finally, and most significantly in our context, Plato gives a display of just this educative power in beginning the conversation in the *Parmenides* with Socrates' response to Zeno; moreover, he makes Socrates remind us of that response at

135e5-7. There Socrates recalls that he was moved to introduce the form/thing distinction precisely

> because it seems to me that this undercuts the difficulty about showing [δοκεῖ γάρ μοι . . . ταύτῃ γε οὐδὲν χαλεπὸν εἶναι . . . ἀποφαίνειν] that things are like as well as unlike and whatever else they may be.[13]

Seen in the light of these passages, Parmenides' contradictions appear as calculated pedagogical provocation. Parmenides knows that Socrates—or, to step back from the dramatic context, Plato knows that his most promising hearers, those who survive the test of their own impatience and become capable of conceptual thinking—will feel the contradictions as a challenge and will seek to undercut them by distinctions.

Just what are the specific distinctions, however, that Plato means to elicit by this challenge? And what is his goal in eliciting them? Though the full answer to these questions requires the whole analysis of the hypotheses in the following two chapters, we can begin by coming back to the perennial question of the meaning of the One. Since the basic contradiction in the hypotheses is that between the characterizations of the One in the first and second hypotheses, the challenged hearer will first wonder if the contradictions can be undercut by identifying distinct referents for these characterizations. But what could they be? When Parmenides first introduces the One as the subject of his exercises at 137b2-3, he alludes to "my hypothesis" (τῆς ἐμαυτοῦ ὑποθέσεως). This would seem to recall the historical Parmenides' proposition, "the all is one," cited at 128a8-b1; if so, then the One would refer to "being as such," τὸ ἐόν, as that in which, according to the revelation of Parmenides' poem, all things are at one and homogeneous. But this is not so helpful as it might first appear. *Plato*'s Parmenides, at least, has disowned the traditional monistic interpretation of this "being"; as we discussed earlier (I.C.2 and I.C.3), both he and the older Zeno as well are represented as rejecting the younger Zeno's defense of him, and both apparently approve Socrates' positing of forms in distinction from things. Yet there are many forms. What, again, can the One refer to?

The key to the riddle is the hearer's grasp of Parmenides' conceptual focus and elicitative posture in the first half of the dialogue. Parmenides focused on the unity of each form, first in the sense of its kind of integriy (130e-131e) and second in the sense of its number (131e-133a). And his arguments pointedly exploited the way that the young Socrates conceives the unity of the form by means of concepts—in particular, whole/part and singular/plural—which properly apply only to participant things. To the hearer who grasps the arguments this way, Parmenides has *all along*[14] been applying the predicate "one" to forms and to things with (implicit, to be sure) systematic ambiguity.[15] Faced with the challenge of Parmenides' contradictory characterizations of the One, the hearer will be moved to try to reconcile them by setting them apart and assigning them to forms and to things as two essentially distinct sorts of "one."[16] This sorting-out will be the hearer's own active exercise, in contrast both to Parmenides' activity in setting forth the hypotheses and to the less acute hearer's passive exercise in simply following and thinking them through. And it will, finally, directly execute the complex task bequeathed by the first half of the dialogue. By thinking through the forms as, in each case, a one, the hearer treats them uniformly, without reference to the particular, peculiar character each is; thus the philosophical voice just birthing in Socrates, the voice which has wondered whether the form/thing distinction might not be "the same in all cases" (περὶ πάντων ταὐτόν, 130d6), gets its proper development. More pointedly, the contrast in the sorts of one-ness proper to forms and things, respectively, is not a perceptual matter; grasping this contrast and thinking through the natures of form and thing in terms of it requires conceptual, nonimagistic thought. This mode of thought, in turn, is just what is needed for an authentic, non-analogical understanding of the constitutive priority of form to thing. Thus the "exercise" turns out to execute, not merely prepare for, the "conversion" the young Socrates has not yet managed.[17]

If these prefatory comments are sound, then our third question seems all the more pressing. Since the task of "conversion" is bequeathed to Socrates, why does Parmenides replace him with Aristotle?

In fact, this problem too dissolves when we bear in mind the mimetic and elicitative character of Platonic drama. In reality, of course, the task is bequeathed not to the *persona* Socrates but to the young Academicians who find themselves at the critical turning-point that Plato re-presents through that *persona*. The replacement of Socrates serves a double function in Plato's communication with this audience. First, it would be utterly out of character for Socrates to remain passively affirmative, as does Aristotle, throughout Parmenides' presentation. But were he to respond along the way with critical questions and objections, the work of "conversion" would be taken out of the hands of the Academic hearer. By having Parmenides replace him with an interlocutor likely to "make the least trouble" (ἥκιστα γὰρ ἂν πολυπραγμονοῖ, 137b6-7), Plato leaves the work for the Academician. At the same time, the pointed contrast between Socrates and Aristotle[18] gives the Academician strong negative impetus. Aristotle's very passivity makes Socrates' absence conspicuous and poignant.[19] Moreover, to the hearer who aspires to Socrates' projected maturity as a philosopher, Aristotle's projected destiny is startling: first introduced as "the man who became one of the Thirty [Tyrants]" (127d2-3),[20] he is the very opposite of a philosopher. The whole effect is to predispose the hearer to be suspicious of Aristotle's responses and to take upon himself the critical inquisitiveness that Socrates would surely have shown.

Thus the displacement of Socrates works harmoniously with Parmenides' contradictions. Plato's pedagogical strategy is rich and complex. In presenting the hearer with Parmenides' Zenonian contradictions, Plato puts him in a position precisely analogous to that of Socrates at the beginning of the conversation, after Zeno's treatise. Yet by replacing Socrates with Aristotle, he incites the hearer to become Socratic *for himself*—and in just the double sense we noted earlier. On the one hand, the hearer is spurred to be thoughtfully critical (as Aristotle is not), to ask (as Socrates did, 127d) to go "back to the beginning" and reexamine the contradictions.[21] This is to become Socratic in attitude.[22] On the other hand, the hearer is given the substantive basis for this reexamination, Socrates' distinction of form and thing; to apply this to the contradictions is, as we have suggested and will try to show, to rethink the distinction itself in a genuinely conceptual mode of thought. So far as he can do this, the hearer will actually accomplish the "conversion" that the mature Socrates will "later" point to as the goal of philosophical education. To go by the dramatic framing of the *Parmenides*, this should enable him to grasp adequately what the mature Socrates could articulate only indirectly and with much opacity in the *Republic*.[23]

THE following analyses are an attempt to work out this interpretation in detail. As we shall see, the critical rethinking that Plato provokes discloses a structure and meaning in the hypotheses that is not otherwise apparent. On the surface we are given four discrete and equally weighted pairs of hypotheses. But at the subsurface level, we shall find that the last three pairs serve to explicate the central substantive implications of the first pair. The following analyses are therefore divided into two major sections treating hypotheses I–II and III–VIII, respectively; the second of these, in turn, is divided into three subsections, addressing III–IV, V–VI, and VII–VIII, respectively.

CHAPTER IV

Hypotheses I, II, and IIa:
Form, the Participant Thing,
and Their Relation
(137c-157b)

A. The Contradictions Regarding
the One (I–II)

In his synoptic statements, as we noted, Parmenides focuses
the contradictions in the hypotheses by gathering them into
tight, complex systems. Though his first such statement follows the fourth hypothesis, it appears to address only the first
two hypotheses, for it takes only the One, not "the others," as
its subject. (We shall come back to this point later.)[1] There Parmenides draws the first two hypotheses into a three-part set of
contradictions. "Thus if there is a One," he says at 160b2-3,

> the One is both everything and is not even one, alike in
> relation to itself and to the others.

First, it follows from the being of a One that it "is not even
one"; this refers back to the contradiction between antecedent
supposition and its consequences in hypothesis I (137c-142a).
Second, it also follows that the One "is everything" or "all
[characters]" ($\pi\acute{\alpha}\nu\tau\alpha$); this refers to the host of apparent contradictories which are established as characters of the One in
hypothesis II (142b-155e). Finally, these two lines of inference
are asserted together, even as a pair;[2] yet they—that is, hypotheses I and II—contradict one another.

Relying on Parmenides' synopsis for organization, let us articulate each part more closely in the order of its initial appearance.

1. Within I: The One Which Is Not, and Is Not One

When Parmenides first concludes at 141e that the One is not even one, this is only one of the culminating steps in a long series of negations. To summarize them, hypothesis I concludes that the One lacks limits (137d), shape (138a), and place (138b); is neither in motion nor at rest (139b); is neither the same nor different with respect to (139e), nor like nor unlike (140b), itself or others; is neither equal nor unequal with itself or others (140d); is neither older nor younger nor the same age with itself or others (141a) nor, on that account, in time at all (141d); neither is at all nor, on that account, is one at all (141e) nor is subject to name, speech, knowledge, perception, or opinion (142a). Though his particular argumentation varies, Parmenides secures all these negations by the same basic line of reasoning. Each of the characters under consideration in some way presupposes whole/part structure and/or plurality in that to which it applies. At the very outset, however, Parmenides establishes that the One, since it is one, cannot be many and that, since it is not many, it cannot have parts (137c-d). Thus he can show that none of the various characters properly applies to the One. This line of reasoning reaches the height of paradox in the denials of being and of oneness at 141e ff. To bring this paradoxicality fully into view, consider Parmenides' argument in reverse, tracing back from conclusions to grounds; (1) the One is not one (141e-142a) because this would imply that it *is*, and it in no sense *is* (141e); (2) in turn, the One in no sense *is* because "is" is temporally determinate, implying present time, and the One is not "in time" at all (141d-e); (3) again in turn, the One is not "in time" because this would imply that it be older and younger and the same age as itself and others, and the One does not have these age characters (141a-d); (4) still again, the One does not have these age characters because this would imply that it has likeness and equality, so far as it is the same age, and unlikeness and inequality, so far as it is older or younger, and the One has none of these characters (140e-141a); (5) in particular, the One does not have the character of inequality because this would require that, as greater or lesser in its number of measures, it have these measures as its parts, and this, in turn, would imply that it is many (140c-d); likewise, the One does not have the characters of likeness or unlikeness or equality because each of these would imply, also, that it is in some respect many (139e-140a, 140a, 140b-c); (6) the One cannot be many, however, since it is one (137c).

Now the paradox in the denial of oneness should be evident: to join the conclusion in step (1) with its ground in step (6), the One *is not* one because it *is* one! If, in turn, we go back one step further, to the ground of step (6), the paradox in the denial of being becomes equally conspicuous. Parmenides could insist that the One be one only after first laying down, as the premise for the hypothesis as a whole, that (7) there *be* a One (137c). Thus, to join the conclusion in step (2) with its ground in step (7), the One *in no sense is* because it *is*![3]

What are we to make of these contradictions? In the face of such logically achieved absurdity, can the hearer help but sympathize with the course chosen by Aristotle?[4] At 142a6-b3, Parmenides asks him for an evaluation and a decision:

> —Well then, is it possible for all this to be the case with the One?
> —I for my part think not.
> —Would you like, then, for us to go back and reconsider the supposition from the beginning, to see whether matters may look different on the second time through?
> —I'd like it very much indeed.

2. Within II: The One Which Has All Characters

On the face of it, however, the very "different" conclusions of hypothesis II are equally intolerable. This time Parmenides' arguments are almost all positive; the One is shown to take on

all possible characters at once. But since every definite character stands in a relation of mutual exclusion with its contrary,
and since Parmenides—in particular, in the summaries with
which he closes each argument—stresses how the One takes
on *both* each character *and* its contrary, the One seems internally contradictory at every turn. To cite the cases (again, with
special reference to Parmenides' summaries), the One is both
one and many, a whole and parts, and limited and infinitely
many (145a), both in itself and in another (see 145b and 145e,
discussed below), both at rest and in motion (146a), both same
and different (147b) and like and unlike (148cd) itself and
others, both in contact with and not in contact with itself and
others (149d), both equal to and greater and smaller than itself
and others (151b), both equal in number to and more and
fewer than itself and others (151e), both older and younger and
of the same age and not each of these, in being and in becoming, with regard to itself and others (155c).

As in hypothesis I, though the particular arguments vary,
most of the double predications[5] turn on the opening characterization of the One. Right away Parmenides establishes that
the supposition—"if a One is" (ἕν εἰ ἔστιν, 142b3, 5)[6]—implies that this One has both being and oneness. And since these
are distinct yet each belong to the self-same "One which is"
(τὸ ἓν ὄν), the One has a dual nature: it is a whole (of being and
oneness as, in some sense, its parts, 142c-d),[7] and it is these
parts. From this duality Parmenides is able to secure most of
his contrary characterizations with dispatch: for example, as a
whole the One is one, but as the parts of this whole it is many
(see 142e-143a, discussed in A.3, below); again, as the parts it
is in itself as the whole (145c), yet as the whole, since it cannot
be in its parts but must be somewhere, it will be in another
(145d-e); and so forth. With the exception of several peculiarly
odd phases of argument (examined in section C, below), Parmenides' long march through the characters of the One thus
takes on the unsettling duplicity of many Socratic arguments:
proceeding in little steps, each in itself relatively reasonable, he
generates a position that, formulated as a whole, seems altogether strange and paradoxical.

3. I vs. II: The Two Ones: The Contrast
in Sorts of Unity

Finally, hypotheses I and II stand in pointed contradiction to each other, both as whole positions and at every particular step. Parmenides makes this conspicuous by repeating the same list[8] of characters in just the same order in the two hypotheses. At each step in hypothesis II the One is said to *be* just what, at the correlative step in hypothesis I, it is said to *not be*. Moreover, in each case, characters are taken up together with their specific contraries. Thus the contrast between positive and negative is intensified: the One in II is said to be *both/and* just what, to put it somewhat awkwardly, the One in I is said to be *neither/nor*. In these several ways Parmenides makes the contradictions between I and II pointed and pronounced.

The preceding remarks on each hypothesis by itself already suggest the seminal point of contradiction between I and II. The lines of reasoning in the opening characterizations of the unity of the One are precisely converse. In I Parmenides begins from the oneness of the One and reasons that, as one and so not many, the One cannot have parts nor, therefore, be a whole.[9] In II, on the other hand, he starts from the presence of (in some sense) oneness and being as distinct parts of the One and reasons that, as having parts and so being a whole, the One must be both one and many. Since it is in the lack of parts and in the dual aspect of being both a whole and its parts that the lines of characterization in I and II, respectively, are sourced, this particular contradiction between I and II is seminal for the whole system of contradictions between them—and a chief focus, as we shall see, in the insight which dissolves it.

Intriguingly, this pointed contrast in whole-part structure and number is even more precisely articulated than we have yet indicated. Whereas there is only the one line of negative reasoning (as just recounted) in I, in II there are *two* distinct lines of positive reasoning from the One's being a whole to its being both one and many. These are presented at 142d9-143a3 and 143a4-144e3. In the first, Parmenides thinks from "the One-being" (τὸ ἓν ὄν, see especially 142e1, 143a2)[10] as a whole to the inner constitution of each of its parts, the characters of "one" (ἕν) and "being" (ὄν). He reasons that each, as a part (see τοῦ . . . μορίον, 142e2), cannot be lacking the other. But this establishes a perfect analogy of whole to part: since "being," as a part, must be *one* and since "one," as a part, must *be*, then just as the whole, so each part will be a "One-being"; and this implies, in turn, that, like the whole, each part is a whole made up of parts in its own right, and so on *ad infinitum*. Thus the "One-being" proves to be one as a whole but "infinitely many" (ἄπειρον τὸ πλῆθος, 143a2) in its parts. The second argument comes to its comparable conclusion by a pointedly different route. Again Parmenides begins from "the One-being," that is, the composite whole of "one" and "being" (see 143a4-6); but he immediately proposes that Aristotle focus on the aspect of "one" apart from that of "being" by an act of deliberate conceptual abstraction (τῇ διανοίᾳ . . . λάβωμεν, 143a7). Thus he asks,

> Now take just this 'one' (αὐτὸ τὸ ἕν) which we are saying has being and conceive it just by itself alone (αὐτὸ τῇ διανοίᾳ μόνον καθ᾽αὑτὸ λάβωμεν) apart from the being which we say it has. Will this 'one' itself be found to be merely one or also a plurality? (143a6-9)[11]

Parmenides then proceeds through three phases of argumentation. First, given that this aspect of "one," precisely in being abstracted from that of "being," differs from "being" and vice versa, and given that this difference is not sourced in or the same as either the aspect of "one" or that of "being," then it follows that "difference" itself must be co-present with "one" and "being" as a third aspect (143b1-8). Second, given that any two of these aspects may constitute a pair, that is, a two, and given that the addition of any one to any such pairing of the others will yield a three, Parmenides next reasons that the co-presence of "one," "being," and "difference" implies the being (εἶναι), too, of number. For two and three are even and odd, and so their various multiples display the four species that exhaust all number: even times even, odd times odd, odd times

even, and even times odd[12] (143c1-144a5). Third, the being of
number is now Parmenides' basis for an intricate demonstration that "this 'one' itself" is many. Since there are "infinitely
many" (ἄπειρος πλήθει, 144a6) numbers and since each, in accord with the being of number as such, itself has being, there
must be an infinite number (i.e. quantity)[13] of beings. But this
is to say, in turn, that being is divided[14] and distributed by
number to infinitely many beings, ranging from the smallest
to the greatest; these latter would thus be the parts of being.
But to be *a* part is to be *one*, and this is of course true of each of
the many parts of being; thus it turns out that just as number
does for being, so being divides and distributes the aspect of
"one"—"this 'one' itself"—to infinitely many beings. But, finally, this means that

> the 'one' itself (τὸ ἕν . . . αὐτό), parceled out by being, is
> both many and infinite in number (ἄπειρα τὸ πλῆθος)
> (144e3-5).

Or, summing up by quoting Parmenides' careful reference to
his different perspectives on the One in the two arguments,

> Thus not only is the One-being (τὸ ὂν ἕν) many, but also
> the 'one' itself (αὐτὸ τὸ ἕν), distributed by being, is nec-
> essarily many (144e5-7).[15]

Once the specificity of their difference is recognized, it becomes clear that the two arguments are not redundant but
complementary; in addition, the contradiction between the
opening characterizations of the One in hypotheses I and II
gets sharply focused. Though both arguments take the One as
a whole of parts, the first concentrates on this while the second
departs from it. Thus there is a difference between just what it
is that each argument shows to be one and many and in what
sense. In the first argument, the focus is on the One-being as
such, that is, on the composite whole of parts. Here the question whether it is many is concerned with its inner constitution
as composite; the plurality of the One is that of its parts, and it
is one in the sense of being the integral whole of these parts. In

the second argument, by contrast, the focus is on the composite precisely not as composite but solely in its aspect of oneness. By his pointed invocation of conceptual abstraction (διανοία) at the outset and by his repeated use of the intensive expression αὐτὸ τὸ ἕν, "the 'one' itself," Parmenides refers us to the form Oneness;[16] but by characterizing the separateness of this Oneness from "being" as a separateness only in διανοία and by establishing the composite of "being" and "one" as the matter or referent from which Oneness is initially abstracted, he makes clear that he is concerned with Oneness specifically in its immanence in "beings." This is confirmed when "the 'one' itself" is said to be "distributed" to many beings as the character that each has precisely as *a*, or *one*, being. Here, therefore, the question whether it is many is concerned with whether the form Oneness recurs in a plurality of cases. Plurality here refers to the number of its instances, and the sense of "one" that pertains to "the 'one' itself," taken in its immanence as a dianoetically distinguishable aspect of the composite, is singularity. It is precisely as *a*—that is, one *qua* singular—"being" that each "being" can be counted and thereby, with all the others, make up the many instances of "the 'one' itself." If we grasp the two arguments together now, their precise harmony becomes clear: the first argument, focusing on the internal constitution of the One *qua* composite whole of parts, establishes that each[17] is many within itself, through its infinitude of parts; while the second, treating the One[18] as an instance of Oneness *qua* singularity and examining the number of such singulars, establishes that there are many of them.[19] This entire twofold characterization, in turn, reflects back upon the corresponding opening characterization of the One in hypothesis I. Parmenides began, as already discussed, by quickly reasoning that the One cannot be many nor, therefore, a whole of parts. Precisely because this denial of plurality is Parmenides' first step, asserted not on the basis of prior argument but as a stipulation, the specific sense of the oneness of the One in I is at first unfocused. The opening arguments in II, however, make it clear. Once the character, being a whole, and its immediate implications are established, then, since the negative of these applies in retrospect to the One in I, the specific sense of its oneness may be inferred. In precise contradiction to each of the two characterizations in II, the One in I will be noncomposite and not pluralizable; or, to put this in positive terms, this One will be simple and unique.

B. Resolving the Contradictions: The Distinction of Form from Thing (I–II)

The preceding analysis is true to the surface meaning of hypotheses I and II, as it is focused by Parmenides' own summations. But if we are correct in taking his contradictions as a pointed challenge to the hearer, then the preceding is only the first step in interpretation. Once understood in their mutually nullifying relations, the hypotheses must be destroyed[20]—that is, converted from this shape and status as merely formal exercise to that of positive, definite ontological insight. This, at any rate, will be the drive of the Academic hearer who takes up for himself the posture of the now silenced Socrates. The work of destruction breaks down into roughly three phases: first, there is the task of finding the basic resolution of the contradictions within and between hypotheses I and II and of articulating the new positive sense that results; this is the task we will address in this section. There will still remain several peculiar puzzles in I and II, requiring particular reflections that partly presuppose and partly develop the basic resolution; we will undertake these reflections in the following section. Finally, once our discussions have distinguished the subjects and theses of I and of II, we shall be prepared to follow the crucial reintegration of them in Parmenides' "third" ($\tau\rho\acute{\iota}\tau o\nu$) approach—we will refer to it as IIa—at 155e-157b; this is the task of the final section of the chapter.

To work out the basic resolution, we should take up each of the three moments, as we have now laid them out, in the system of contradictions in hypotheses I and II.

1. Within I: The Specificity of the
Negation of Being; Timeless Being

Aristotle's desire to abandon the first hypothesis (142a-b) is understandable. A One whose very being implies its utter lack of character, including unity and being, is absurd. But it is also clear that Aristotle, the youngest person present (137b) and a future tyrant, is conspicuously *not* that man "of wide experience and natural ability" who will be able "to follow [Parmenides] through [his] host of very remote arguments" (133b). Aristotle's desire to reject rather than reflect upon the contradictions within I should therefore spur the hearer to do just the opposite. What is more, Plato makes precise use of the hearer's wariness toward Aristotle to indicate the point of focus for this reflection: the key step in establishing the contradictions is made by Aristotle, not by Parmenides. To be sure, Parmenides does the pedagogical work. He sets the stage, putting Aristotle to the test as he did Socrates earlier; and he goes out of his way to develop the contradictions out of Aristotle's error. Nonetheless, it is Aristotle's, not Parmenides' own position that he thus elicits and exposes.

Let us consider the text. At 141d4-5 Parmenides concludes his argument that the One is not temporal or "in time." Then at 141d7-e3 he establishes the specifically temporal sense of each tense—imperfect, perfect, future, and present—of the verbs "to become" (γίγνεσθαι) and "to be" (εἶναι). In the course of this, he links "is" and "is becoming" (see τὸ . . . ἔστι καὶ τὸ γίγνεται, 141e2-3) and associates both, as present tenses, with time "now present" (τοῦ νῦν παρόντος), in contrast to time past and future. He then tests and exposes Aristotle in the following exchange:

—If, then, the One (τὸ ἕν) in no way partakes of time, then it never has become nor was it becoming nor was it ever nor has it now become, nor is it becoming nor is it (ἔστιν), nor will it become nor will it be becoming nor will it be.
—Very true.

—Well then [Parmenides *asks*], is it possible that something partake of being (οὐσίας . . . μετάσχοι) in any
other way than these?

—*It is not possible.*

—In no way, *consequently* (ἄρα), does the One partake of
being.

—It seems not.

—In no way, *consequently* (ἄρα), is the One (ἔστι τὸ ἕν).

—Apparently not.

—Nor, *consequently* (ἄρα), is it even to the extent of being
one; for then it would already be [a] being (εἴη . . . ὄν)
and [a] participant in being. But as it seems, the One
neither is one nor is, if it is necessary to believe such an
argument (141e3–142a1).[21]

But it is not necessary. The conclusions rest upon the fundamentally preemptive assumption that being as such, or
every sense in which a being "is," is temporally determined.
What is the warrant for this position? To the one listening to
the hypotheses with the first half of the dialogue in mind, Aristotle's answer at 141e8 ("It is not possible") represents the
most extreme form of Socrates' earlier error: Aristotle as-
sumes that the sort of being proper to things—being that, in
association with becoming, is either past, present, or future—
is universal. More particularly, he fails to recognize the difference between the "is" of time present and the tenseless "is" of
what transcends temporal determination.[22] But this destroys
just what Socrates, and now the critical hearer in Socrates'
stead, wants to preserve: the timeless forms.[23] Thus the hearer
cannot help but object.

The implications of the objection are significant. Not only
does it resolve both contradictions in I, it transforms them into
specifications of the One's transcendence of the order of
things. Aristotle is justified in denying *not* being as such but
only temporally determinate being, being in time, to the One.
Thus the basic contradiction—if a One is, it is not—turns into
the revelation that this One, if it is, has timeless being! And
since the other contradiction—that the One is not one—fol-

lows from the denial of being, it undergoes an analogous transformation. If "to be" is understood in Aristotle's presumptive way as 'to be in time,' then "to be one" (ἓν εἶναι, 141e11, also e12) must mean 'to be one in time.' But to be one—or a one—in time is to belong to the spatio-temporal order of physical-sensible things, the order of "the visible" that, in *Republic* VI, makes up the lower half of the divided line. Hence the denial of unity to the One turns out to be, instead, a denial only and specifically of that sort of unity that belongs to things in time. This sort, Parmenides establishes in the corresponding arguments in II (see 151e ff.), is the unity of a whole of parts. Thus the denial takes on the positive sense—confirming the opening characterization, in the process—of affirming the partlessness or simplicity of the One.

2. Within II: The Dual Nature of the Composite; a Categorial Study

In its mechanism of pedagogical provocation, the second hypothesis is a precise analogue to the whole system of hypotheses. As we have noted, Parmenides punctuates his argument by periodic summations; both within hypothesis II and at key junctures (160b, 166b) within the whole system, he weaves his various results together to give contradictory characterizations of the One. In direct proportion as his particular arguments are a "remote host"—and this is most extreme in hypothesis II—these summations exercise a crucial pivotal function. To the hearer dizzied by the complexity and density of the arguments, they provide points of rest, compressing the parts into a compact, retainable whole. But at the same time, precisely because they render the One contradictory, the critical hearer will be moved to take them as a point of departure; like Socrates after hearing Zeno's treatise and unlike—indeed, in resistance to—the passive young Aristotle, this hearer will want to turn back to the particular arguments in order to free the One from contradictions.

What this hearer will find is that all the contradictions dis-

solve under scrutiny. In several cases, the arguments arc pedagogically ironic, and their ostensible conclusions are really
puzzles that point to otherwise hidden issues (see C.2, below)
and to quite different conclusions (see C.3, below). Generally,
however, Parmenides reproduces the same kind of seemingly
contradictory attributions that Socrates earlier penetrated in
Zeno's treatise (129cd): he does predicate contraries of the
One, but since they belong to it in different senses, there is no
real contradiction. We have already seen the most pervasive
way Parmenides does this, playing on the dual nature of the
composite One as whole and as parts; the real point of his double predications, as pedagogical provocation, is evidently to
show the hearer how this dual nature both enables and is reflected in the various characters of the One. Thus to cite several
striking instances, it is as a whole that the One has location "in
another" but as the parts of this whole that it is "in itself"
(145b-e); in turn, it is as "in another"—and hence as a whole—
that the One "moves" but as "in itself"—and hence as the
parts—that it is "at rest" (145e-146b). Or again, it is as "in another" that the One has contacts with others but as "in itself"
that it has contacts with itself (148de). In these and other cases,
Parmenides gives the appearance of contradiction by dropping
the qualifying "as . . ." phrases;[24] but these qualifications are
implied by the arguments and so make the contradictions *only*
apparent. Just as being a whole and being the parts are distinct
respects of the composite, so must the characters derived from
them belong to the composite in distinct respects.

Insofar as the hearer bears this distinction in mind, the
whole of hypothesis II makes new sense. Just as Socrates dissolved Zeno's paradox by pointing out how things may be
both like and unlike, both one and many, etc., so the hearer,
dissolving its contradictions, will find in II an extensive enumeration of the complementary contrary characters to which
any composite One is subject. But this is not all. Through several structural features, hypothesis II goes beyond a merely
particularistic enumeration. First, Parmenides' pairing of
characters with their contraries suggests a higher level of generality. Contraries call for each other and together constitute a

unified range of possibilities. This range, in turn, relates to the contraries themselves as encompassing kind or genus to sub-kinds or species. Thus by working through pairs of contraries, Parmenides raises the hearer's attention from particular characters to the general kinds of character to which the composite One is subject. Second, Parmenides groups these pairs of contraries suggestively. At the lowest level, there are striking appositions of similar kinds of character; such appositions suggest still higher, more encompassing genera, to which the encompassed kinds would then be subordinated as species. On the other hand, there are equally striking contrapositions that relate and set into relief the emergent encompassing genera. Indeed, apposition and contraposition seem to work together as structural features, the one suggesting, the other focusing the basic kinds of character. To see this more precisely, consider the series of contraries in its entirety:

(1) whole-part structure
(2) singularity/plurality
(3) limits
(4) shape
(5) located in itself/in another
(6) at rest/in motion
(7) same/different with respect to itself/others
(8) like/unlike itself/others
(9) having/not having contacts with itself/others
(10) equal/unequal (greater/smaller) in magnitude to itself/others
(11) equal/unequal (more/fewer) in multitude to itself/others
(12) in time
(13) is and becomes/is not and does not become older/younger than itself/others
(14) has temporal modes (past/present/future)
(15) subject to name, propositional speech, knowledge, opinion, and sense-perception

(1) and (2), of course, are clearly appositive; as we have already observed, they express different senses of the unity proper to

the One. Beyond this, (7) and (8) are clearly a pair, both describing the relatedness of the One to others and to itself. But "relatedness" is too vague, for (10)–(11), also a clear pair, also express the One's relatedness, yet in a contrasting sense. (9) serves a key role in focusing the contrast: "having contacts" is like sameness/difference and likeness/unlikeness in being essentially relational, but it is like equal/unequal in magnitude and in multitude in its focus on things as extended and quantitative. (In his arguments for (9), Parmenides goes out of his way to focus on the question of the *number* of contacts between the One and others.) Thus (7) and (8) are set in relief as modes of relatedness in identity and quality, in contrast with (9)–(11) as modes of relatedness in extension and quantity. This specification of (9)–(11), in turn, both associates and distinguishes them from (3)–(6). Both groups treat the spatial being of the One, but (3)–(6) focus on the One by itself: limits,[25] shape, location, and rest/motion are characters that, while they may imply the possibility of relatedness, themselves bear directly on the One's own spatiality without regard for others. (Note, in particular, that Parmenides' argument for "being in another" strongly suggests that this "other" signifies not another One thing but, rather, space or place. The key step in his reasoning is the thesis, introduced at 145d, that the One "must be either in something else or nowhere at all"; since "nowhere" is the contradictory to 'somewhere,' that is, 'in space' or 'in (a) place,' and since the necessity ["must"] of the thesis requires that "in something else" and "nowhere" relate as contradictories, "in something else" must signify simply 'somewhere' or 'in space.' Thus the character, "being in another," does not refer to relatedness to other things, as do the characters in [7]–[8] and [9]–[11], but to the general status of spatial location.)[26] Still further, this unification and inner distinction of (3)–(6) and (9)–(11) sets (12)–(14) into relief, revealing *their* basic unity and distinction. In contrast to spatial being as the notion common to (3)–(6) and (9)–(11), (12)–(14) all address the temporal being of the One; and in analogy with the distinction between (3)–(6) and (9)–(11), the characters in (13) describe the temporal relatedness of the One to others and to itself, while those of (14) focus on the One by itself, presenting its modes as a distinct being, without regard for others. Finally, these two basic associations—of (7)–(8) with (9)–(11), as aspects of relatedness, and of (3)–(6) and (9)–(11) with (12)–(14), as spatial and temporal aspects of existence—set (15) into relief. In (15) Parmenides wants to know whether the One can be the referent of any relation, "that *to* which" (ἐκείνῳ) and "*of* which" (ἐκείνου) there may be relation; and he has temporally determinate relations (subject to "was" and "is" and "will be") in mind (155d4-5). But he is concerned not with the relatedness in its being that the One has with other things but rather with the relations in consciousness that the mind has toward the One as its referent. Thus (15) stands paired with (3)–(14) as a (complex, to be sure) whole: whereas (3)–(14) expose the spatiotemporal being of the One by itself and in its relatedness, (15) exposes the intelligibility, the accessibility for consciousness, of the One.

As a result of such reflections, the hearer initially dizzied by hypothesis II as a host of contradictory particular characters can now recognize a system of interrelated kinds of character. We might represent it as in the accompanying diagram.

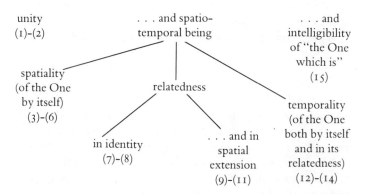

Grasped this way, hypothesis II presents a genuinely *categorial* analysis of the composite One. Much more than an enumeration of particulars, it articulates the most basic *kinds* of character to which such a One is subject, and it suggests the interrelations of these kinds. To this degree, it is prototypical for (the philosopher) Aristotle's later doctrine.[27]

3. I vs. II: The Form's Prescinsion from the Categories of the Thing

By dissolving the contradictions internal to hypotheses I and II in these ways, the hearer has already done the groundwork for the dissolution of the contradiction between I and II. That the One both has "all [characters]" (II) and lacks even being and unity (I) is contradictory just insofar as "the One" refers to the selfsame subject. Yet the preceding reflections make this questionable. In I, on the one hand, the real point of the denials is to set the One beyond the order of spatio-temporal existence; if it "is" at all, the One has the timeless being of the forms. In II, on the other hand, Parmenides shows how the One is subject to the categories, the basic kinds of character, proper to spatio-temporal existence. Thus the two hypotheses appear to examine two distinct sorts of unit, Ones that belong to essentially different orders of being.

For the critical hearer who has recognized the basic issues in the elenchus and Socrates' limits in dealing with them, Plato makes this ambiguity precise and pointed by several deft touches in the opening argumentation of II. In the third step of the second argument for the plurality of the One (143a-144e, outlined and discussed in A.3, above), Parmenides makes a sound case for the distributedness of the forms being (οὐσία) and Oneness (αὐτὸ τὸ ἕν) to many particular beings. But his characterizations of the mode of distribution and its impact on the forms are more than questionable. At 144b4-c1 he says of being that it is κατακεκερμάτισται, "parceled out" or "broken up into bits," and so μεμέρισται, "divided into parts." This language presupposes just what he earlier exposed as an error in Socrates' thinking of the forms: being is treated as if a physical composite, a whole of separable parts. When Aristotle says nothing, Parmenides raises the point still more directly. Now with regard to the form Oneness, he confronts Aristotle with the same dilemma he earlier (131a ff.) put before Socrates:

Tell me then, can [Oneness], being one, be in many places at the same time as a whole? Reflect on this (τοῦτο ἄθρει).

—I am reflecting, and I see that it is impossible.

—*Consequently* (ἄρα), if not as a whole, then it must be divided into parts; for I suppose (γάρ που) there is no other way for it to be present by all the parts of being at the same time.

—Right. (144c8-d4).[28]

As before, Aristotle's pointed failure to "make trouble" when the very coherence of the theory of forms is at stake should only spur on the critical hearer. Aristotle accepts without discussion what Socrates earlier struggled to circumvent (130e ff.), the characterization of the participated form as a whole of parts. Thus he misses the lesson that was implicit in the elenchus, that the notion of whole and part, proper as it is to the physical-sensible, cannot be applied to the form; as the conundrums at 131c-e made vivid, this would reduce the form to the status of its participant things. The hearer who has understood this will therefore take seriously Parmenides' pointed invitation to "reflect on this" and will object both to the terms of the question and to the inference Parmenides draws from Aristotle's answer. Precisely because it is not a thing, he will insist, the form cannot be understood as a whole of parts.

With this thought, however, the hearer is put into just the right position to grasp the specific ambiguity of "the One" in I and II. Consider his experience as he ponders the argument in II. Just as he comes to complete the twofold characterization of the One as—in retrospective contradiction of I—a composite that is but one of many such singulars (144e5-7), Parmenides provokes him to object that the form differs in kind from its many participants in being a partless or simple one. This substantive connection of the elenchus with I and II makes the ambiguity pointed and transparent. In II "the One"[29] must refer to each of the many composite *things*, considered in its purely exemplary character as a typical physical-sensible unit or one.[30] In I, by contrast, "the One" must refer to the *forms*, taking each in its exemplary character as a simple, unique one.

Heard this way, hypotheses I and II cease to be contradictory and take on a new, positive significance. This significance, in turn, reflects the basic integrity of the *Parmenides*. Both pointedly in the opening arguments and more generally in the subsequent argumentation, the first two hypotheses serve to mediate Socrates' predicament in the first half of the dialogue. In I–II Parmenides offers Socrates—or better, Plato offers the critical hearer—the key help he needs to grasp and preserve the theory of forms. The young Socrates had thought he could transcend the limitations of δόξα simply by positing forms in distinction from things; but because he was unself-conscious of the essential features of things *as things*, he proved unable to avoid projecting these onto forms and thus undermining his own distinction. In particular, Socrates failed fully to grasp the sort of one a form is, letting it be treated as a whole of parts (130e-131e) and a singular among many others (131e-133a); both times he was forced to admit that such a one would be many, a plurality. Now we can see precisely why Parmenides goes to such lengths to devise his two distinct arguments for the plurality of the One in the opening phase of II. By stressing the composite structure and the plurality in number, respectively, of the One, he reiterates and makes explicit Socrates' own conceptions—but with this conspicuous difference: Parmenides ascribes these characters only to the One in II, while denying them to the One in I. Thus he pointedly corrects Socrates. It is only the physical-sensible thing that is composite and singular; the form is simple and unique. Beyond this, the subsequent argumentation in I and II constitutes a full (if perplexing and provocative) account of the form's prescinsion from the categories proper to things. Hypothesis II, we have seen, exhibits these categories. Thus it provides just what the youthful Socrates, still under the sway of presumptuous δόξα, lacks and needs: a conceptually articulated account of the general nature of the physical-sensible thing. But each affirmation in II is retrospectively paired with a denial in I. Thus the two hypotheses together also exhibit, point for point, just what are the kinds of character to which forms, in their essential difference from things, are *not* subject. In this way Parmenides helps Socrates—or the critically attuned hearer—to make a genuinely self-accountable transcendence of δόξα for the first time.

Needless to say, it is only such a hearer who is likely to find this significance in hypotheses I and II. It is a feature of Plato's pedagogical rhetoric of problem-posing that what serves as a bridge for those inwardly ready to understand also serves as a barrier for those unprepared. In the *Parmenides*, as we noted at the very outset, the standard of readiness is high. The hearer must, in the substance of his insight, share the fundamental intuitions regarding the distinctive nature of the form that are implicit in the youthful Socrates' similes of "day" (131b3) and "models" (132d2); in the form of his understanding, in turn, he must be ready to transcend simile itself, able to raise its content to conceptual form; and in his philosophical motivation, he requires that Socratic keenness that seeks out contradiction as the occasion for critical thinking. Given these qualities, the hearer will find the hypotheses a rich territory. As a conceptual distinction of form from thing, the basic significance of hypotheses I and II works to initiate a thinking of forms that is genuinely appropriate to them in its mode. The hearer who reaches this subsurface meaning makes the crucial advance in the "conversion" of the soul toward being; he has achieved the second beginning, as we called it, in Platonic theory.

C. Puzzles along the Way:
Implications and Anticipations

Interpreting Parmenides' subject "the One" as systematically ambiguous, referring to each one form in hypothesis I and to each one thing in hypothesis II, does resolve the contradictions and reveal the positive sense of I and II as a whole. At the same time, several particular passages remain puzzling; indeed, thinking their subject as the form or the physical-sensible thing seems even to intensify their obscurity. As we shall see, in each of these cases, full explication is impossible without reference to hypotheses III–VIII; such explication, in fact, is a primary function of III–VIII. Still, it is important to take note of these riddling passages as they first occur. There are three in particular: the denial of both difference and sameness to the One (form) in I, 139b-e; the attribution to the One (thing) in II of both difference and sameness with "the others," 146c-147b; and the attribution to the One (thing) in II of both equality and inequality in size both with itself and with "the others," 149d-151b.

1. The Isolate Form (139b-e)

As soon as "the One" in hypothesis I is interpreted as referring to each one form, all the denials in I—except for those of sameness and difference—make compelling sense. Since all the characters but these presuppose spatial or temporal being, none can apply to the One; for the forms prescind from spatio-temporality. Given the context, this is the sense even of the denials of name, speech (λόγος), and knowledge (ἐπιστήμη) at 142a. Taken on its face, Parmenides' reasoning is that, since whatever is subject to these must have being and since being has just been denied to the One (141e), the One cannot be subject to them; but of course, since "being" here is unwittingly conflated with temporal being, the real force of these denials is to express the One's prescension from the sort[31] of name, speech, and knowledge—as well as opinion and sense-perception (142a)—to which temporal things are subject.

But what of sameness and difference? These do not presuppose spatiality or temporality. Evidently, the oneness *qua* uniqueness of the form makes it impossible for the form to differ from itself or be the same with another. (See Parmenides' arguments at 139b.) But the very lack of these characters would seem to imply, conversely, the possession of sameness-with-itself and difference-from-others. Indeed, hasn't it been already established that each form differs from all other forms (recall Socrates' distinction of forms from one another, 128e-129b) and stands, in contrast to its diversity of instances, as "one and the same" (132d9-e1, also 132a3)? Strikingly, when one looks from the closing summary at 139e4-5 to the arguments themselves at 139c3-e3, one sees that Parmenides does *not really* deny these characters after all; his real point is some-thing else. At 139c3-d1, first, he establishes that being "other than another" (ἕτερον . . . ἑτέρου) does not follow or derive in any way from "being one" (τῷ . . . ἓν εἶναι). Since each form is precisely a simple and unique character, being one—that is, simple and unique—is essential to it; but being different is not entailed by being one; hence, being different is not, in contrast to being one, essential to the form. Similarly, at 139d1-e3, Parmenides argues only and specifically that being "the same" (ταὐτὸν) does not coincide with being one: since in the case of being the same as "the many" (τοῖς πολλοῖς), being the same is not incompatible with plurality, while being one *is* incompatible with it,[32] "the same" and "one" must be distinct characters. The argument shows that sameness—or sameness-with-itself, here treated as a special case of same-ness—does not belong to the One—that is, to the simple and unique form—*as such*. But at the same time, Parmenides has not shown that sameness-with-itself or difference-from-an-other cannot belong at all to the One. What is a distinct char-acter from oneness is not therefore necessarily incompatible with it; again, what is not essential to the form as such is not thereby precluded from belonging to it inessentially. Parmen-ides makes no attempt to argue the latter. Indeed, in curious ways Parmenides seems even to oppose any such argument—and, therefore, any reading of the passage that would take it in this way. At 139d6 he states (in a counterfactual formulation) that the characters "one" and "same" "*differ*" (διαφέρει): does this not suggest what is also implied by the *distinction* of "one" from "other than another," namely, that a One may be "different" or "other," even if this is not directly consequent upon its being one? Likewise, Parmenides' key example in his second argument has a suggestive irrelevance: that sameness with the many is impossible for the One follows from its being one and not many, and this would hardly be undercut by at-tributing sameness-with-itself to the One; on the contrary, since it is one and not many, to be the same as itself would im-ply that it is *not* the same as the many. Thus Parmenides, by his choice of this example, seems to underscore the limited reach he intends for his argument: even while distinct from self-sameness, the oneness of the One is by no means inconsistent with it.

Why does Parmenides argue with such subtlety, hedging his conclusions in these ways? Not until later, in hypothesis V, will he return to the question of the sameness and difference of the simple and unique One and make his basic insight clear. At this stage we can only formulate the puzzle: for the hearer who penetrates the surface contradictions to their subsurface sense, the argument works both to distinguish each one form from every other character and at the same time to preserve self-sameness and difference-from-another as characters that each one form, even if not by inner necessity but only in some contingent context, may nonetheless have.[33]

2. The Thing and "the Others" (146d–147b)

Parmenides first introduces the notion of τὰ ἄλλα ("the others") or τὰ μὴ ἕν ("what are not one") at 146d. As if these purely negative names did not render them obscure enough, he gives expressly contradictory arguments to show that the One is both different (ἕτερον, 146d1–5) and the same (ταὐτόν, 146d5–147b8) with these "others." Thus the hearer is pressed simultaneously by the question of the reference of "the others" and the task of resolving the contradiction. Consider first the explicit lines of argument Parmenides proposes. The argument for difference is direct and short: difference—the relation of "another to another" (ἕτερον ἑτέρου)—is reciprocal; "whatever are *not* one" are thus different from the One; therefore, the One in its turn will be different from them. The argument for sameness, on the other hand, is indirect and involved. Parmenides constructs an elimination. Earlier (146b2–5) he had established that anything must relate to anything else either as same or as different or as part to whole or as whole to part. He now proceeds in two steps. First he shows that the One and "what are not one," since neither participates in difference,[34] cannot be different from each other; this directly contradicts his preceding argument for difference, of course.

Next he argues that "what are not one," since this "not" implies that they lack number and wholeness, can be neither the parts of the One nor a whole of which the One is part.[35] This leaves sameness as the only remaining possibility; the One, Parmenides concludes paradoxically, must be the same as "what are not one."

Even apart from the obvious issue of the compatibility of difference and sameness, Parmenides' way of arguing raises a new dilemma. How, if not by "difference," can "what are not one" still be "*not* one"? And how, if these "others" *are* "not one," can they then be the same with the One? In a striking way, Parmenides appears to address just this dilemma by his next set of arguments. In itself this set—the two arguments in affirmation of the likeness and unlikeness of the One at 147c1-148c2—is both problematic[36] and superfluous; to Aristotle's[37] relief, Parmenides replaces it with the much more straightforward, internally sound derivations of likeness from sameness and of unlikeness from difference at 148c3-d4. But to the critical hearer still pondering the preceding dilemma, this set is of great value. Parmenides proposes, first, that precisely insofar as the One and "what are not one" are different, each from the other, they are like (ὅμοιον) (147c2-148a6); he then argues, conversely, that, since sameness is contrary to difference and should lead to the contrary character, as the same the One and "what are not one" will be unlike (ἀνόμοιον) (148a6-c1). These combinations are signal. They bring to view that there are *two* sorts of difference. The first argument, referring back to the reciprocal difference established at 146d1-5 and deriving likeness from it, in this way brings to the fore the reciprocal distinction between terms on par or of equal status; this is the difference that holds between entities the same in kind. The second argument, by contrast, refers back to the sameness established between terms *not* reciprocally different, at 146d-147b. As not different in this sense from the One, "what are not One" must also be not like or the same in kind with the One. Hence, the unlikeness or difference the second argument establishes must have the radical character of incommensurability or difference in kind. What is more, the emergence of this second sort of unlikeness or difference implies as well the emergence of a second sort of sameness. Terms that are radically unlike and so not the same in kind may, for just this reason, coincide or be integral; as not commensurate, they are also not mutually exclusive or incompatible. It is therefore possible, in principle, for such terms to constitute an identity.[38]

These reflections partly clarify, partly compound the basic riddle of the whole passage. On the one hand, they suggest a resolution to the contradiction between the predications of difference and sameness. The negative ("not") in the notion of "what are *not* one" may be equivocal, shifting between the two sorts of difference just noted. In one sense, "what are not one" would refer to what differ *as likes* with the One; this sense fits perfectly with Parmenides' affirmation of reciprocal difference. Here "what are not one" would be other Ones—just those many other singulars that are required and implied by the second of Parmenides' opening characterizations of the One as one and many in II ($143a4-144e3$). In the other sense, "what are not one" would refer to that which is so unlike the One as to somehow coincide or be integral with it. Whatever this would be, 'it' would be "unlike" in the specific sense of lacking just that unity—hence, both wholeness and number— which essentially characterizes the composite; thus 'it' could not be the parts of the One or a larger whole of which the One would be a part. This sense does fit, of course, with Parmenides' denial of difference and of whole-part relations and his consequent affirmation of the sameness of the One and "what are not one."

Just what, however, would "what are not one" really be, taken in this second sense? *At this stage* in the hypotheses, there is no basis for answering this question. Once again, we must be content for the present just to formulate the puzzle. We will have occasion to return to the question when we come to hypotheses III and IV, however: there Parmenides examines "the others" both in their relation to the One and in themselves, and he sorts out the several senses of "what are *not* one" more explicitly.[39]

BEFORE continuing, it is worth noting that Parmenides plays on the equivocal sense of "not one" once more in II. In the next argument he holds that the One does (148d8-e1) and does not (149a-d) have contact with "the others" (τὰ ἄλλα). The argument for contact—that the One is, as a whole, "in" or "among the others" (ἐν τοῖς ἄλλοις)—requires that the latter be understood as other Ones, other singular things; the relation of spatial inclusion or bordering indicated by ἐν is possible only between physical things with shape, location, and size, that is, only between Ones that, as different, are all alike. The argument against contact, by contrast, plays on the other sense of "not one." Parmenides begins by reasoning that the number of contacts must be one fewer than the number of terms involved; then he shows that, since "the others" *as "other"* (εἴπερ ἄλλα ἐστίν, 149c6) lack oneness and, so, number altogether, the total number of terms involved in their relation with the One can only be one; thus there will be no contacts. Here he takes "what are not one" in the sense of what is essentially *unlike* the One. Since the two senses are basically distinct, once again the contradiction dissolves.

In all the remaining arguments involving "the others," however, Parmenides restricts himself to the first sense. This is necessary. In these arguments Parmenides seeks to show the relatedness of the One to "the others" in size, number of measures, and age. But only things that are each singular and composite can have size, number, and age in the first place. Thus Parmenides takes "the others" consistently in the sense of other Ones.

3. The Forms of Size (Revisited) (149d-151b)

Perhaps the oddest, most perplexing passage[40] in all of hypothesis II is the treatment of the characters of size, largeness (μέγεθος) and smallness (σμικρότης) and equality, at 149d-151b. Not only are Parmenides' conclusions contradictory, but the arguments by which he reaches them materialize the forms and participation at every turn. Young Aristotle, as usual, does not object. Indeed, just as he earlier collapsed being as such into temporally determinate being, so here he collapses being as such into spatially extended being; in both cases he fails to grasp the transcendence of the forms. The critical hearer, therefore, will find it necessary to object all along the way—and as before, he will transform the sense of the whole passage as a result. To work out this transformation, we need to consider the argument in its three main divisions: Parmenides establishes first that the One is equal in size to "the others" and to itself (149d-150e); next that it is larger and smaller than itself (150e-151a); and finally that it is larger and smaller than "the others" (151a-b).

(*149d-150e*) Parmenides' remarkable argument for equality proceeds in three basic steps to its conclusion. First, that the One and "the others" be related as equal or as larger or smaller requires both the being of the corresponding forms, equality and—as mutually relative terms—largeness and smallness,[41] and the participation of the One and "the others" in them. This is so, Parmenides reasons, because nothing in the nature of being one or of being "others than the One"[42] can itself account for these relations (149d9-150a1). But, second, it is impossible for either smallness or largeness to be in the One. Such being-in would imply a host of contradictions. In a word, whether in the One as a whole (150a3-b2) or in only a part of the One (150b2-5), in either case smallness would be not small, as it above all should be (150b7), but either equal or larger; for to be in something implies either "being extended through the whole of it" (δι' ὅλου αὐτοῦ τεταμένη, 150a4) and, so, being equal to it or "containing it" (περιέχουσα αὐτό, 150a4-5) and, so, being larger than it. But, in turn, if smallness is not in the One, neither can largeness be; for if it were, then something—the One—would be larger without anything being smaller, a patent impossibility (150b7-c3). From these two steps, finally, Parmenides goes to his conclusion by a striking substitution: if the One, not partaking of largeness and smallness, cannot be larger or smaller, then it cannot exceed or be exceeded by "the others"; but what neither exceeds nor is exceeded by another is equal to it (150d4-8)! Just the same reasoning holds as well for the One's relation to itself (150e1-4). Hence it is equal to "the others" and to itself.

In a number of ways, the argument seems designed to provoke thought about materiality and immateriality. In the final step, first of all, the form of reasoning works against the content. To argue for one term (equal) by eliminating its determinate negation (unequal, understood as, positively, larger or smaller) presupposes that both are real possibilities to begin with; thus the hearer is moved to reflect that anything that can be equal to others[43] in size must also have the *possibility* of inequality. This not only undermines Parmenides' conclusion, since he had reasoned to equality from the *impossibility* of inequality, but it also calls attention to the internal relations that make one complex structure of large, small, and equal. Parmenides has already asserted directly that largeness and smallness call for one another as mutually relative contraries (ἐν-αντίω . . . ἀλλήλοιν, 149e10); now he is indirectly showing how equality stands to them both (as the aspects of inequality) as their contrary and forms with them a conjunction of alternatives.[44] This reflection relates to the size relations of things, of course; probably more important in the context of the dialogue as a whole, the argument is also designed to generate reflection on size and the forms. In the second step, in particular, Parmenides leads the hearer back to Socrates' "abyss of nonsense,"[45] giving a new version of his earlier conundrums at 131c-e.[46] The contradiction he reveals—that smallness would be equal or larger, not smaller—presupposes that the form itself has the size character that it causes in its participants; that is, the argument works only if it is assumed that smallness, as it is "in" the One that partakes of it, is itself *a small thing*. For the hearer who did not see the point of Parmenides' earlier conundrums, Parmenides' argument here provides a second chance. Since this hearer will initially accept the contradiction as genuine, he will find himself in a bizarre position: as a consequence of the size properties of the participated forms, it is unreasonable for their participant things to have such properties (specifically, large, small) at all. The very bizarreness of this position makes it thought-provoking; and its content will guide the thought toward a comparison of form and thing. For the hearer who *did* get the point of Parmenides' earlier conundrums, on the other hand, this comparison is already well underway, as the basic thrust of hypotheses I and II, and Parmenides' contradiction serves rather to stress one of its key points, made in the correlative passage in I (140bc): the forms for size are themselves sizeless.

For the critical hearer, then, both the second and third steps are fallacious. This has manifold implications. On the one hand, the concluding attributions of equality and, as well, the denial of participation that leads to them must all be withdrawn. On the other hand, this withdrawal leaves secure and free from challenge the purely hypothetical content of the first step: *if* the One and "the others" are to have the various possibilities of relativity of size, the corresponding forms must be and be participated by them.

(*150e-151a*) Parmenides next argues for the self-contradictory characterization of the One as both larger and smaller than itself. The argument is as terse as it is problematic. As "in itself," already established at 145c, the One must itself "be around itself from the outside" (περὶ ἑαυτὸ ἂν εἴη ἔξωθεν) or "contain" (περιέχον) itself; as containing term to contained, it is larger than itself, and as contained to containing, it is smaller than itself. The reasoning is plausible if the hearer thinks of the relation of containment that holds between discrete things: for one thing to be "in" another thing, they must be of different sizes. (Parmenides will use just this point in his next argument.) But problems arise when he thinks the One by itself this way. It was "in itself," Parmenides earlier argued, in that the parts are "in" the whole. Does *this* sort of containment permit a difference in size between the terms, the parts and the whole?[47] Would not that part of the whole that "is around" the parts and by which it contains them be just that—namely, a part? And if so, would it not belong to the parts as well as (like all the other parts) to the whole? But if so, there could be no difference in size between the parts and the whole.

The critical hearer thus dissolves Parmenides' contradictory conclusion and at the same time restores one of the characters lost with the collapse of the preceding argument at 149d-150e. Reflected upon, Parmenides' reasoning suggests not that the One is larger and smaller but rather that—*qua* the whole and all the parts[48]—it is equal to itself. Beyond this, the argument raises a new line of questioning. To dissolve the contradiction, the hearer must distinguish the containment of one thing by another from self-containment: what is obvious in the first sort, the difference between the terms, becomes obscure in the second. Specifically, if the whole and the parts are equal in size, then how do they differ? Even more pointedly, if, as the reflection on the containing part suggested, they coincide completely insofar as they are considered in their physical-sensible character, does their difference lie in some non-physical-sensible respect? Precisely because the argument at 150e-151a is restricted to the physical-sensible aspect of the One, it can only raise, not respond to, these questions; but in doing so, it points to crucial reflections to come in the consideration of hypotheses IIa and III.[49]

(*151a-b*) Finally, Parmenides argues for the characterization of the One and "the others" as larger and smaller than each other. We might mark the key steps as follows: (1) "Is this necessarily so, that nothing *is* (μηδὲν εἶναι) besides (ἐκτὸς) the One and the others?" "Indeed," comes Aristotle's rhetorical assent, "how could it not be so?" (2) "But, too, it is necessary that what is always be somewhere (εἶναι που)." "Yes." (3) "Accordingly, will not what is in something be as a smaller in a larger? For one thing would not be in another (ἕτερον ἐν ἑτέρῳ) in any other way." "Indeed not." From these points Parmenides makes his way to the conclusion. Given only the observation that to "be somewhere" is to "be in something," Parmenides can reason that, given (1), the One and "the others" have only each other to "be in"; and if each is in the other, then from (3) it follows that each is both smaller and larger than the other.

What will strike the critical hearer in this is less the unsound-

ness and contradictoriness than the superfluity and—in the superfluous portion—the irony of the argument. Once it has become clear that "the others" refers to other Ones, that is, other
composite things, step (3) alone is enough to reach a noncon-
tradictory sense of the conclusion. The composite thing, Parmenides has reminded us, is "in another," and for different
things, the being of any one in another implies the relation of
smaller to larger. Whether as a part (for Parmenides has shown
how each part is itself a composite One, 142e) in a whole or
simply as spatially enclosed by something else, each One will
be smaller than another One; and conversely, that other will be
larger than it. Thus the relations "larger" and "smaller" may
be established between the One and its "others."[50] But if this
suffices, why does Parmenides go out of his way to present
steps (1) and (2)? The question becomes acute when we note
that, for the critical hearer who has recognized Aristotle's
preemptive conflation of being as such with temporal being,
(1) and (2) present a variation on that preemption. "Besides[51]
the One and the others," precisely because these are only the
physical-sensible, there *are* ($\varepsilon \tilde{\iota} \nu \alpha \iota$) the forms. That Aristotle
unwittingly lets these pass for "nothing" ($\mu \eta \delta \grave{\varepsilon} \nu$), nonbeing,
in (1) only reflects his presumption, made manifest by (2), that
whatever *is* "is somewhere" ($\varepsilon \tilde{\iota} \nu \alpha \iota \pi o \upsilon$), that is, is a spatial
thing. Why, though, does Parmenides choose this time to
ironize on Aristotle's fixation on the spatio-temporal?

In fact, the question leads to and exposes the unity of the
whole three-part discussion of size relations in its subsurface
meaning. Aristotle's preemption of nonspatial being will immediately recall to the critical reader the implicit positive content of the first part: by his ironic contradiction Parmenides
stressed that the forms for size are themselves sizeless and so
nonspatial (see 150a-c); and by his opening argument he established that *if* the One and "the others" are to have the various
characters of relativity of size, the corresponding forms must
be and be participated by them (see 149d-150a). In light of these
points, the positive content of the second (150e-151a) and third
(151a-b) parts takes on a new significance. By showing that the
One and "the others" actually do possess these characters of

relativity of size (equal, larger, smaller), these parts constitute the secondary premises for a *modus ponens* proof of the being of the nonspatial forms of size. Concisely stated, the proof runs as follows: if things are equal and larger and smaller, then the forms equality, largeness, and smallness must *be* and be participated by these things; things in fact are self-equal and larger and smaller than one another; therefore, the forms of size relations *are* and are participated.

THE arguments at 149d-151b treat the characters of size exclusively in terms of magnitude; "large" and "small" describe the relative bulk or spatial extent of things. Distinct but akin to this, there is the sense of size as number; a thing may be "more" (πλεῖον) or "fewer" (ἔλαττον) than another in some number of units of measure. Parmenides expresses his awareness of this kinship by immediately following the predications of the characters of size as magnitude with the correlative predications of the characters of size as number (151b-d). And in his arguments he makes the latter directly dependent on the former: insofar as the One is larger and smaller and equal to itself and "the others," his argument runs, it will be more and fewer and equal, too. Given this dependence, it is not necessary to repeat the preceding analyses point for point; the critical hearer will modify the conclusions regarding size as number to correspond to those regarding size as magnitude. It is worth noting, however, that by ordering his predications as he does, Parmenides calls attention at once to the generic unity and the specific differentiation of the notion of size. This is a case in point of the way the exposition goes beyond a particularistic examination of characters and calls to mind the categories, that is, the kinds of character proper to things.

D. Relating the *Distincta*: the Founding of Thing in Form (IIa)

By the close of hypothesis II, the critical hearer should be partly satisfied. By taking up Plato's implicit challenge and dissolving the contradictions in I and II, he will have worked his way through a conceptual distinction of form and thing. Thus he will have purged himself of Socrates' basic error, the thinking of the forms on the model of composite, singular things. But he will not yet have begun the key analysis that, precisely because of this error, Socrates omitted from his presentation of forms. Now that form is distinguished from thing, the hearer will want to know how the two are related. That is, just what is the constitutive role the form, understood as different in kind from things, has for them?[52]

For the reader whose understanding remains on the surface, however, the situation is quite different. For him as for Aristotle, hypothesis I was self-defeating and had to be abandoned for a new start. The results of that start, however, are hardly less problematic: at every turn, as Parmenides' summations bring out, the One appears to be characterized by contradictories. Unless some way can be found to reconcile these, this second version of the One will have to be abandoned as well, having proven equally self-defeating and contentless. The whole of the two hypotheses will thus remain a purely formal exercise.

Plato is an astonishing teacher. The wonder of his dense, brief excursus on "the instant" (τὸ ἐξαίφνης) at 155e-157b is not only that in the same words he speaks at once to both hearers, on both levels of significance; beyond this, the meaning of the passage on the surface level contains implications that, if properly grasped, lead directly to the meaning on the deeper, critical level. Thus, as we shall see, the discussion of "the instant" (we will call it IIa)[53] both responds to the separate issues of the two levels and provides a pathway from the one to the other.

CONSIDER first the issue as it appears on the surface level. Parmenides' compact opening sentences frame the argument:

> Let us take up the argument yet a third time (τὸ τρίτον). If the One is (τὸ ἕν εἰ ἔστιν) as we have described—both one and many and so not one and not many (καὶ μήτε ἓν μήτε πολλὰ) and partaking of time—, then tell me, is it not

necessary that insofar as it is one, it sometime partakes of
being, and insofar as it is not [one], it also sometime does
not partake of being? (155e4-8)[54]

The "third" attempt is needed because the second has apparently generated internal contradiction: the One of II is, above
all, both one and many, and this means that it is also, as many,
not one and as one, not many. Likewise, as one it is, but as not
one—since being one is essential to it—it is not. But even in
articulating the problem for the not-yet-critical hearer, Parmenides suggests the solution. The One of II also "partakes of
time"; hence the contradictory characters may be distributed
to different moments ("sometime") in the temporal history of
the One. "Sometime" the One may be and be one, and some
other time it may not-be[55] and be many.

In the first phase of argument (through 156c3) Parmenides
expands this solution to the problem of the contradictories in
two directions. First, he introduces processes (or "motions,"
see κινήσεων, 157a2) between these contradictory characters
(or "states," see στάσεων, 157a2). Thus, if the one sometime is
and sometime is not, it must sometime pass from being to
nonbeing, or "perish" (ἀπόλλυσθαι, 156a6), and sometime
pass from nonbeing to being, or "come into being" (γίγνεσθαι, 156a5); likewise, if it is sometime one and sometime
many, it must sometime "be integrated" (συγκρίνεσθαι,
156b5) and sometime "be disintegrated" (or "dissolved,
parted," διακρίνεσθαι, 156b5). Second, he universalizes his
solution within the framework established by II. One/many
and being/not-being (in both cases, of course, in time) represent the first (unity) and the fifth (temporality) of the emergent
categories in II. To represent the intervening categories of spatiality, relatedness in identity, and relatedness in spatial extension (as we earlier titled them), Parmenides now introduces
"in motion"/"at rest" (156c1-3), "unlike"/"like" (156b6-7),
and "larger"/"smaller"/"equal" (156b7-8); and in each case he
also introduces contradictory sets of processes: "being set in
motion"/"coming to stand" (156c1-3), "dissimilation"/"assimilation" (156b6-7), "increasing"/"diminishing"/"becom-

ing equal" (156b8). In all these cases, the solution to the contradiction is the same: the One that is in time is in one state or
process at one time, and it is in the opposite state or process at
another time. Thus Parmenides seems to save the One of II
from the sort of self-negation that befell the One of I; "the
third" is savior, appropriately enough, to the second hypothesis and its One.[56]

The solution has implications, however, that are far more
troublesome than the original problem. In particular, the transition (μεταβάλλειν) from one state or process to another is
much more obscure than it first appears. Parmenides focuses
on motion and rest to bring out the difficulty (156c1-e7).
Clearly, to have the two opposite characters the One must
undergo a transition *from* (ἐκ) one *into* (εἰς) the other. This implies, in the first place, that in the transition it possesses neither
its old character (e.g. in motion) nor the new one (e.g. at rest).
For if it were still in motion, it would not be able to take on the
character, at rest. And if it were already at rest, it would have
no transition to make, no change to undergo, to begin with. In
the moment of transition, therefore, the One must be neither
in motion nor at rest. But, on the other hand, there can be no
such moment *in time*. Parmenides says flatly, "There is no time
at which a thing can be at once neither in motion nor at rest"
(156c6-7). Although he is not explicit, the reason for this is,
presumably, that rest and motion exhaust their relevant genus;
hence, anything which is subject to them must always, at any
point in time, have one or the other as its character. But this
means that the transitional moment must be out of time, nontemporal. Parmenides names this paradoxical 'moment' τὸ
ἐξαίφνης, "the instant." And he points out that the argument
that has disclosed it holds equally for all the sets of states and
processes of the One (156e7 ff.).

We have called these implications both "troublesome" and a
"pathway" to the subsurface meaning of the hypotheses. They
are troublesome, first, because they reintroduce and intensify
the contradictoriness the argument had seemed to resolve.
Parmenides shows, in sum, that to have each of its opposite
characters at different times, the One must, in a 'moment' out

of time, have neither of these characters: it may have *both* only if it also has *neither*, and it has both *in time* only if it also is *not in time*. Of course, being "neither/nor" in every regard and being "not in time" were characteristic of the One of I—the *nonbeing* One that the uncritical hearer abandoned at the close of I. The trouble Parmenides reveals may therefore also be put in terms of the relations of the hypotheses: "the third" turns out to save the One of II only by rooting it in the abandoned One of I; the One of II can be only insofar as, in the non-temporal "instant," it is the One of I!

For the uncritical hearer, there are two possible responses here. The first is to abandon II and IIa together with I: since II and IIa depend on the contradictory and absurd I, they too must be absurd. For this hearer, the hypotheses at this point lose all possible content; their value can lie only in the formal thinking they provoke. The second response, by contrast, is to rethink I in light of the dependency of II upon it. For the One of II to "be" the One of I is for the One of I to *be*; but the trans-temporality of the "instant" requires that this be *nontemporal being*; this requirement, in turn, overthrows Aristotle's unwitting identification of being as such with being in time. Thus the uncritical hearer is led to the basic discovery provoked for the critical hearer already at 141e, and more: he is introduced to nontemporal being and, through the express content of IIa, to the foundedness of temporal being upon it.

FROM what has been said, the general thrust of IIa for the critical hearer should already be largely apparent. He has already rejected Aristotle's preemption of nontemporal being; when he hears Parmenides' characterizations of the One in the "instant," above all that

> at that point[57] it neither is [temporally] nor is not [temporally], neither comes-into-being nor perishes (157a2-3),

and

> neither is one nor is many, neither is disintegrated nor is integrated (157a5-6),

he will recognize the reference to the nontemporal, non-integral form. Hence he will find in the central point of the argument a direct, albeit seminal response to his question of the relation of form to thing. In showing that the temporal, integral One must—in order to be itself—in some sense be the One that prescinds from time and integrity, Parmenides makes the thing essentially relative to the form. In some sense the thing, in its very being as a thing, depends upon the form.

To begin to specify this, we need to take up the argument as it appears on the subsurface level of meaning, that is, with its implicit reference to thing and form explicitly in mind.

Note, first, that the critical reader has earlier penetrated the apparent contradictions in II and has recognized the compatibility of the opposite characters predicated of its One. For him the problem of their contradiction must therefore be *regener*-ated, and this will require some respecification of the senses of the various characters. To announce this is the function of the qualification—"and so not one and not many," καὶ μήτε ἓν μήτε πολλά, 155e5-6—which Parmenides interjects into his opening sentence in IIa. Each character is now[58] to be taken in a sense that excludes its contrary; thus the One will be "one . . . and so . . . not many," on the one hand, and ". . . many and so not one . . . ," on the other. For the characters drawn from the emergent categories of spatiality, relatedness in identity, and relatedness in spatial extension, the only modification of sense required is that each character be predicated of the One in the same respect; thus, the One must be understood to be moving and to be at rest in the same respect, and likewise for like/unlike and greater/smaller/equal. With regard to the basic characters of unity and temporality the modification of sense is more extensive. First, Parmenides introduces the contrary to "being" as a character of the One for the first time; since "being" is temporal being, i.e. the being in time that characterizes that which "comes-into-being," (see γίγνεσθαι, 156a5), "not being" must also be temporal; it refers to the non-existence *in time* of what "perishes" or "passes away" (see ἀπόλλυσθαι, 156a6). Second, "one" and "many" must be reconstrued as exclusive rather than complementary. Since at the outset reflection is directed solely toward the One of II—the One which, as Parmenides says at 155e6, "partakes of time"— and since this One is essentially "one" *qua* composite, the burden of the reconstrual must fall on "many." The One can be "many and so not one" only by being *merely* many, a sheer non-integral plurality;[59] given this, it can be "one . . . and so . . . not many" just insofar as it is integral, a one-of-many in which its *mere* plurality is suppressed. Parmenides' formulation of the processes correlative to these states makes clear that these are just the senses of "one" and "many" he has in mind: "to become integrated" or "compounded" ($\sigma\nu\gamma\kappa\rho\acute{\iota}\nu\epsilon\sigma\theta\alpha\iota$, 156b5) is to become a one-of-many, composite, while "to become disintegrated" or "dissolved" ($\delta\iota\alpha\kappa\rho\acute{\iota}\nu\epsilon\sigma\theta\alpha\iota$, 156b5) is to be decomposed, reduced to mere plurality.

It is in light of these reconstruals and the structure of the One thing they reveal that the role of the form begins to emerge. As contradictory, the various characters of the thing must be distributed to different times in its history. Though this in itself is not problematic, it raises a critical question: if the thing is characterized at different times by mutually exclusive states and processes, how is it that it is *one* thing in the first place? If, to use Parmenides' own central example, there is a thing at rest at one time and a thing in motion at another, the natural presumption would be that these are two distinct things, not two phases in the continuous history of one self-same thing. Nothing in these characters themselves, since they are mutually exclusive, nor in their times, since these are different, entails or even suggests that they qualify the same term in its temporally continuous existence—quite the contrary. The same natural presumption holds for the other four sets of characters as well: in each case it is a question how the thing's *identity through difference* or, since this difference is expressed in time, how the *continuity* of its existence is first established. In the cases of one/many and (temporal) being/not-being, moreover, the presumption against identity is especially great. To be *merely* many is to not be *a* thing at all, nor, therefore, to *be* at all; this is the thrust of Parmenides' correlation of "being one" with "being [in time]" in his opening sentence (155e6-8, quoted above). Here the question pertains not merely to the identity and continuity of the thing during the course of its history; rather, this history itself is now only one phase within the larger compass of time, to be distinguished into the periods before, of, and after the thing's existence. In this context the question is: how is it established that it is the same one thing that at one time exists and is an integral whole but that, before and afterward, is merely many, a non-integrated plurality, and as such is either not yet or no longer existent as that integral whole at all? To violate the abstractness of the hypotheses: think, for example, of the dispersed elements that constitute a living being or, again, of its scattered, decomposing limbs after death. The question is *how*—or, to ask this in a Platonic way, by virtue of *what*—we are able to make such identifications.

The disclosure of the "instant" not only provides the basis for an answer to this question, but also, in the course of doing so, begins, at least, to open up the question of the way in which the thing depends for its being upon the form. In the "instant," we have said, the One of II (that is, the thing) *is* the One of I (that is, the form). This "is" signifies a complex structure. To bring it into focus, consider the relation of the "instant" first to the ongoing existence of the thing, then to the form that defines the thing. With regard to the ongoing existence of the thing, the presence of the "instant" may be regarded from either of two perspectives. On the one hand, the existence of the thing appears as a differentiated temporal stretch, a time line marked at every point by various changes. At the center of each of these changes we shall find the "instant" as the non-durative moment of transition from one state to its contrary. Thus regarded, there will be countless "instants" in the course of the thing's existence. On the other hand, we can also consider how the thing, by virtue of its physical-sensible nature, is constantly changing in a host of ways; since, again, change requires the "instant" as moment of transition, the "instant" will be constantly present throughout the thing's existence. Thus what first appears as the saturation of the temporal stretch by countless "instants" also appears, regarded from the second perspective, as the everpresence of the "instant."[60] With regard, second, to the form, the "instant" bears a striking affinity in kind with it. Because the "instant" is not a stretch of time, it implies neither duration nor, since this presupposes duration, age for what is situated within it. Thus the "instant" presents itself as, so to speak, a 'place' appropriate to the form's own nature. As situated in the "instant," the form has just that prescinsion from temporal determinateness that the closing arguments of I (140e-141e) established for it.

For the form to be situated in the "instant," however, is, according to our first consideration, for it to saturate the temporal stretch of the physical-sensible particular[61] or, to shift to the second view, to be everpresent through the course of its existence. Parmenides thus provides the elements for understanding how the temporal continuity of the thing is rooted in the presence of the form. If it were not for the form, there would be nothing more to the thing than a sequence of mutually exclusive characters; hence there would be no self-same thing, no "One" of the sort described in hypotheses II and IIa, in the first place. By virtue of its presence as what, to recall Parmenides' earlier phrase, "is ever the same" (τὴν αὐτὴν ἀεὶ εἶναι, 135c1) through that sequence of characters, the form provides an underlying stability and point of reference. Because the thing remains self-same in its form, it retains a basic unity through its constant change of states and, so, is first able to stand as that which underlies and has these states as its own.

To violate the abstractness of the hypotheses once again: in a host of ways, any living being—say, for example, an oak tree[62]—is constantly changing. It grows from being smaller to being larger than "the others" around it; in its seasonal turnings it becomes unlike itself; in its rhythm of summer growth and winter dormancy, it alternates between motion and rest. Because it is constantly transiting between contrary states in these and other ways, it is also constantly passing through the "instant." In the "instant," however, it has neither of any of the contraries as a character but, rather, *is* the atemporal One of hypothesis I; that is, in the "instant," the form—in this case, Oak—is present in the particular. This presence gives the particular a fund of self-identity throughout its various changes, and it is this self-identity that gives its temporal being the unity of a continuous temporal history.[63] In the same way, moreover, the form even accounts for the thing's identity beyond its existence, through the transitions pertaining to its being-in-time ("temporality") and "unity." It is the unchanging form, itself indifferent to these transitions, by virtue of which a thing that has perished and is now a mere plurality may be identified as the same one thing that once existed and was an integral whole. Even after the oak has perished and begun to decompose, to lapse, so to speak, back to earth, nonetheless its form, Oak, lets us grasp it in its nonbeing and disintegrity, lets us, that is, recognize and remember it as an oak that once was but now no longer is.

If this line of interpretation is well taken, then IIa stands as a crucial complement to I–II. The basic point of I–II is the form's transcendence of the spatio-temporal order of things. IIa, in turn, shows how the form is immanent: the form is that in the thing which, situated in the "instant" and unchanging through the thing's change of states, lets it be one self-same thing in the first place. In a striking reversal of one of Socrates' basic errors, it is now clear that transcendence and immanence are not contradictory; quite the contrary, transcendence is the necessary precondition for immanence. Earlier we noted that it was Socrates' treatment of the form as a thing that required him, in order to preserve its status as $\kappa\alpha\theta'\alpha\dot{\upsilon}\tau\dot{o}$ ("in and for itself"), to deny its presence $\dot{\epsilon}\nu$ $\dot{\eta}\mu\hat{\iota}\nu$ ("in our domain"). (See 133c3-6, discussed in II.B.3.) Now to reverse this, once the form is grasped as transcending thinghood itself, nothing prevents it from being present in things. The key is the way the notion of the "instant" allows us to think the intimate relation of atemporal form and temporal thing. For the form not to be-in-time but, rather, to be timeless—the subsurface point of the closing arguments in I (140e-141e)—is not for it to exist in a realm outside time, a separate world. To think this would be to repeat Socrates' mistake, for such a realm, both as "outside" and as a "realm," would be a second spatio-temporal order fashioned in the image of ours. Instead, as situated in the "instant," the form exists at the very core, so to speak, of that which is in time—not, however, as subject to but, rather, as foundational for the temporality of the latter. As in and for itself indifferent to the determinations of time, the form is that unchanging presence that lets the thing have its temporal continuity—and, so, be the thing that it is—in the first place. Thus conceived, the transcendence of the form makes possible its immanence: because it is radically different in its nature from things, it is fit to function as the immanent basis for them. [64]

THUS understood, hypotheses I-IIa accomplish, in their essentials, the central project of the *Parmenides*: the "conversion" of the soul from its initial, perceptually oriented understanding of the forms on the model of things to a conceptually articulate understanding of forms in their constitutive function for things. I and II have made the distinction in kind between forms and things that Socrates failed to achieve. And IIa has indicated how the form, precisely as different in kind, can be the basis for the continuity and, so, the being of the thing as *a* thing in time. Thus Socrates' theory of forms is, in principle, "saved." At the same time, however, this accomplishment brings with it the need for yet another beginning. The reflections and recognitions by which thinking first reaches the level of the forms are not sufficient to keep it there; on the contrary, in overcoming one set of obscurities, largely the consequences of the limits of δόξα, they disclose another set, more intrinsic to the forms themselves. Identifying these deeper obscurities and beginning the work of penetrating them is, as we shall see, the underlying task of hypotheses III-VIII. [65]

CHAPTER V

Hypotheses III–VIII: The Explication of I–IIa (157b-166b)

THE ontological relativization in IIa of the One of hypothesis II (the thing) to the One of hypothesis I (the form) raises key questions about the founding relation itself and about each of its terms, form and thing. First, in exposing the temporal sense in which the thing, self-same through different stages, is one *qua* continuous, Parmenides' analysis stops short of accounting for the deepest level of its unity; to expose the way in which the thing retains its specific identity through the gain (i.e. "integration") and loss (i.e. "disintegration") of composite unity is not yet to disclose just how it has that composite unity in the first place. For the hearer who reflects on this, it will be provocative. In the argumentation of hypothesis II, composite unity was the first character established for the thing, and all the other characters attributed to the thing directly or indirectly depend upon it. If, as IIa has begun to show, the form is the basis for the thing, must it not somehow give rise to the basic and fundamental character of the thing? Thus the hearer will ask for more radical exploration of the constitutive relation first exposed in IIa. Is the form responsible not only for the temporal continuity of the composite thing but also for its composite unity as such, its being as a whole of parts, a one "out of" many, in the first place? Second, as a result of the negative character of I, the ontological relativization in IIa has a paradoxical look to it: what both "is" and is the referent of consciousness in all its modes, namely, the One of II, is made dependent upon what "is not" and is not intelligible in any way, namely, the One of I. Of course, the paradox dissolves when the specificity of the negations in I is understood: the One *qua* form is denied only the sorts of being and intelligibility proper to the One *qua* thing. Nevertheless, nothing has been said explicitly of the sorts of being and intelligibility which, as proper to forms, are not denied. What, then, is the kind or sense of being proper to forms? And just how are they, as simple and unique, properly intelligible? Finally, the positive character of II also gives the relativization in IIa an odd look. In II, "being" in the only sense so far entertained, namely, being in time, was asserted of the One (see 151e-152a); likewise, the One was said to be intelligible in every possible way (see 155d). Once he grasps the specificity of the being and intelligibility which, proper to forms, differ from and are prior to the being and intelligibility of things, the critical hearer will want to reevaluate the latter. That is, he will want to know: what is the status or specificity of the being and intelligibility of things, grasped in light of their dependence on and difference from the (now properly understood) forms?

On the surface, hypotheses III–VIII simply execute the last three of the four phases of inquiry originally projected by Parmenides at 136ab. He first concludes the exploration of the consequences of there *being* a One by turning, in III–IV, to "the others" (with respect both to themselves and to the One); then he takes up the consequences of there *not being* a One, first, in V–VI, for this One (with respect both to itself and to "the others") and second, in VII–VIII, for "the others" (with respect both to themselves and to the One). At the subsurface level, however, Parmenides continues to present a rich philosophical content in III–VIII. For the hearer who interprets their formal subjects, "the One" and "the others," in accord with the several senses of these in I–IIa, each pair of hypotheses will come to light as discussion of one of the nexus of basic issues just noted. III–IV explore the participatory relation of form and things; V–VI address the intelligibility and being of forms; and VII–VIII review the status of things. Moreover, the direct contradictions between the members of each pair continue to serve a constructive, if somewhat different, function in the subsurface argument. As we shall see, in each pair the first of the two hypotheses works out some set of consequences implicit in the ontological distinction and relativization in I–IIa; the second then performs a *reductio*, showing that a rejection of the distinction and relativization yields absurd, unacceptable consequences. Thus the pairings serve two purposes at once: Parmenides both continues the "conversion," explicating the theory of forms at a new depth, and he shows—by displaying the predicament of philosophy without the theory—the necessity of accepting it.

A. Participation: πλῆθος and πέρας (III–IV)

1. The One and "the Others"

From the premise that "a One *is*," Parmenides derives directly contradictory consequences for "the others" in III (157b-159b) and IV (159b-160b). In III he asserts a relation of "participation" between "the others" and "the One"; on the basis of this relation he is able to argue that "the others" are many wholes of parts and "suffer all the opposite characters" (159a6-7) studied in II. In IV, by contrast, he gives an argument that "the others" must be "separate" from "the One" and as such "deprived [of it] in every way" (159e1); and on the basis of this privation,[1] he is able to deny all of the various "characters," even including unity, to "the others."

To the hearer attuned to the form-thing distinction in I–IIa, the reference of "the One" and "the others" will be transparent. First, "the One" is described both in III, through a contrast with "the others" (157c), and explicitly in IV (159c) as being without parts; and in another contrast in III, it is also denied plurality (158ab).[2] Moreover, there is a striking passage in the middle of III in which Parmenides, attempting to reveal the nature of "the others" prior to their "participation" *in the One*, discloses "the nature different *from the form*" (τὴν ἐτέραν φύσιν τοῦ εἴδους, 158c6)![3] Thus the hearer is confirmed in interpreting "the One" throughout III and IV as the simple and unique One of I and (if it should not be clear already) in interpreting this latter as the form. This suggests, in turn, that "the others" refers to the physical-sensible, the things which, in accord with the distinction expressed by I–II, are "other"[4] than the forms. Parmenides has already used τὰ ἄλλα with this reference repeatedly in his elenchus of Socrates (see 130e6, 131e4, 132a6, 132c9, 133a5, also 132d2). But the real confirmation comes from the predications made in the course of III: "the others" are shown as wholes of parts (157c), as many in number (158b), and as subject to precisely the contrary characters of the One of II, that is, of the physical-sensible thing.

That these same characters are denied to "the others" in IV is no objection to this interpretation, for the basis of the denials is the more fundamental denial of participation. The issue in III–IV is the foundedness of things in forms, which was first disclosed in IIa; now, however, it is to be explored at a new depth. Here the focus is not temporal unity or continuity but, rather, the most basic characters of the thing, the composite structure and, as well, the plurality that distinguish it as a physical-sensible thing in the most elemental sense. Is the form—or the thing's participation in the form—responsible even for these? III and IV fit together as positive and negative demonstrations of the same point: whereas III shows that and how the form and participation do found the thing at this ultimate level, IV shows that without participation there can be no thing in any sense.

THIS interpretation of the reference of "the One" and "the others" in III–IV lets us resolve a small puzzle we noted earlier (p. 80): when Parmenides gives the first of his two general synoptic statements at 160b2-3, right after hypothesis IV, he takes only the One, not "the others," as a subject; and this gives the sentence the appearance of addressing only I–II, not III–IV. He says,

> Thus if there is a One, the One both is everything [or, all characters (πάντα)] and not even one, alike in relation to itself and to the others (160b2-3).

Once we recognize, however, that "the others" in III and IV refers to the One of II, the remark takes on a precise double meaning, and the difficulty disappears. That "the One . . . is all characters" refers at once to the One of II and to "the others" of III; and that "the One . . . is not even one" refers at once to the One of I and—since they are denied all of the various characters, even including unity—to "the others" of IV.

2. That and How the Thing Participates (III)

Hypothesis III has a complex inner organization. Parmenides begins with a deductive argument that establishes the whole-part structure and the plurality of "the others" (things) as consequences of their "participation" ($\mu\acute{\varepsilon}\theta\varepsilon\xi\iota\varsigma$) in the One (the form) (157b-158b). Here he is thinking through the responsibility of the form for the fundamental characters of the thing. It appears, however, that he finds the deductive mode an obstacle; since it treats as given what is only first constituted through the participatory relation, it fails to expose the inner working or constitutive action, so to speak, of participation. This seems to be why he shifts into a more exploratory mode at 158b-d and attempts a sort of *reduction*[5] of the composite thing back to its ultimate, constitutive elements and their relation. It is here that the hearer is given the deepest—albeit compact and unelaborated—account of the basis of part-whole structure. Parmenides then concludes with a resumption of the deductive argument (158e-159b); it is here that he attributes to "the others" "all the opposite characters" studied in II, though his focus (for reasons we shall consider later) is on likeness/unlikeness. Our exposition of III will take up each of these subphases in turn.

a. The Deductive Characterization of the Thing

The basic line of reasoning in 157b-158b is straightforward; it consists of two basic steps, each of which may be further analyzed. (1) Parmenides begins with a terse, elliptically stated elimination argument to show that "the others" must "participate" in the One (157bc). (i) On the one hand, they cannot simply "be" (ἐστι, 157b9) the One, for this would contradict their status as "others" (ἄλλα) than it (157bc). (ii) But neither, Parmenides says, can they be "completely deprived" (στέρε-ταί γε παντάπασι) of it (157c). (At this point he gives no explicit argument to support this second denial; what is left out here, however, is supplied later by IV, which considers the state of "the others" precisely as "in every way deprived" [πανταχῇ στέρεται, 159e1] of the One. There Parmenides will show that if "the others" are thus deprived, they will have no characters at all. Yet this, both in itself and in light of II, is absurd. Thus, as we shall see more fully in the next section, IV gives a basis for rejecting the possibility of utter deprivation.) (iii) All that remains as a possible relation is the intermediate between identity and utter privation: Parmenides concludes that "the others" "participate in some way" (μετέχει πῃ, 157c2) in the One. (2) But "in what way (πῇ)?" Aristotle asks. Parmenides' second step is to show how "the others" can have or share in, yet still differ from, the One (157c-158b). The argument has two parts. (i) First he ascribes whole-part structure to "the others" (157c-158a). (a) By "having parts" (μόρια ἔχοντα, 157c3) "the others" can differ from the One, which alone is "completely one" (παντελῶς . . . ἕν, 157c4), that is, a simple unity (157c). (b) Yet parts belong not to a "many" (πολλῶν) but to a unified and intelligible whole (157c-e). (c) Thus "the others," if they have parts, will each[6] be a whole and in this approximative sense share in the One: each will be a "one consisting of many [parts]" (ἓν ἐκ πολλῶν, 157c6). (d) What is more, "the same reasoning" (ὁ αὐτὸς λόγος, 157c6) applies to each part: since it by itself is "one" yet must differ from the One, it too must be composite[7] (157e-158a). (ii) Parmenides next turns to plurality in number (158ab). (a) As sharing in the One, "the others" will differ from it, that is, will not be one (158ab). (b) But if they were neither one nor more than one, they would "be nothing" (οὐδὲν ἂν εἴη, 158b4), which is obviously impossible. (c) Thus "the others" must be many in number (πολλά). As presented, the argument seems clearly elliptical. In IV Parmenides will observe that what is "in no way one" (οὐδαμῇ . . . ἓν, 159d3) cannot be many either: for to be many is to be many ones. But if this is so, then step (c) must implicitly assert singularity as well as plurality of "the others": in a word, they are many singulars. And step (a), in turn, must be interpreted to deny not oneness *qua* singularity but only oneness *qua* uniqueness to "the others." Of course, since uniqueness is a sense of "one" proper only to the One (the form), this restriction is pointedly appropriate. Once this interpretation has been made, moreover, (ii) stands in striking analogy to (i). Plurality is to the uniqueness of the One just what "having parts" is to its simple unity: to be many ones is to approximate the uniqueness of the form in just the same way that being a whole of parts is to approximate its simplicity. Further, precisely as ways of approximation, these express very well the status of "participation," asserted by (1), as an intermediate between identity and complete deprivation.

EARLIER, in the course of analyzing one of Parmenides' puzzles in II regarding the thing's self-containment (150e-151a), we came to the question of the difference between the thing *qua* whole and the thing *qua* all of its parts. Our analysis showed that, regarded merely as physical-sensible quantities, the two are equivalent; this suggested that the difference must lie in some nonphysical factor. Our interpretation of the subsurface meaning of IIa has now suggested what this factor might be: the One of I, or the thing's defining form. Only in III, however, does Parmenides make this explicit and so address the questions he provoked at 150e-151a. The key passage (though its content is not developed until the second part of III) is a short stretch of subordinate argumentation at 157c8-e2.

The argument is intended to establish the point, marked as (2)(i)(b) in the preceding analysis, that parts belong not to a "many" but to a whole. Parmenides proceeds in two steps. First he shows why a part cannot properly be said to be part of a "many" in the sense of a sum of parts; then he shows what makes a whole different from such a sum. His argument for the first step is as follows: what is a part of many will be, since it is itself amongst these and since it is a part of "all" of them (see εἴπερ καὶ πάντων, 157d2), a part both of itself (d1) and "of each one of the others" (d2); yet to be part of itself is "impossible" (d2), and an item-by-item examination of each of the others will only show—since, presumably, they are *other*—that it is part of none of them; thus the part will be part of none of the "many," a consequence that renders "impossible" (d7) the very characterization of it as a "part" (d6-7) in the first place.[8] From this Parmenides concludes and proposes that

> the part, then, is part not of the many or all [sc. of the parts]; rather it is [part] of a certain unitary character, that is, of a definite one (μιᾶς τινὸς ἰδέας καὶ ἑνός τινος) which, as a complete one composed of all (ἐξ ἁπάντων), we call a "whole"—it is of this that the part would be part (157d8-e2).

The grammar here is somewhat ambiguous,[9] but the basic point seems clear enough: it is the presence of μία τις ἰδέα, a unitary character or form, that lets "all" stand not merely as a "many" (πολλά) but as a "whole and one" (157e3). The key but puzzling term is τέλειον, which we have translated as "complete" (e1). What is τέλειον is perfect, finished, in need of nothing further. The ἰδέα or form, then, in some sense perfects or finishes the "many," transforming it from a mere aggregate to a self-sufficient one; or, to put this in terms of the part-whole relation, it turns the "many" into a whole to which each one of them somehow properly belongs as a part.

As just noted, however, it is only in the following passage, the "reduction," that Parmenides focuses these suggestions.

b. The Reduction to πλῆθος and πέρας

In several respects Parmenides' argument in 157b-158b is very satisfying. The dependence of the One of II upon the One of I, first shown in terms of temporality in IIa, is now revealed within the more basic category of unity. Moreover, he has made the basic characters of the thing, whole-part structure and singularity/plurality, consequences of its participatory relation to the form; thus what he earlier derived from a merely conceptual analysis of the notion ἕν ὄν, a "One being," he has now shown in its ontological basis. In another respect, however, the argument is not satisfying: while it is clear what follows from "participation," the conception itself is still opaque. Speaking crudely, how does "participation" work? Granted that it designates the constitutive role of the form, just what does the form do and—if to anything—to what? It is apparently in order to open up the conception that Parmenides drops his deductive manner of argument and, at 158b ff., takes up a more exploratory, probing posture.

The basic aim of Parmenides' reduction is to recover the constitutive elements of the thing. He asks Aristotle to focus on the moment, as it were (see τότε, ὅτε μεταλαμβάνει, 158b9), of participation and to consider what "the others" are "just in themselves" (αὐτά γε, 158b7); thus he is able to separate out, if only in conceptual abstraction (τῇ διανοίᾳ, 158c2), that element or "nature" in the participant thing which is "different from the form" (τὴν ἑτέραν φύσιν τοῦ εἴδους, 158c6). And bringing this "nature" to mind, in turn, enables him also to isolate or set in relief the counter-character of the form: to see what the thing would be without its form is also, considered conversely, to see what the form "provides" (παρέσχε, 158d5), or how it functions, in first giving rise to the 'formed' thing. This is an ingenious exploratory reflection,[10] and its results here are both basic and obscure. Keying from step (b) in (2)(ii) above, that "the others" are "more than one" (πλείω ἑνός, 158b3, b5), Parmenides suggests that "just in themselves" they must be πλήθει ἄπειρα, "without limit in quantity" (158b6), or, more directly, πλήθη, "quantities" or "multitudes" (158c1). Thus, both each of "the others" and also each of its parts would be, "just in itself," a πλῆθος, "quantity" or "multitude" (158c4), and will have the character of ἀπειρία, "lack of limit" (158d6). It is the form, in turn, that "provides" πέρας, "limit" (158d1-2, d5), to each such πλῆθος.

These notions, πλῆθος and πέρας, are hardly self-explaining. Each carries a rich nexus of connotations and—especially in the case of πλῆθος—close associations from other parts of the dialogue.

Consider first Parmenides' reduction back from the participant thing to its 'pre'-participatory "different nature." What does it mean for the thing to be, "just in itself," $\pi\lambda\tilde{\eta}\theta\sigma\varsigma$? Parmenides' phrase $\pi\lambda\dot{\eta}\theta\epsilon\iota$ $\ddot{\alpha}\pi\epsilon\iota\rho\alpha$ ("without limit in quantity") at 158b6, repeated as $\ddot{\alpha}\pi\epsilon\iota\rho\sigma\nu$ . . . $\pi\lambda\dot{\eta}\theta\epsilon\iota$ at c6-7, seems to echo if not reiterate the key expression, $\ddot{\alpha}\pi\epsilon\iota\rho\alpha$ $\tau\dot{\sigma}$ $\pi\lambda\tilde{\eta}\theta\sigma\varsigma$, used three times earlier in the dialogue: meaning "infinitely many," "infinite in number," that expression was applied to the plurality that each form suffers according to the regress argument, at 131b1-2, to the plurality internal to each thing through its infinitely many parts, at 143a2, and to the plurality of things as many singulars, at 145e3-5. But closely considered, the echo is misleading. These senses all presuppose a one, a countable unit—whether we think of the one thing as a singular or of each one of its parts, the plurality ($\tau\dot{\sigma}$ $\pi\lambda\tilde{\eta}\theta\sigma\varsigma$) they describe is a plurality of ones. The "other" or participant thing here in III, by contrast, is thought apart from its participation; and since, as we have traced in section a above, it has its oneness—in whole, in part, and in number—only as a consequence of its participation, that means that it is thought apart from its oneness. As such, it can be only a *mere* many, a many to be thought not as a number of singulars but, on the contrary, as what lacks any intrinsic enumerability. The real reference of Parmenides' term $\pi\lambda\tilde{\eta}\theta\sigma\varsigma$ is therefore not that notion of plurality which is interdependent with singularity (the notion dominant in II, 142d-145a, and in III, 157b-158b) but, rather, the barely effable notion, first proposed indirectly in IIa, of a sheer nonintegral plurality. Parmenides now brings this notion up to the surface for consideration. How, then, is it to be understood? To begin with, in its general meaning, quantity, the Greek term $\pi\lambda\tilde{\eta}\theta\sigma\varsigma$ connotes both multitude and magnitude (bulk, extent). That Parmenides intends to call both to mind becomes evident when he focuses on the inner constitution of the "different nature," the $\pi\lambda\tilde{\eta}\theta\sigma\varsigma$, at 158c2-4. He says,

> Should we want to take away from such [sc. $\pi\lambda\dot{\eta}\theta\eta$, "manies"], in thought, the smallest portion ($\dot{\sigma}\lambda\dot{\iota}\gamma\iota\sigma\tau\sigma\nu$) we can, wouldn't that amount too, since it would not partake of the One, necessarily be a many ($\pi\lambda\tilde{\eta}\theta\sigma\varsigma$) and not one?

The direct point of this, of course, is to deny that the "manies" are composed of definite ones or units as parts. The notion it conveys is that of a mass without internal structure or articulation. The aspect of multitude occurs in the closing contrast: each portion, no matter how small, will be many rather than one. The aspect of magnitude or extent, in turn, is suggested by the thought-operation Parmenides proposes: to "take away" (ἀφελεῖν) a "smallest portion"[11] presupposes that we have something of volume to work with, a certain bulk that stands in contrast to the portion taken away as large to small.[12] At the same time, all of this needs to be qualified in an important way. When we think of a mass or bulk, it is hard not to think (or even picture) a definite quantum; but this would be a mistake here and mislead us. Parmenides' characterizations, ἄπειρον πλήθει and ἀπειρία ("without limit in quantity" and "lack of limit"), make clear that the πλῆθος is to be thought as indeterminate or indefinite both in number and magnitude. Really, this is already indicated by the passage just quoted. What has no minimal one or unit cannot be counted, except by reference to altogether external standards of measure; although as many "and not one"[13] it invites us to apply the notion of plurality, it in itself has no definite number. Likewise, nothing warrants our thinking the πλῆθος as having some definite volume or extent. That the portion taken away is "smallest" reflects only our limits (cf. "the smallest portion *we can [take away]*," (158c3); and that the mass from which it is taken stands to it as large to small is only a relative character. In and of itself, it has no definite magnitude. These observations, in turn, bring another along with them: since every existent magnitude or bulk is determinate (if only at each point in time), the πλῆθος Parmenides means to evoke is not something that, by itself at least, exists. Rather this "nature" is a component term; arrived at by dianoetic abstraction (cf. "in thought," 158c2), it exists only *with* that apart from which it is now being thought, the One in which it partakes. Now, this set of characters—lack of inner structure, indeterminate multitude and magnitude, and lack of independent existence—points clearly to the identity of the "nature" Parmenides seeks: the sheerly material element or medium of things, conceived in its purity as apart from and unspecified by any intelligible structure (any One or form). Having come this far, however, the critical hearer will want to go one step further. Earlier, in presenting his arguments regarding things (the One of II) and size, Parmenides established that having the various features of size—largeness and smallness in magnitude and multitude—depends on participation in the sizeless forms, the great and the small. This point has definite implications for the present passage. Even as the "nature different from the form," the πλῆθος will not be self-subsistent; rather, it will be that in a thing which *is* through partaking of the great and the small. The thing itself, in turn, is thus disclosed as the result of a combination of two distinct participations, that in the great and the small and that in the One. The first of these provides it its physical element, its aspect, albeit in itself indeterminate, of size. What, in turn, does the second provide?

Parmenides comes to this, the second major revelation of the reduction, at 158c7-d6; the One or form, he suggests, gives πέρας to the πλῆθος. He says:

—And further, when each one part first[14] becomes a part, from the beginning (ἤδη) they have πέρας in relation to one another and in relation to the whole, and the whole [has πέρας] in relation to the parts.
—Quite so.
—For the others than the One, then, the consequence of their communing (κοινωνησάντων) with the One is, it seems, that something different arises within them, which gives them πέρας in relation to one another; the nature they have by themselves (καθ' ἑαυτὰ) gives them, by contrast, a lack of πέρας (ἀπειρίαν).

The concrete sense of πέρας is boundary. A boundary, in turn, is the property line which first delimits—and so makes definite, determinate—an otherwise indefinite terrain; hence the conceptual sense of πέρας is limit, and it carries the connotation of definiteness. Note, further, that Parmenides speaks of "πέρας in relation to . . ." (πέρας πρὸς . . .). A boundary, of course, defines the terrain on both sides, differentiating an area into definite regions and relating these to one another within that area as a whole. Or, considering it from the point of view of the particular regions, each is not only bounded-off, made a distinct entity for the first time; each is also set into relation, as the distinct entity it is, with the other region for the first time. If we bear all this in mind, Parmenides' terse remarks become clearer. To begin with, in his closing observation that "the nature which the others have by themselves gives them a lack of $\pi\epsilon\rho\alpha\varsigma$," he is referring to their character as $\pi\lambda\tilde{\eta}\theta\sigma\varsigma$, "mere many." As such, each is indefinite, both in extent and number. Moreover, each lacks any definite inner structure: no portion of the $\pi\lambda\tilde{\eta}\theta\sigma\varsigma$ has any more inner unity than the entirety. Hence there is no sense in which there could be distinct and interrelated parts composing a definite whole. Rather, all this is first made possible by the "communing" of the $\pi\lambda\tilde{\eta}\theta\sigma\varsigma$ "with the One." Just how a bulk or extent is structured, how it is articulated into parts, depends upon just *what* it is the bulk or extent of. Conversely, this *what*—the essential or defining character of a thing—calls for a certain definite arrangement of material parts. The "something different" ($\tilde{\epsilon}\tau\epsilon\rho\acute{o}\nu \tau\iota$) that "arises within" a thing from its "communing" or partaking of the One (the form) is just such a *what*. The form in its immanence, it differs in kind from the many items, the physical parts, that make up the thing; yet these are what they are, bearing the relations to one another that they do, in direct response to its presence. Only thus does the indefinite $\pi\lambda\tilde{\eta}\theta\sigma\varsigma$ become a "complete" or "finished" thing. $\Pi\epsilon\rho\alpha\varsigma$ as limit is in play here in all the several senses Parmenides goes through at 158c7-d6. Most obviously, the form requires a distinction of the $\pi\lambda\tilde{\eta}\theta\sigma\varsigma$ into various parts in a determinate organization; thus the parts are bounded-off or have $\pi\epsilon\rho\alpha\varsigma$ "in relation to one another" (158d1-2). Every composite thing is, as such, a network of internal boundaries that define parts and so set them into determinate relations with each other, always in accord with the essential form. Such relations between parts, second, implicate the whole. On the one hand, to be this particular part in each case means to have a definite and delimited place within the whole, hence to have πέρας "in relation to the whole" (d2). On the other hand, the whole is itself delimited by the parts: their boundaries toward one another define its physical structure, shape, and size completely; hence the whole has πέρας "in relation to the parts" (d2). Finally, just this latter delimitation of the whole by its parts implies a πέρας that relates the thing as such outside itself toward other things: as a definite order of parts, the whole is distinguished or bounded-off from other such wholes and, so, set into various possible relations with them; in this way "the others," many distinct composite things, each have πέρας "in relation to one another" (d5).

Thus Parmenides addresses the question left hanging in his deductive argumentation in section a, above; and in doing so, he goes a considerable distance in explicating the founding relation of form and thing he first exposed on the level of temporality in IIa. The deed of the form is to exact a definite distinction and arrangement of parts; and that to which it does this is the πλῆθος, the otherwise indefinite material element of things. In this way the form is responsible for the whole-part structure, as such, of the thing.[15]

IF ONLY in passing, it is important to underscore a certain convergence—and a puzzle it raises—between points of subsurface meaning in II and in Parmenides' reduction in III. In treating the forms of size at 149d-151b in II, Parmenides stressed the thing's dependence upon them: if the thing is to have size, this can only be through its participation in the forms, the great and the small. The reduction, in turn, suggests a certain qualified dependence of the great and the small on the One (the thing's defining form): if size is to have being in space and time, it requires the defining form; as we just noted in a somewhat different context, every existent magnitude or bulk is determinate. If we draw these points together, they suggest that the One, at least in its function as defining the thing, and the great and the small, at least in their function as the basis of size in things, must have some collaborative connection, some interrelation. In light of hypothesis I, however, this is puzzling; there Parmenides apparently denies to the One both the basic

relational characters (139b-e) and the capacity to stand in any
sort of relation (142a). We shall return to this issue later, for
Parmenides brings us back to it in hypothesis V.

c. The Unlikeness of the Self-same

In the final passage in hypothesis III, 158e-159b, Parmenides
resumes the deductive manner and argues that "the others" are
both like and unlike themselves and one another (158e1-
159a6), same and different from one another (a6), in motion
and at rest (a7), and have "all the opposite characters" (a7). For
all but the first of these attributions he gives no argument.
They offer "no difficulty" (οὐ χαλεπῶς, a8) as he says; in fact,
since "the others" of III are each a composite one among many
in just the manner of the One of II, the arguments for these attributions have already been given in the course of II.

But this being so, why the disproportionately lengthy, altogether new argument for likeness and unlikeness? In fact,
Parmenides responds to a key question he earlier left hanging.
By his odd arguments for likeness and unlikeness at 147c-148c,
Parmenides established the possibility in principle that "what
are not one" (τὰ μὴ ἕν), understood as lacking wholeness and
number, be both radically "unlike" and yet the "same" as (that
is, coincident or integral with) the One thing. But this raised
the question: what could "what are not one," understood this
way, actually be? Now, in hypothesis III, Parmenides takes as
his point of departure the discovery that "the others" are "both
limited and without limit" (πεπερασμένα τε . . . καὶ ἄπειρα,
158e5-6) in character. If "the others" are considered with regard to only one of these characters, then they are like themselves and one another. But if they are considered with regard
to both characters at once, then, since these characters are "opposites to each other" (158e6), each of "the others" emerges as
unlike itself and (if considered in one character and compared
to any "other" considered in the other character) unlike one
another. Thus he exposes, *within* each self-"same" One of "the
others," just that radical "unlikeness" which his argument at
147c-148c first suggested, and he in effect identifies "what are
not one" as the unenumerable, indefinite πλῆθος. As his pre-

ceding reduction brought out and he now underscores, each of "the others" is at once a One composite thing and this indefinite πλῆθος. The mediating factor, that which, by integrating the πλῆθος, lets it be the "same" as the thing and so harmonizes the "unlikes," is the defining form.[16]

3. The Necessity of Participation
(IV)

Hypothesis III reveals that and how, given their participation in forms, things have their fundamental characters as things; or repeating the stronger language used earlier, it shows the necessity, given participation, of the fundamental characters of things. There is still the question, however, whether participation is itself necessary. Showing this necessity is the main subsurface function of IV. Parmenides' approach is indirect, to say the least: first (159b-c) he gives an argument against participation; then (159c-160b) he derives the consequences of nonparticipation for "the others," consequences directly antithetical to those of participation in III. Nonetheless, for the hearer who has recognized Parmenides' persistent ironic mimicry of δόξα earlier in the dialogue, his real point and strategy in IV are clearly signaled.

To begin with, the opening argument is pointedly flawed; Parmenides rehearses several of Socrates' most basic earlier errors. In the first step of the argument, for example, he concludes that the One and "the others" must be "separate" (χωρίς, 159b6) since, given that nothing is omitted or not included by the disjunction the One/"the others," there can be no third entity "in which" (ἐν ᾧ) they could both be (159b6-c4). This not only treats the One (form)[17] and "the others" (things) as entities on par, but by taking the togetherness of two things in a common place as the proper alternative, it also reduces "separateness" and, so, the One (form) itself to spatial significance. Strikingly, Parmenides next denies that "the truly one" (τὸ ὡς ἀληθῶς ἕν, 159c5) can have parts. But he is only intensifying the irony: he goes on to conclude that the One cannot be "in the others" (ἐν τοῖς ἄλλοις, 159c6) either as a whole—for it has been shown to be "separate"—or in part—for it has no parts (159c5-7). Beyond its reiteration of the errors just noted, this mode of argument also presupposes that the One is in principle subject to the categories of whole and part, just what the denial of parts should tell against. To the hearer still under the sway of δόξα, the hearer for whom the divisible physical-sensible thing is the paradigmatic being, there may be nothing objectionable here. But to the critical hearer, the argument is through and through unacceptable: in its repetition of Socrates' earlier materialization of form and participation, it shows only that both are inconceivable within the framework of δόξα.

On the other hand, the argument has an underlying positive function. By serving as a pretext for denying participation, it gives Parmenides the occasion to conceive the consequences if things "are utterly deprived of the One" (159e1). These are disastrous and absurd. Since, as the reduction in III has shown, a thing gets its unity from its defining form, "the others" would lack unity in every sense (159d3-4). This entails also that they will not be many—not, at least, insofar as each of a many must be one (159d4-7).[18] To lack unity and plurality, in turn, is to lack enumerability or number (159d7-e1). And this last denial rules out the possibility that "the others" have any discrete characters at all, not like/unlike (159e2-160a3), same/different, moving/resting, coming-into-being/perishing, greater/lesser/equal, or "any other such characters"; for in every case, to have this or those discrete characters is to be enumerable, to be in some number of ways (160a4-6). These conclusions are disastrous in the sense that they demolish the physical-sensible things of ordinary experience. This, in turn, is absurd: were there not such things and such experience, there would be no discussion of forms—indeed, no discussion at all!—in the first place.

Parmenides does not make any such judgments explicitly. Maintaining the pedagogical detachment he has assumed from his opening speech, he leaves the surface meaning of the hypothesis intact. For the critical hearer, however, IV contains the elements of a cogent *reductio*; and construed that way, it serves to ground and confirm the basic points of III. In short, except as being first constituted through participation in (or by the immanent presence of) immaterial forms, physical-sensible things would be impossible; and far from being impossible, such things are everywhere at hand; there *must*, therefore, be such participation in such forms.

B. The Form: Intelligibility, Communion, Being (V–VI)

1. "The One Which Is Not"

In hypotheses V–VIII Parmenides turns to the consideration of the nonbeing of the One: V–VI work out the consequences of this for the One itself, while VII–VIII (to be discussed separately in C, below) work out the consequences for "the others." Thus Parmenides obeys his own methodological counsel, expressed at 135e-136a: to be "thoroughly exercised," he told Socrates, one must investigate the implications of the nonbeing as well as of the being of the chosen subject. Especially for the youth whose passion for philosophy is not yet freed of φιλονικία, the contentiousness and competitive zeal of the advocate, there is an important lesson here: genuine inquiry must investigate all sides of an issue, not merely back up one point of view against another. As we observed earlier, this one-sidedness was a mutual failing of the young Zeno and of his eristic anti-Eleatic opponents. It is also a danger for Socrates; as the earlier sequence of his aggressive challenge to Zeno and his helplessness before Parmenides exposed, his affirmation of the forms has not yet been tempered by genuinely open and general reflection.[19] By requiring one to investigate the not being as well as the being of the subject at hand, Parmenides' method serves to check one-sidedness and to free the aspiring thinker from the sorts of blindness—to his own position as well as to the possible alternatives to it—that this can produce.

Beyond this, however, Parmenides has even more pressing subsurface motives for his turn to "the One which is not" (τὸ μὴ ὂν ἕν) in V–VI. As we have seen, IIa makes the many composite Ones of II (things) depend for their temporal continuity upon the One of I (the form); and III–IV serve to deepen this dependence by tracing it back to the prior level of the thing's composite unity as such. If we look back to I, however, this seems paradoxical at the very least: there the One was apparently denied any sort of relation (see especially 139b-e, 142a), being (141e), and knowability (142a). The critical hearer, of course, will have penetrated this paradox to a significant degree. Provoked by Parmenides' irony, this hearer will have already recognized the hidden specificity of the negations: what is denied the One is not (to take the most basic character) being as such but only that sense of being—namely, being in time, temporally determinate being—which is proper to things. Nonetheless, this recognition is only a first step. It depends for its significance on the presumption that there is another sense of being that is not denied, a sense that is proper to forms. But *that* there is—and if so, *what* it is—remains to be shown. The same point holds for relation and knowledge. That the One (the form) lacks those relations and that intelligibility proper to things does not, in and of itself, imply that it has some other sense or sort of these; this remains to be established. Until this second step is taken, the value of the first must be problematic and the ontological relativization must stand as incomplete.

In turning to "the One which is not" in V (160b-163b) and VI (163b-164b), Parmenides is really returning to the One of I (the form). The pivotal question for V and VI is whether there is a distinction in the sense of being, such that "the One that is not" may nonetheless, in some other sense, also *be*. And associated with this are similar distinctions between senses or sorts of intelligibility and of relation. Thus V and VI respond pointedly to the issues left hanging in I; what is more, between them they exhaust the basic possible alternatives. In direct contradiction, V argues *for* such distinctions, thus offering an account (compact and introductory, to be sure) of the positive characters of the One (the form), while VI, focusing on being, denies any such distinction in sense and thus rejects any such One altogether. In this way V and VI relate as a pair analogously as did III and IV: the first works out the inner implications of the ontological relativization while the second reveals the consequences of denying it.

2. The Characters Proper to the Form (V)[20]

As we shall see, the subsurface argument in V is compact and carefully structured. At its surface, however, it is a riddling mass of contradictory attributions. As before, the hearer must make his way from surface to subsurface by puzzling through these contradictions, with the distinction between form and thing as his guiding light. Cuing from the mutual reference of contradictory attributions and the several major shifts in topic, we can divide the hypothesis into three parts. Parmenides begins by establishing the intelligibility of the "One which is not" as a distinct referent for discourse (160b-161a). This leads him to the question of its relatedness "to the others" ($\pi\rho\grave{o}\varsigma\ \tau\grave{\alpha}$ $\mathring{\alpha}\lambda\lambda\alpha$, 161a6, $\tauο\hat{\iota}\varsigma\ \mathring{\alpha}\lambda\lambda o\iota\varsigma$, c3) (161a-e). He closes by taking up the major issue, the sense of being proper to "the One which is not" and, especially in light of the first two parts, its implications.

a. Securing the Subsurface Point of I

Parmenides opens V with arguments to show that the "One which is not" is a genuine referent of discourse ($\lambda\acute{o}\gamma o\varsigma$) and knowledge ($\mathring{\epsilon}\pi\iota\sigma\tau\acute{\eta}\mu\eta$). By the particulars, even the wording, of the arguments, he directly recalls the closing passage in I, in which the nonbeing One is judged ineffable (142a).[21] But the relation of V to the close of I is complex: since the latter passage means one thing on the surface and another beneath the surface, the impact of V upon it is also twofold.

Consider first the opening arguments in V. Parmenides begins with a reflection on the new basic supposition: for "someone" ($\tau\iota\varsigma$) to "say" ($\lambda\acute{\epsilon}\gamma\epsilon\iota\nu$) that "[a] One is not" presupposes that he can distinguish his subject term from its "opposite," what is "not one" ($\mu\grave{\eta}\ \mathring{\epsilon}\nu$); that is, it presupposes that he can distinguish "the One" from "the others." But this means that the One must have two basic characters: it must be "knowable" (γνωστόν τι), a referent or subject of knowledge (cf. αὐτοῦ ἐπιστήμη), and it must differ—strikingly, Parmenides says it must have "difference *in kind* (ἑτεροιότης)²²—from "the others" (160b-d). Moreover, all of this presupposes that it can stand in, or be a referent term for, many relations; otherwise it could hardly be "that" (ἐκεῖνος) which or "what" (τι) is referred to in discourse, and "*from* which" (τον)²³ "the others" are different, and "*to* which" there belongs ([εἶναι] αὐτῷ) a knowledge which, in turn, is "*of*" or "*about* it" (αὐτοῦ), and so forth (160e-161a).

This reasoning directly controverts the surface significance of the closing passage in I. There Parmenides developed the final consequences of the denial of being to the One. Focusing on its capacity to stand in relations, he *asked*,²⁴

> But that which is not, can anything belong *to* it (εἴη ἄν
> . . . αὐτῷ)? or can there be anything *of* it (αὐτοῦ)?
> —How could there be?
> —*Consequently* (ἄρα), it *has* no name, nor is there speech
> *of* it nor any knowledge nor perception nor opinion.
> —Apparently not (142a1-4).

Taken at face value, this is turned against itself by the arguments in V. These latter make what I denies—in particular, that the One is knowable—a necessary condition for the premise of the denial: according to the full concatenation of V and I, one must first know the One in order, through denying it being, to deny it knowability! The result is a baffling dilemma. On the one hand, one cannot deny the knowability of the nonbeing One, for this proves self-defeating. On the other hand, how can what has no being stand as a referent or subject for knowing?

The dilemma can be dissolved only by moving, with the critical hearer, to the subsurface level. Here the two passages dovetail rather than collide. For the critical hearer, the inexplicit specificity of the being that was denied to the One in I alters the sense of the closing denials: what lacks being-*in-time* must be denied those relations and the sorts of presence for consciousness proper to things in time, but this is all. Thus, the closing passage in I is correct in denying that the One (the form) is subject to "perception" (αἴσθησις) and "opinion" (δόξα); but the denial cannot extend to "knowledge" (ἐπι-στήμη) and the "discourse" (λόγος) associated with it. Indeed, as the opening arguments in V now serve to point out, the very act of denying these latter evidences how the "One which is not" is subject to them. Precisely as "different in kind" from things, the form is given not to the sense- and time-bound modes of consciousness (conspicuously unmentioned in V) but only to unchanging "knowledge" and "discourse." Inter-preted in this way, Parmenides' arguments in V are making ex-plicit what he left implicit earlier; or, more precisely, they as-sert positively what was—to the hearer attuned to the irony and hidden specificity of I—earlier not negated.[25] Thus Par-menides begins to establish the positive characters of the forms and so to secure and complete the subsurface point of I.

But the first set of arguments are only a bare beginning. The critical hearer more than ever needs to learn the positive sense of being proper to the forms; and the brief, unexplicated attri-butions of knowledge and discourse can only incite, not sat-isfy, his interest in their manner and possibility; finally, he will want to understand more about the sort of relations, indicated by discourse, which the forms may have. That these issues are raised, even stirred up, by the opening arguments in V is all to the good. They are the implicit themes for the next two phases of argument. Bearing them in mind helps to open up the otherwise perplexing nests of contradiction in these phases, and their clarified content, in turn, helps to illuminate the is-sues.

b. Relations: "To the Others" and Among Forms

Parmenides now turns to the question of the relatedness of the One, explicitly "to the others"(πρὸς τὰ ἄλλα, 161a6, τοῖς ἄλλοις, c3). By two distinct series of arguments, he generates a twofold contradiction. (1) In the first series (161a-c), he es-tablishes that the One has both (i) "unlikeness toward the others," in the reiterated sense of difference *in kind* (ἑτεροῖα,

161a7, 8) and otherness *in kind* (ἀλλοῖα, a8),[26] and (ii) "likeness to itself," since if unlike itself, it would be an unstable referent for discourse. (2) Then in the second series (161c-3), Parmenides gets Aristotle's assent that, since (i) "not . . . equal to the others" (οὐδ᾽ . . . ἴσον . . . τοῖς ἄλλοις, 161c3), the One must (ii) "partake of inequality" (ἀνισότητος . . . μετέχει, c9); and since "greatness and smallness" (μέγεθος τε καὶ σμικρότης, d2) are modes of inequality, and since, further, equality is their "mean" (μεταξὺ, d5-6) and as such is co-implicated as equally proper, with them, to whatever partakes of them, the One must also (iii) "have a share in equality and greatness and smallness" (e1-2). This final step contradicts both (1)(i) and its own starting-point in (2)(i). How, the puzzled hearer must ask, can "the One which is not" both be different in kind from existent things and yet take on the characters of physical greatness and smallness? And how can it both be not equal to "the others" and yet partake of equality?

Once again, the key to resolving the contradictions is the inexplicit specificity of the being that is attributed to "the others" and denied to the One. It is precisely because they exist spatio-temporally, whereas the One does not, that things and the form are different in kind. Parmenides underscores this incommensurateness in his arguments for both (1)(i) and (2)(i). Thus attuned, the critical hearer should find the ease of (2)(ii)—the step that enables (2)(iii) and so generates the contradictions—striking and unwarranted. Presumably to encourage the hearer's objections, Plato once again has Aristotle make the troublesome move, in responses to Parmenides. The exchange goes as follows:

> But since [the One] is not equal to the others, mustn't it also be that the others are not equal to it?
> —Necessarily.
> —But are not what-are-not-equal (τὰ μὴ ἴσα) unequal (ἄνισα)?
> —Yes. (161c).

Aristotle's "yes" absolutely requires qualification. In its common sense meaning, "unequal" applies to things greater or smaller than one another, that is, to the spatio-temporally existent "others"; precisely because the One lacks this sort of being, it is "not equal," as established in (2)(i), and so *not* "unequal" in the ordinary sense.[27] Thus the hearer should be moved to object. The attribution of inequality (ἀνισότης) can be accepted only if it is meant in some extraordinary sense, specifically, only if there is some *nonspatio-temporal* way in which the One can "partake of inequality." And the same holds for the attributions of the other forms of size in (2)(iii) as well.

That there *is* such an extraordinary sort of partaking should not be completely surprising; the hearer will have been ready to learn of it since he reflected on the relation between the defining form and the great and the small in the course of the reduction in III. This partaking does not give the One (the defining form) the physical characters of size, as if it were a thing; nor does it relate the One directly to "the others" as, e.g., greater or smaller with respect to them. Note the precision of Parmenides' language in these regards: in the attributions of (2)(ii) and (iii), he drops all mention of "the others" and all use of the verb "to be" with adjectival forms (e.g. ". . . is great," ". . . is equal");[28] instead he restricts himself to the construction, ". . . partakes of . . ." (μετέχει τινος, μέτεστί τινί τινος), together with general substantives (μέγεθος, "great*ness*," σμικρότης, "small*ness*," ἰσότης, "equal*ity*"). Thus he suggests a relation entirely between forms, a "partaking" quite apart from physical-sensible existence. This is the so-called "communion" (κοινωνία) or "blending" (σύγκρασις) of forms with one another. Though he will not give a full explication of this relation until the *Sophist*, Plato has several pressing reasons for introducing it here. The most immediate is the one just noted: the constitutive function of forms for things is impossible without such a communion. The thing derives its material element, its physical magnitude, from the great and the small; but this element requires determination by the One (the defining form). Thus, for either the great and the small or the defining form to exercise its constitutive function for the thing, each must combine with the other.[29] This is not to say, of course, that the defining form gets size, nor that the forms of size are in themselves defined by that form. Rather they commune so that "the others," existent things, partaking of the forms in this community, may derive their own proper size and character from them.[30]

Interpreted in this way, the contradictions once again dissolve; or better, they cease to be obstacles and articulate, instead, the ongoing motion of understanding. That the One is different in kind from existent things and yet partakes of greatness and smallness, and again that it is not equal and yet partakes of equality, expresses a basic shift in the level of discourse. Whereas the first phrase in each pair, reiterating the negative motion of I, denies to the form the sorts of relations proper amongst things, the second phrase is positive, disclosing the quite different sorts of relations proper amongst forms.

c. The Being and Intelligibility of the Forms

In the final part (161e-163b) of V, Parmenides addresses the question of the "being" (οὐσία) of the One. And as before, he constructs a formidable set of contradictions. From the outset, of course, he is involved in an apparent contradiction: how can "the One which is not" "partake of being in some sense" (οὐσίας . . . μετέχειν πῃ, 161e3)? But this is only the beginning. As if to compound this negation of nonbeing by being, he goes on to introduce a second sense of nonbeing as well, correlative with the new sense of "being." What is more, he attributes both being and nonbeing (in the new senses) not only to "the One which is not" but, as well, to "what is" (τὸ ὄν). On the surface, the whole system of attributions appears soundly reasoned in its argument and hopelessly contradictory in its conclusions (161e-162b). Parmenides turns next to the equally contradictory consequences of these conclusions. What has contrary conditions must "transit" (μεταβάλλον) from one to the other, and this is a sort of motion; thus the One, transiting between its conditions of being and nonbeing, must move. But at the same time, as "the One which is not," it partakes of none of the species of motion, neither "alteration of character" (ἀλλοίωσις) nor local motion (as, in turn, revolution in place or change of place); thus it must be at rest (162b-e). This second contradiction, finally, gives rise to a third: as moving, on the one hand, the One must "alter in character" (ἀλλοιοῦσθαι, 162e4), and altering in character it must both come-to-be, in "becoming different" (γίγνεσθαι . . . ἕτερον, 163a8), and cease-to-be, in "passing out of [an] earlier character" (ἀπόλ-λυσθαι . . . ἐκ τῆς προτέρας ἕξεως, a8-9); on the other hand, insofar as it does not partake of any motion but is, rather, at rest, the One cannot "alter in character," and as not undergoing any such alteration, it cannot come-to-be or cease-to-be either (162e-163b).

Being and Nonbeing. For the critical hearer, of course, the initial contradiction—that "the One which is not" nonetheless "partakes of being in some sense"—is merely apparent. Since hypothesis I denied only that sense of being proper to things, temporally determinate existence, it has only set the stage for the affirmation of the quite different sense proper to forms. But what is this new "eidetic" sense? As with his opening attribution of knowability, Parmenides begins by reflecting on the basic supposition. The One, he says,

> . . . must have the character [namely, nonbeing] which we assert of it. Otherwise, when we assert that it is not, we would not be saying true 'things' (ἀληθῆ).[30] But if we are saying true 'things,' then it is evident that we are saying 'things'-which-*are* (ὄντα). Isn't this so?
> —It is so.
> —But since we do claim to be saying true 'things,' then necessarily we claim also to say 'things'-which-*are* (ὄντα) (161e5-162a1).

Parmenides gives us several primary features of the new sense of being here. First, it arises in the course of our seeking the truth: it is 'things' that are "true" (ἀληθῆ) that "*are*" (ὄντα).[32] This seeking, in turn, takes the form of discourse, λέγειν. This is important, for it suggests the basic context for construing Parmenides' ambiguous ὄντα. To speak the truth discursively is to say what the subject of discourse "is," to predicate certain characters of it: we say, X "is" Y. This "is," moreover, extends also to the characters—the forms—that are said of the subject. In its participial form ὄντα, the finite "is" has been converted to a modifier, and it refers to *what*-"are," to *that which* the subject is said to "be." That all of this gives a distinct new sense of "being" seems clear. "Being" in this new context refers not to temporal existence but, rather, to the having or partaking of certain forms and to these forms as such, as making up or characterizing the true nature of the participant. That X *is* Y, and that Y belongs to *what* X "is" and so to its "being," may be so whether X "is," in the sense 'exists at some present time,' or not.[33]

Beyond this non-contradictoriness between the two senses, moreover, there is a manifold interplay. To show this, is the basic point of Parmenides' remarkable exegesis of being and nonbeing at 162a-b. He begins innocently enough, formulating the positive implication of the denial of being to the One: "the One which is not *is*" (Ἔστιν . . . τὸ ἓν οὐκ ὄν, 162a1-2) in the sense that it "*is* not-being" (i.e. non-existent).[34] Thus the eidetic sense of being is itself presupposed by and is at play in the denial of being as temporal existence. Parmenides expresses this by calling the "is" a "bond" (δεσμὸν, a4)—a metaphor that nicely signifies both the copulative function of "is" in the syntax of the assertion and the substantive necessity, inherent in the very nature of the One (as the form), that it be non-existent. Indeed, with proper explication we could even say that non-existence is itself a true character and, in this sense, one of the ὄντα, the " 'things'-which-*are*," with regard to the One. In any case, for Parmenides this first combination of being (in the eidetic sense) and nonbeing (in the temporal-existential sense) is only the beginning. "In the same way" (ὁμοίως, a5) that "the One which is not" needs *be* not-being, so "what is" (τὸ ὄν, a5) must *not be* not-being, if it is to be (a5-6). And to round this out, it must also *be* being (a7-8), while "what is not" (τὸ μὴ ὄν) must also *not be* being (b1-2). To the hearer who has distinguished the senses of being, this fourfold play has several striking implications. To begin with, for "what-is to *be* being" implies that this being—temporal existence—is a true character (again, one of the ὄντα) of "what-is"; and this, in turn, shows that being in the eidetic sense (the "*be*") applies to existents (things) as well as to forms. What begins to emerge here is the subsurface point of Parmenides' assertions at the close of hypothesis II that "the One which is" is subject to "knowledge" (ἐπιστήμη, 155d6) and "discourse" (λόγος, d8). Just insofar as these focus on what a thing *is*, not on the thing as such in its transience and instability as a particular in space and time but rather on its true characters, the timeless forms, by themselves, then the thing is subject to them.[35] (Conversely, knowledge and discourse cannot grasp the thing in its perspectivally shifting presence as a sense object. For more on this, see the discussion of hypothesis VII in C.2, below.) Second, Parmenides' combination of eidetic nonbeing with eidetic being is striking: the same subject may both "be" and "not be." This would have been impossible with temporal-existential being and its negation; since these are contradictory, they can be attributed to the same subject only if distributed to different times. (This was a key point in IIa, of course.) But eidetic being and its negation are not contradictory; indeed, eidetic nonbeing appears both to presuppose and to complement eidetic being. Plato will not go into this issue focally until the *Sophist*; nevertheless, Parmenides' exposition pointedly anticipates the discussion there of the sense of nonbeing as difference.[36] What *is not* such-and-such *is* different from it. Thus as hypotheses I–II have shown so extensively, and as Parmenides' comparison of what "is not" with "what is" here formulates, the form has a character different from "existent," while the thing has a character different from just that different character of the form. Of course, if Parmenides were to drop his general reference and pick out particular forms or even things (always with reference to their forms, however), he could greatly expand his illustrations of this new sense of nonbeing. The differences of each one form from the others are vast and manifold, as the *Sophist* will show. But he restricts himself to introducing the new conception.

Motion and Rest. For the hearer who has grasped the distinctively eidetic being and nonbeing of the One (the form), the second (162b-e) and third (162e-163b) sets of attributions will be puzzling and provocative. Parmenides begins by asking,

> Well then, would it be possible for something which is of a certain character (τὸ ἔχον πως) to not have this character without transiting (μεταβάλλον) out of it (162b9-10)?

When Aristotle unhesitatingly accepts such "transiting" ("It would not be possible," b10), Parmenides has no difficulty showing that this means the One must have motion. "Transiting" (μεταβολή, c1, 2) is a motion, after all, and the One has just been shown as "both being and not being" (ὄν τε καὶ οὐκ ὄν, c3); thus it must move in the sense of transiting between being and not being. But there are difficulties here. Parmenides is repeating the same basic line of reasoning that he used earlier in IIa—with the key difference that there he was discussing the physical-sensible One, the thing that has contrary states at different times; here the subject is the nonphysical One (the form). Can the necessity of transition be established when the characters in question—being and nonbeing—are neither contradictory nor located in time? Strikingly, Parmenides' following arguments seem designed to force this issue into the open. Taking up the several sorts of physical motion earlier attributed to the existent One of II, he now denies each to "the One which is not." Precisely because it "is not," it has no place—literally, "no where"—in relation to things that are (μηδαμοῦ γε ἐστι τῶν ὄντων, 162c7), and this makes change of place inapplicable to it; again, since it has no "contact" with and cannot be spatially "in" any being, revolution in place is impossible for it (162d1-5). Both arguments stress that the One has no physical being.[37] Nor, Parmenides goes on at 162d6-8, can the One "alter in character"; for if it were to alter, then "the discourse" (ὁ λόγος, d7) about it—including, presumably, this very assertion, that it alters—would no longer be about *it*. This argument stresses the constancy, indeed the "likeness with itself" established at 161b5-c2, which characterizes the One (the form) as object for the intellect and as in no way physical-sensible. Thus the One is shown to lack the basic ontological status prerequisite to every sort of motion considered so far, that is, every sort of motion applicable to the physical-sensible existent. But can there be any other sort? Parmenides as much as *asks* this explicitly in concluding the whole argument at 162d8-e3:

> But if it neither alters in character nor revolves in the same [place] nor changes place, tell me, then, could it still move in some sense?
> —How indeed?
> —Well then, what is unmoving (τό γε . . . ἀκίνητον) must hold still, and what holds still must be at rest.
> —It must be.
> —The One which is not, *accordingly*,[38] must both be at rest and move.

Needless to say, for one who—like Aristotle—knows only the physical-sensible, no other sort of motion is possible; and since any physical thing that is unmoving is, *ipso facto*, at rest, the One *qua* "unmoving" would be at rest. But to the critical hearer, the attribution of rest is precisely as problematic as the arguments for it have shown the initial attribution of motion to be. Parmenides' question at 162d8 must be taken up as real, not rhetorical, and answered affirmatively before the attributions can be meaningful, much less accepted. Unless there is a genuine nonphysical sort of motion and of rest, the nonphysical One can have neither character.

Alteration in Character and Coming-to-be/Ceasing-to-be. By his final set of attributions Parmenides both compounds and focuses the basic issue. The compounding is obvious enough. On the one hand he derives as a consequence of its motion that the One must undergo "alteration of character" (162e4-163a3). There is a certain plausibility to this: the One's motion consists in its "transiting" between being and not being, and this may be considered as an altering—in the literal sense of "other-ing," ἀλλοί-ωσις—of character. However, the attribution also directly contradicts the denial of alteration Parmenides just made at 162d5-8; such alteration would give discourse about the One an instable, indeed evanescent, subject. As if to insist on this contradiction, Parmenides conjoins to the attribution a new denial of alteration. Since the One "in no way" has motion, it "in no way" alters in character (163a3-4). And he then goes on to expand the contradiction in terms of "coming-to-be" and "ceasing-to-be." Note, however, that just as with being and not being at 161e-162b, so here he takes these terms as predicative, not existential, in syntax and meaning:[39] as altering in character, the One "comes-to-be different from [what it was] before" and "passes out of [its] earlier character"; and as not altering, it does neither (163a7-b5). The importance of this compounding consists in the way it focuses the underlying question. In particular, the hearer now has a considerably more precise notion of the kind of nonphysical motion and rest that can provide sense and positive content to Parmenides' closing contradictions. What is required is an alteration in the character of the One that does not undermine the stability of discourse about the One. Again, since the One is to have both motion and rest, alteration and no alteration, this nonphysical alteration must somehow be accompanied—however paradoxical this sounds at first—by its own lack. Does the One undergo such a combination of alteration and the lack of it? Does it transit between being and not being, yet also not transit (remain unmoving), in some way?

In fact there is such a combination, and it is just the function of the contradictions, once again, to provoke the hearer to grasp it for himself. He knows, to begin with, that any properly nonphysical motion must belong to the soul ($\psi\upsilon\chi\acute{\eta}$);[40] and if, in turn, it involves the One (the form), it will be the motion of mind or—in the language of the *Republic*—$\tau\grave{o}$ $\lambda o\gamma\iota\sigma\tau\iota\kappa\acute{o}\nu$, that part of the soul that seeks to know the form by way of $\lambda\acute{o}$-$\gamma o\varsigma$, discourse. But just what is the movement in this knowing? And just how does it involve the One (the form)? Once again, Plato does not go into these issues focally until the later Eleatic dialogues.[41] Parmenides gives only the seminal elements of the full Platonic responses. Nonetheless, these elements are clear; the searching hearer has only to ponder Parmenides' introduction of the eidetic senses of being and not being. To know the being of a subject, we saw, is to know *what* it "is"; that is, it is to grasp the defining forms in which the subject partakes. And

since the subject is itself a form,[42] this will be a knowledge of
the other forms in which it "partakes" in the special sense, just
introduced, of "communion" or "blending." But in the discursive process of knowing, such a grasp requires the painstaking work of drawing distinctions. Since the initial recognition
of the subject quite properly[43] subsumes it, in its specificity,
under a more encompassing form, the mind must distinguish
within the latter what the subject "is not" from what it "is." In
its explicit and developed form as the method of definition by
bifurcatory[44] diairesis, this process of distinction involves
many steps, of course; with each distinction, the mind pro-
gressively narrows what the subject "is," until finally it arrives
at a grasp that includes nothing the subject "is not." But the
basic rhythm of each step is essentially the same: attention
shifts from the being of the subject (i.e. the encompassing
form) to what, within this being, the subject "is not" (i.e. the
other forms, specifically different from the subject, that also
partake of the encompassing form); and conversely, recognizing what the subject "is not" sets into relief, with new specificity, just what it "is." Thus the One (the form) *as the object of
knowing* undergoes precisely the motion Parmenides has described, a transiting back and forth between its being and its
not being (or difference); in the course of each such transiting,
it alters in character in the sense that its being—that is, "what"
it is known to "be"—becomes ever more specific. At the same
time, however, it is a basic precondition of the whole process
of discourse that the subject remain constant and unchanging,
self-same throughout; in terms of the syntax of assertions,
while the predicate term alters with each new distinction, the
subject term remains unaltered. In this sense the subject "holds
still" or is at rest even as it undergoes motion; indeed, there
could be no intelligible discursive knowing without both at
once.

THE discovery of the nonphysical motion of the One serves
both to integrate V as a whole and to complete its function as
the positive complement to the negations in I. With respect,
first, to V by itself: whereas its first two parts introduce the

nonsensory knowability of the One (160b-161a) and its "communion" with other forms as distinct characters (161a-e), respectively, its third and final part (161e-163b) explicates the former in terms of the latter. To know the One (any one form) is to distinguish it, within the encompassing forms with which it communes, from those others from which it differs. The key to this explication is the new eidetic sense of being and not being. With respect, second, to V and I together: V serves as the positive fulfillment of the promise implicit in the denials in I. The subsurface thrust of I was to purify the hearer's thinking, to purge from his conception of forms the various spatial and temporal characters of things. But this purgation implied a corresponding restoration. To put this in terms of the new sense of being and not being: once we grasp what the form "is not," we are both capable and in need of learning what it "is." By investing terms once restricted to things (e.g. "motion," "alteration of character") with new meanings proper to forms, V begins this higher, positive learning. It opens up the inner relations of the forms, and it provides the basic elements of the method for systematic inquiry into the forms through these relations.

But it is important to proceed cautiously at just this point. How far along the way of this "higher" learning can the sort of "knowing" suggested by V carry us? There is still one apparent disparity between I and V, and reflection upon it raises a striking prospect. In our earlier discussion of I we noted Parmenides' ambiguous position regarding the basic characters of relation, self-sameness and difference-from-others: he denies that they are proper or innermost characters essential to the One (each one form), yet he lets the One have them as inessential, in some sense contingent characters. (Recall ch. IV.C.1.) In V, by contrast, the One must be self-same and different-from-others. Insofar as it is the subject term in discursive knowing, it must have "likeness with itself" (161b5-c2) and be unaltering in character (162d5-8); and in order that what it "is," its being, be disclosed, it must both have and be disclosed in its nonbeing in the sense, precisely, of difference-from-others. Likewise, in its function (in communion with the great and the small) as the constitutive basis for things, the One must have "difference-in-kind" (ἑτεροιότης, 160d8, 161a7, a8) from them. But if all this is so, then neither discursive knowing nor participation reach to or exhaust the innermost character of the One. Since they require of the form what is not ultimately characteristic or essential to it, they fall short of it. In one respect, this should not really be surprising. To put it in more familiar, thoroughly Platonic terms, the form is prior to, not dependent upon, being known and being participated. To the pre-Kantian perspective, at any rate, this priority is a guarantee against, not the source of, epistemological and ontological problems. Precisely because the object is independent of being known and the knowing process itself, true knowledge is possible; and because the transient particulars in time derive from causes quite indifferent to them, existence is securely founded. In another respect, however, the shortfall presents a striking possibility. It is only and specifically that knowing which proceeds by λόγος, discursive knowing, which approaches the self-same form by exploring what it "is not," its difference-from-others. Thus the question arises whether there could be some *non*discursive knowing that, just as discursive knowing overcomes the limits of δόξα, overcomes its limits in turn. This would be an insight that, transcending discourse, would thereby transcend the analytic framework of sameness and difference: a noetic 'vision'[45] that would penetrate to the form in its full and innermost character. Is there such an insight? The *Parmenides* leaves this an open possibility. For the time being, the best the hearer can do is to formulate and preserve the question.[46]

3. The Necessity of Eidetic Being (VI)

In its relation to V, hypothesis VI (163b-164b) has the same ironic double function that IV had in relation to III. On its surface, VI is the direct contradictory to V: it begins from a denial of the central thesis of V (that "the One which is not" nonetheless has being in another sense), and on the basis of this it denies as well all the other characters attributed to the One in V. But the critical hearer, pressing to resolve the contradiction, will find that this is *only* the surface. Guided once again by Parmenides' irony, his reflections on the arguments will show him that VI actually leads in a circle back to V. Only apparently denying, it really attests the necessity of the eidetic sense of being for the One.

On its surface, the argument in V is straightforward. Parmenides begins with a blanket rejection of any sense of being for the "One which is not." In the key exchange at 163c4-7, he *asks*,

> Now tell me whether, when we assert that something is not, we are asserting that in one sense ($\pi\omega s$) it is not, in another it is—or does this "is not" mean simply ($\dot{\alpha}\pi\lambda\tilde{\omega}s$ $\sigma\eta\mu\alpha\acute{\iota}\nu\epsilon\iota$) that what is not neither is nor partakes of being in any way at all?
> —Simply and absolutely, that, certainly. ('$A\pi\lambda o\acute{\upsilon}\sigma\tau\alpha\tau\alpha$ $\mu\grave{\epsilon}\nu$ $o\mathring{\upsilon}\nu$).

Taking this as his premise, Parmenides then considers all of the characters in V, showing that each is impossible for a "One which is not." Strikingly, he takes up these characters in the same groupings they had in the three parts of V—but in just the reverse order. Thus VI has the look of an orderly dismantling, step by step, of what was accomplished in V. To recapitulate briefly: At 163d1-e6, Parmenides denies coming-to-be/ ceasing-to-be (since these are ways of "partaking in" and "losing being"), alteration of character (since this would imply coming-to-be/ceasing-to-be), and motion (since this would imply alteration of character); and he rules out rest, too, since this would imply "being in the same [place]." Then at 163e6-164a1, he introduces a general application of the blanket denial of being:

> Nor can any of what-are ($\tau\iota$ $\tau\tilde{\omega}\nu$ $\check{o}\nu\tau\omega\nu$) belong to it [sc. a One which is not]; for to partake of such would be at once ($\check{\eta}\delta\eta$) to partake of being ($o\mathring{\upsilon}\sigma\acute{\iota}\alpha s$).

This rules out, first, all of the relative characters attributed in the second part of V, both those of size ("greatness and smallness and equality," 164a1-2) and those of identity ("likeness and difference-in-kind,[47] both toward itself and toward the others," a3-4, also a6-7).[48] It also eliminates all the characters discussed in the first part of V; but at this point Parmenides expands his list to include others as well, in particular, those which were treated in the closing negations of I. Thus the One is denied the capacity to stand as the referent or subject for any sort of relational character, in particular,

> as that *of* which or *to* which or as a 'something' or a 'this' or this *of* which or as *of* another or *to* another or as at sometime past or as later or as now or as [the subject of] knowledge or opinion or perception or discourse or name or anything else of what-are (ἄλλο ὁτιοῦν τῶν ὄντων) (a7-b2).[49]

In sum, as Parmenides concludes at 164b3, "A One which is not does not have any sort of character at all."

To the hearer who is critically attuned, however, this cancellation of V will not stand close scrutiny. As before, Parmenides' pointed rhetoric suggests the way for critical reflection. There are three key points to note. To begin with, Parmenides neither gives arguments in support of the premise nor even asserts it himself. On the contrary, he *asks Aristotle* whether the meaning of "is not" allows for the preservation of being in some other sense; and it is Aristotle, not himself, who rules this out—indeed, with a conspicuous emphasis (see 163c7, quoted above). This gives all that follows a striking twist. Parmenides is examining the consequences of Aristotle's rejection of the distinction between spatio-temporal existence and the eidetic sense of being. Secondly, Parmenides himself tacitly invokes this distinction in the course of the arguments. In the first part of his denials (163d1-e6, correlative with the third part of V) he takes being in the sense of the spatio-temporal existence proper to things: as ways of "partaking in" and "losing being" (163d1-3), coming-to-be and ceasing-to-be have an existential, not a predicative, function[50] and refer specifically (as in II, 141d-e) to temporally determinate being; and the "being in the same [place]" that rest implies is "being" in the specific sense of spatially determinate existence.[51] But then in applying generally the denial of being at 163e6-164a1 (quoted above), Parmenides refers to τῶν ὄντων, "what-are." As the following arguments illustrate, this is just the same notion of being that he introduced in V at 161e: these ὄντα are those characters, e.g. "greatness," "likeness," etc., which are "what" a subject "is." There is, thus, a compound irony to Parmenides' arguments. To understand the consequences of what is, really, not his own but Aristotle's rejection of any sense of being for the One requires making just the sort of distinction between senses of being that Aristotle denies. Moreover—and this is the third point—the irony goes deeper still. As we noted, in his final set of denials at 164a7-b2, Parmenides goes beyond a retraction of the correlative attributions in V. He secures as well the closing negative characterizations of the One in hypothesis I: the One is incapable of standing as referent for any sort of relational character, including all of the modes of consciousness and—to quote again—"anything else of what-are" (τῶν ὄντων). To the critical hearer, however, this involves and repeats the same self-contradiction that Parmenides, in the first part of V, has just exposed in I. To assert that the One is unknowable presupposes the contrary; the speaker must *know* the One in its *difference-in-kind* from the "others" in order to make it the referent of this very discourse. Now, however, we can go one step beyond the argument of V. As Parmenides' deft phrase suggests, knowability and difference-in-kind are among "what-are," τῶν ὄντων; thus "the One which is not" *is* knowable and *is* different-in-kind. But this is to say, finally, that it "*is*" in just the eidetic sense of being introduced in V.

Heard critically, then, VI dissolves as the contradictory to V; indeed, it returns us, through a reiteration of the undermining of the surface point of I by the arguments of the first part of V, to precisely the central thesis of V. The hearer who has sufficiently transcended Aristotle's position to follow VI as an examination of it can see that it is finally self-defeating. Insofar as it is articulated, this position, bound to the being proper to things, must finally affirm just what it initially precludes: the distinctively eidetic sense of being as proper to the One (the form).

C. The Phenomenality of Things
(VII–VIII)

1. "The Others" and the Nonbeing
of the One

In hypotheses VII (164b-165e) and VIII (165e-166c) Parmenides works out the consequences for "the others" of the nonbeing of the One. The last of the four subphases he outlined for Socrates at 135e ff., VII and VIII mark the formal completion of the dialectical exercises.

On the subsurface level, in turn, VII-VIII constitute a substantive and pedagogic completion. Substantively, they are the third and final step in his explication (III-VIII) of the ontological relativization (I-IIa): since he has treated the participatory relation (III-IV) and forms (V-VI), it remains only to take up the nature of things. Nor is this a repetition of II; on the contrary, it is pedagogically crucial to come back to the topic of things here. Parmenides' basic aim is to guide the "conversion" of mind from the general orientation of δόξα, in which the physical-sensible dominates, to that of philosophy, in which the forms are prior. Essential to this "conversion" is the double movement we have been observing; forms must be purged of the characters proper to things (I–II) in order to be reconceived according to their own positive characters (V). But it is equally important, once this is accomplished, to re-think things. Now that the "conversion" has revealed the essential priority (IIa, III) and the distinctive sorts of being and intelligibility (V) proper to the form, the initial, pre-"conversion" understanding of the thing (II) must be revised. Precisely because the thing is posterior, its proper being and intelligibility must be reconceived in light of the form.

That this is Parmenides' basic project in VII-VIII will become clear to the critical hearer through a reflection on their relations, first, to V and VI and, second, to each other. V and VI, to begin with, have shown the ambiguity of the supposition that the One "is not" ($\mu\grave{\eta}$ ἔστι, 165e3). Insofar as they are thought as participants in the One, this ambiguity should bear directly on "the others." If the negation of being refers only to spatio-temporal existence, not to the eidetic sense of being, then it establishes the very difference-in-kind that is the precondition for participation; but if the negation precludes every sort of being, then the One is reduced to nullity, and there can be no participation. In fact, VII and VIII appear to correlate with V and VI, respectively, and to spell out just these two possibilities. In the course of the opening argument of VII, first of all, Parmenides establishes that "the others" cannot be "different" ἕτερα) from or "other" (ἄλλα) than the One, since the One "is not" ($\mu\grave{\eta}$ ὄντος γε, 164c5). While he leaves open the force of "is not," he goes out of his way to indicate the sort of difference and otherness he intends:

> We call 'different' what is different from [what is reciprocally] different (ἕτερον . . . ἑτέρου) and 'other' what is other than [what is reciprocally] other (ἄλλο . . . ἄλλου) (c1–2).

Thus it is only and specifically difference between terms on par, between "likes"[52] or commensurates, that is denied; this leaves conspicuously undenied the "difference-*in-kind*" (ἑτεροιότης) that, we saw in V, holds between the non-existent but eidetically "being" One and "the others," that is, between the form and participant things. Thus VII seems to presuppose the subsurface content of V. Its later attributions, in turn, confirm this. "The others" are granted just the same characters—most notably, whole-part structure, plurality and number, and limit and unlimitedness—that were attributed to them in II and III. But III (going beyond II, in accord with IIa) showed these characters to be consequent on participation in the One (the form). For "the others" to have them in VII, therefore, the One must *be* in a sense sufficient to let it be participated by "the others"—just what V established. In direct contrast to this,

VIII presupposes the total negation of being studied in VI. At 166a1-3 Parmenides declares,

> In no way at all can the others have a share (κοινωνίαν) in any of what are not (τῶν μὴ ὄντων οὐδενὶ), nor can any of what are not be present by (παρὰ . . . ἔστιν) any of the others.

The restricted or partial denial of being in V did not prevent a One or form from being participated; conversely, the total denial of participation in VII implies that the forms, or "what are not," are denied being in every sense, reduced to nullity as in VI.

Obviously, these connections of VII to V and VIII to VI have a direct bearing on the relation between VII and VIII. Without presuming the substantive analyses to come in sections 2 and 3 below, we may make the following schematic and anticipatory observations. VII-VIII function as a pair analogously with III-IV and V-VI. On the surface, they derive contradictory consequences for "the others" from the nonbeing of the One; as IV to III and VI to V, VIII argues for the simple negation of the (relatively) positive attributions made in VII. But once again critical scrutiny dissolves the contradiction. Since, on the one hand, the analysis of VI has already shown its total rejection of the One to be self-defeating, and since VIII begins from VI, there will be a presumption against VIII from the beginning. On the other hand, we shall also see that the claims of VIII are in themselves self-defeating and absurd; thus the contradiction transforms—much as occurred, in particular, in IV—into a *reductio* that shows the necessity of VII.

Taken together, these several reflections point to the place of VII and VIII in Parmenides' project of "conversion." In supporting VII as, further, presupposing the subsurface content of V, Parmenides presents the implications for "the others" (physical-sensible things) of his positive account of the One (the form). Initially presented in their own terms and as if self-sufficient (II), things must now—precisely because they are really dependent upon the forms (III)—be reconceived in their secondary and posterior status. And because we have now begun to grasp the forms in their own proper terms (V), such a rethinking is a genuine and significant possibility for the first time.

2. The Secondary Status of Things: "Seeming" and "Appearance" (VII)

The real point of Parmenides' opening argument regarding otherness is both subtle and important. Precisely as "others," Parmenides reasons, "the others" must differ from something; since this cannot be the One (for it "is not"), "the others" must be different from one another (164b-c). But it is not difference in its specificity as a particular character that interests Parmenides here—indeed, only later on does he treat it this way, pairing it with sameness and setting the pair in its proper place in the whole series of characters of things (see 165d1-5). Here he takes up difference as the basic and minimal relatedness between terms on par. By denying this between "the others" and the One and asserting it of things with one another, Parmenides reminds his hearer that the One neither is nor is to be found among things. And this, in turn, implies the basic thesis that he will elaborate in various ways throughout VII: things are not Ones; they only seem to be, and really are not, true unities. Rather, he argues, things are $\pi\lambda\acute{\eta}\theta\eta$ ("multitudes") or, more specifically, $\acute{o}\gamma\kappa o\iota$ ("masses"), and as such, they are essentially aggregative in nature and limitlessly divisible (164c7-d6). In the opening part of hypothesis VII,[53] Parmenides focuses on two aspects of this, the number and size properties of "the others." First, since "a One is not," there will be many such things (164d6-8). And since plurality implies number, they should have number as well. But in a sense they do not. Number requires stable units for counting, but each "mass," though "seeming to be one, is really many" (164d3, also d7). Thus, by extension, things only "appear to be, and are not truly" ($\acute{o}\nu\tau\alpha$ $o\dot{\upsilon}\kappa$ $\dot{\alpha}\lambda\eta\theta\tilde{\omega}\varsigma$ $\phi\alpha\acute{\iota}\nu\epsilon\tau\alpha\iota$, e2-3), enumerable (164d-e). Second, each such thing, precisely as essentially aggregative, can only "seem" to have a "smallest" part (cf. $\tau\grave{o}$ $\sigma\mu\iota\kappa\rho\acute{o}$-$\tau\alpha\tau o\nu$ $\delta o\kappa o\tilde{\upsilon}\nu$, 164d1-2). In truth, any such part is no more

small than it is "immense" (παμμέγεθες, d4): though small in
relation to the entire thing, it also "appears" large relative to
each of its own still smaller parts (164e-165a). Moreover, these
very relations imply equality as well: in Parmenides' formulation, whatever can pass from seeming larger (a thing relative
to any of its parts) to seeming smaller (a thing *qua* part, relative
to that of which it is part) must pass through the "appearance
of equality" (φάντασμα ἰσότητος) as an intermediate (a thing
relative to the sum of its parts, "the many smalls" that make it
up)[54] (165a).

The divisibility of things has definite implications, in turn,
for the sort of "limit" (πέρας) or limitedness they can have. Insofar as there is no smallest part, there is no stable one that
could be finally identified as a bounding feature, whether as
"beginning" (ἀρχή) or "terminus" (τελευτή) or "middle"
(μέσον).

> Though to someone looking from far off and dimly, such
> must appear as one, to someone looking from up close
> and sharply each one appears as indefinitely many (πλήθει
> ἄπειρον) . . . (165b7-c2).

No matter what we might select as the boundary of a thing,
therefore, the identification must always fail: it will be not
'that' but its outermost or centermost part which is the real
boundary—and again not this latter but *its* outermost part, and
so forth, *ad infinitum*. And this means that there can be no such
real boundary; rather, limit can only be relative, as a function
that each composite one performs for each neighboring other
(πρὸς ἄλλον), and apparent (φαίνεσθαι) (165a-c).

Parmenides concludes the argument in VII by generalizing
this reflection on perspectivity to cover all the other characters
attributable to things. What "appears" like—or one and of the
same character—from far off, "appears" unlike and heterogeneous from close up. And the same holds for touching/sepa-
rate, motion/rest, coming-to-be/ceasing-to-be and not doing
so, and "all the other characters of this sort." "The others"
"will seem to be" (δόξει εἶναι) in each of the opposite conditions (165c-e).

As we noted, the particular characters Parmenides treats here are not new; rather they are just those asserted of things in II and made consequent on participation in III. Thus, Parmenides' attributions of apparent number and size properties reiterate the two key aspects of the imperfect unity that he showed in both II and III to be proper to things: their singularity/plurality as many ones and their composite structure as material wholes of analogously structured material parts. His attribution of relative and apparent limit, in turn, recalls his account in III of the way in which neighboring ones serve, each for the other, as a differentiating boundary. And in his concluding generalization he picks out characters from each of the middle four categories studied in II: spatiality, relatedness in identity, relatedness in spatial extension, and temporality; thus (as before in III) he effectively re-presents the whole series of characters. What is new, on the other hand, is the *status* of all these characters. In II Parmenides asserted simply, in the case of each character, that the One thing "is" such-and-such. Now, by contrast, Parmenides introduces the same basic qualification for every attribution: things only "appear" (φαίνε-ται) and "seem" (δοκεῖ) to "be" (εἶναι) such-and-such, and the characters, in their presence in things, are only "appearances" (φαντάσματα).

The notion of "appearing" or "seeming" has both positive and negative aspects, and these serve aptly to suggest the special epistemic and ontological status of things. In its positive sense, to "appear" or "seem" is to be *manifest to the senses*. Things stand as objects for "perception" (αἴσθησις) and the "opinion" (δόξα) associated with it; as Parmenides' reference to "looking" (ὁρῶντι, 165c1) indicates, they are "visibles." In its negative sense, on the other hand, to "seem" or "appear" is to *not really be*; the terms suggest a contrast between the merely partial or passing and true, unequivocal being. In his treatments of the characters of things in VII, Parmenides stresses such partiality and evanescence. Precisely as objects for the senses, things are subject to perspectivity; and changes in perspective bring changes in character. What is manifest as one— or as small or homogeneous or in motion or touching another, and so forth—from one point of view in space and time will show itself as just the opposite when seen from another.[55] Thus each of the characters, in its presence in the thing, is partial and unstable, ceasing-to-be and giving way to its contrary when the perspective for which it is present changes.

The timeliness of the qualification, moreover, should be clear. In V Parmenides first introduced the sense of being—the *is*—proper to forms in the context of discursive knowing. Being in this sense is not subject to any perspectivity: a form *is* what it is, through the communions that knowing articulates, timelessly and unequivocally. The contrast suggested by "appearing" or "seeming" refers back to just this "true" (ἀληθῶς, 164e3) being. Thus Parmenides' qualification serves to subordinate things to forms. In effect, he lets the being and intelligibility of the forms stand as the measure for those of things, and he finds things lacking. "Appearing" and "seeming" are his pointed recharacterizations of the way things are, and are perceived to be, what they are. As a revision of the simple "is" of hypothesis II, this nicely expresses the secondary ontological and epistemic status of the physical-sensible.

3. The Necessity of the Ontological Relativization as a Whole (VIII)

On the surface, VIII contradicts VII by making its qualified negations absolute. In his opening argument (165e), Parmenides begins by reiterating the first major claim in VII, that "the others" cannot *be* one or many. For if there is no One, they cannot be a One either collectively or individually; and if none of them individually is a One or singular, then—since a plurality is a plurality only of singulars[56]—they cannot be many either. In his second argument (166a), however, Parmenides goes on to contradict the positive side of his claim in VII: "the others," he now asserts, cannot even *seem* or *appear* to be one or many. He establishes this by beginning from the denial, noted above, that "the others" can in any way "share in," or have as "present by" themselves, anything that is not (166a1-3). Since *ex hypothesei* it is the One that is not, and since Par-

menides' now unqualified denial precludes even that any
"seeming" (δόξα) or "appearance" (φάντασμα) "of what is
not" (τοῦ μὴ ὄντος) can be "present by" the others (166a3-6),
it follows that "the others" cannot in any way "be supposed,
from their appearance, to be one" (δοξάζεται . . . ἓν εἶναι);
moreover, since "without a one the notion of many is impossible" (166b1-2), it also follows that "the others cannot be supposed, from their appearance, to be many" (166a7-b2). Once
he has established this, Parmenides is in position to contradict
every other positive claim in VII as well. Since the appearance
of being one and many was the basis for all the subsequent attributions in VII, the denial of the former implies the denial of
the latter. Hence Parmenides can declare at 166b4-7,

> if a One is not, then the others neither are nor appear [to
> be] the same or different, touching or separate, or any of
> the other characters which we just described them as ap-
> pearing (ὡς φαινόμενα) [to be].

Thus VIII ends in a total negation. As Parmenides says point-
blank, summing up: "If a One is not, there is nothing at all"
(ἓν εἰ μὴ ἔστιν, οὐδέν ἐστιν, 166c1).

As before with III–IV and V–VI, however, the contradiction
between VII and VIII transforms under critical reflection; appearances notwithstanding, hypothesis VIII turns out to have
a positive significance with quite extensive implications. This
is clearest if we lead up to it gradually, by a series of observations. First of all, as we observed in section C.1, the premises
of VII and VIII differ. Well attuned by now to the ambiguity of
the denial of being to the One, the critical hearer will surely
distinguish the denial of spatio-temporally determinate existence in VII from the denial of being in every sense in VIII; as
we noted, this is implied by the tacit assertion and express denial of participation in VII and VIII, respectively. This difference in their premises, in turn, significantly changes the apparent relation between the hypotheses: rather than deriving
contradictory consequences from the same thesis, they compare the different consequences of different theses. Second,
and within the new context of such a comparison, the conse-

quences of VIII are patently absurd. The very fact that Parmenides and Aristotle and the silent others are engaged in this
conversation gives the lie to the remarkable conclusion that
οὐδέν ἐστιν, "there is nothing at all." This absurdity has a
twofold effect. On the one hand, because the reasoning that
leads to these consequences is sound, the premise is undermined; thus VIII serves to reiterate the subsurface significance
of VI, standing as a *reductio ad absurdum* of the denial of every
sense of being to the One. On the other hand, the absurdity is
pointed, suggesting not only what should be rejected but also
what should be affirmed in its place. To Parmenides' οὐδέν
ἐστιν ("there is nothing at all"), the hearer can hardly help but
object that *there are, at the very least, the appearances of many
things*. That is, quite apart from the philosophical consideration of their basis or significance, the "appearances" (φαινό-
μενα, 166b6) deduced in VII are incontestably present, everywhere at hand. By denying them in argument, VIII only calls
attention to their presence in immediate experience. Moreover, in the context of the contrast between the lines of argument in VII and VIII, this existential demonstration does take
on specific philosophical significance. Parmenides' denial of
appearances in VIII was a direct consequence of his denial of
participation, and that, in turn, was consequent on the unqualified nonbeing of the One. To now assert that *there are* appearances, therefore, has important implications: we must also
retract the denials of participation and of the distinguishing of
a sense of being proper to the participated One. In positive
terms, we must return to the alternative position partly tacit
and partly articulated by VII, that the plurality of phenomena
is constituted through their participation in the forms which,
in turn, *are* in the eidetic sense that is proper to them.

In its subsurface function, VIII thus makes a proper end for
the whole set of hypotheses. Like IV and VI, it really attests
what it first seems to contradict. But it has a distinctively synoptic reach. In referring beyond phenomena (VII) to their
foundations in participation (III) and forms (V), VIII recollects
and attests the ontological relativization (I–IIa) as a whole.

Connections and Possibilities

BECAUSE this study has concentrated on the long-standing problems of the reference and function of the hypotheses and the internal coherence of the *Parmenides* as a whole, we have only occasionally considered other texts. As we have observed, however, the *Parmenides* refers beyond itself in at least two specific ways: it is framed as a critical reappropriation of the *Republic*, and hypothesis V, in particular, introduces several of the central new teachings of the *Sophist* and the *Statesman*. It is hardly possible to do justice to these connections here; this will require several whole new studies in the future. Still, it is appropriate, in closing, to take note of some of the issues and difficulties that these studies will need to address. Such remarks should serve to remind us of the larger Platonic project of which the *Parmenides*, however synoptic, is but one phase. They should also help to sustain certain critical uncertainties about the unity and stability of that project.

A. The *Parmenides* and the *Republic*: Reappropriation or Departure?

There are, first of all, questions to be raised about the status of the *Parmenides* as a second beginning in philosophy. In Chapter I we considered in an anticipatory way the subtle interplay between the elements of criticism and reappropriation in Plato's dramatic framing of the dialogue: by his stage-setting and selection of *personae*, Plato appears to set Socrates' mature (and, aptly, Eleatic) insight in the *Republic* as a goal; the means, however, is critical and conceptual inquiry of a depth not possible in the *Republic*. The task Plato projects for this inquiry, I argued, is to rethink Socrates' insight at its own level, freeing it from formulations that (however appropriate originally) ultimately fall short of its true content and priorities. Now that we have worked our way through the body proper of the *Parmenides*, we are in position to pose two different sorts of questions about this. The first proceeds within the context of the expectations Plato establishes by his dramatic framing. How well has the *Parmenides* accomplished its projected task? How comprehensively and radically have Parmenides' refutations and hypotheses enabled a saving clarification of the mature Socrates' theory of forms? The second sort of question, by contrast, asks whether the expectations Plato establishes are in fact appropriate to what he actually does in the *Parmenides*. That is, how fully does what the *Parmenides* actually accomplishes conform to what Plato projects as its task? This is the question I suspended earlier (Ch. I, n. 18). It is always possible, I noted, that even while he designates Socrates' mature insight as the goal, Plato is actually recasting it. Here the issue is not how fully he reappropriates his own earlier theory but whether the dialogue really is a reappropriation—and not, rather, a departure—in the first place.

To try to resolve these questions here would be inappropriate. This would require, in addition to our study of the *Parmenides*, a separate and equally comprehensive study of the *Republic* and a comparison of the results of both. At this point, therefore, we must settle for some provisional remarks on the contribution that our study would be likely to make to this larger inquiry.

These remarks fall into two distinct sets of observations. On the one hand, I hope to have brought into focus a number of ways in which the argument of the *Parmenides* really does fulfill Plato's dramatic projection. Here it should suffice just to recall these four: First, by his repeated recourse to sensible similes and by his inability, when pressed, to explicate their content in nonimagistic language, the youthful Socrates shows that he still thinks his new notion of forms in terms proper to physical-sensible things. His similes of the day (131b) and of model and likeness (132d) recall—or, in terms of his dramatically projected life history, anticipate—similes central to the elder Socrates' exposition of the forms in *Republic* VI, VII, and X. (See, in particular, τὸ ἡμερινὸν φῶς, 508c5; the simile of shadows and things at 509e ff. and as it is reintroduced in the context of the allegory of the cave; and the treatment of the levels of imitation at the beginning of Book X.) By having Parmenides expose the incoherence that results from relying on these similes, Plato in effect shows that the content of the *Republic* requires a higher mode of understanding: the aspiring philosopher needs to learn to think the forms in conceptual, rather than sense-perceptual terms. Second, by virtue of their unremitting abstractness, the hypotheses provide just the sort of intellectual "gymnastic" that will enable this learning. Thus, the surface argument of the hypotheses by itself occasions the "conversion" of soul from becoming to being that Plato has the elder Socrates call for at *Republic* 518c ff. Third, in their subsurface argument, the hypotheses provide a determinate pathway for this "conversion." The decisive first step, as we have seen, consists in the manifold distinction, accomplished in hypotheses I–II (and then explicated in III, V, and VII), of the sorts of unity and of being proper to forms from those proper to their physical-sensible participants. As we noted in Chapter I, the elder Socrates' first presentation of the doctrine of forms, at the close of *Republic* V, is dangerously ambiguous on just these points: by contrasting the form and its participants as one and many (475e-476a), Socrates leaves open the possibility of thinking the form as a "one" of the same fundamental sort as each of the many physical-sensible things that participate in it; and again, by contrasting the form and its participants as "being purely" (εἰλικρινῶς ὄν) and as both "being" and "not being," respectively, what they are, Socrates seems to suggest that it is only the addition of "not being" that differentiates the participant from the form—in which case, however, the participant will not differ from the form in its kind of "being." By its manifold distinction, therefore, the *Parmenides* clarifies and saves the elder Socrates' presentation in the *Republic*. As simple and unique, each form is "truly one" (ὡς ἀληθῶς ἕν, 159c5), while each of the many participants, as composite and singular, is only "apparently" or "seemingly" one (164d6 ff., 165b7 ff.). And since, as hypotheses I and II show in negative and positive fashion, composite structure is necessary for an entity's being subject to temporal and spatial determinateness, the being of the form must transcend such determinateness altogether, whereas the being proper to things is essentially subject to it. This, in turn, implies that the being of the form is different in kind[1] from that of its participants: as not spatio-temporal, the form is in principle not subject to the sorts of physical transformation or shifts in viewpoint that cause the impurity, the mixing of what it *is* with what is contradictory of this, that characterizes the participants. To repeat the formulation offered by hypotheses V and VII, what the form *is*, it is "truly," not in a partial or fleeting "seeming."[2] Fourth, the distinction of form and thing in hypotheses I–II sets the stage for the penetrating reflections, in IIa and III–IV, on their relation of participation. In the *Republic* the elder Socrates was able only to assert the fact of participation (see, e.g., 476a) and to offer the simile of model and likeness (or original and shadow, etc.) for it. Parmenides, by contrast, can offer several versions of a powerful transcendental argument for the fact of participation, showing, in essence, that it is only by means of participation that physical-sensible things can have their temporal continuity (IIa) and, more broadly, all of the various characters (IV) that they do, at the very least, "appear" to have (VIII). And in his "reduction" at 158b-d, Parmenides is able to explore in pure or abstract thought (cf. τῇ διανοίᾳ 158c2) the workings of participation; it is here that he offers the new, albeit terse and rudimentary account of how the form provides πέρας, internally and externally delimiting structure, to the sheer πλῆθος, the "mere many," that is all there would 'be' of the thing apart from its participation in its defining form. Thus Plato again clarifies the *Republic*, providing argument to ground its mere assertion and replacing its sensible simile with an act of διάνοια.[3]

On the other hand, these very observations serve to provoke important reservations. In effect, the more clearly our study brings into focus moments in which the *Parmenides* clarifies and recovers the *Republic*, the more sharply it throws into relief other moments of apparent departure or omission. This is the second part of our provisional remarks on the larger inquiry. There are three key areas of reservation, quite different from one another, to note and preserve as topics for the future.

(1) Taken in earnest, the interpretation of the *Parmenides* as critical reappropriation of the *Republic* has far-reaching consequences for the way the *Republic*, just in itself, should be read. To put this in its strongest and most striking form, if the array of insights enabled by the subsurface argument of the hypotheses is really the true content of the *Republic*, then we must be ready to find it implicitly present in the *Republic* from the beginning. This will not only (we shall have to be ready to say) be what Plato later, on rethinking, retrospectively discovered as a potential content; it must rather be *the* definite meaning that Plato intended from the outset. Is such a "unitarian" view of the two dialogues really plausible? Note, to begin with, the extraordinary sustained irony that we would then have to impute to the *Republic*. We would have to say that the elder Socrates possesses all along the conceptual understanding of the forms that, for us, the subsurface argument of the hypotheses first articulates; that he chooses, presumably for pedagogical reasons, to withhold this understanding from the not yet philosophical Glaucon and Adimantus; and that, in giving instead a substantively defective but pedagogically fitting presentation, he leaves the way open for—indeed, himself establishes the tensions and problems that will motivate—the critical reappropriation of this presentation that the *Parmenides* enables. The difficulty of this, moreover, comes home even more sharply when we step back from the *dramatis persona* of the elder Socrates, a Platonic construction, to Plato himself. The conceptual understanding, self-limitation, and forethought to be credited to Socrates must really, of course, be credited to Plato. Again, is this plausible? Can we really affirm that he constructs the argument of *Republic* V–VII and, in particular, the great figures of the sun, the line, and the cave as pedagogically provisional? If so, we must find in the *Republic* the same sort of distance between surface and subsurface, the same sort

of concealment with the aim of provocation to discovery, that we have found in the hypotheses of the *Parmenides*.[4]

(2) As the elder Socrates introduces it at *Republic* 518c-d, the "conversion" of the soul is not just toward "what is" (τὸ ὄν) but also, in particular, toward "the brightest of beings, . . . the Good." The Good, he earlier proposed in offering the simile of the sun, is in some sense the source both for the knowability and for "the existence and being" (τὸ εἶναι τε καὶ τὴν οὐ-σίαν, 509b7-8) of the forms. Given this, it is striking that the hypotheses, even as they occasion the "conversion," make no reference at all to the Good. One might have thought that this would be a primary focus for Parmenides. How, then, should this silence be interpreted? Needless to say, we are not now in position to try to decide this matter; any answer would presup-pose an interpretation of the Good, and this, in turn, requires as its context the autonomous study of the *Republic* that I have deferred. For now, it is appropriate to note two general lines of interpretation that our study of the *Parmenides* leaves open. At least *prima facie*, these are basic alternatives. On the one hand, the silence may signal that the doctrine of the primacy of the Good has been dropped. This would imply, in turn, what many hold for other reasons as well, that the *Parmenides* marks at least a partial turn away from the conception of forms in the *Republic*.[5] If, in particular, it is by virtue of the Good as their ground that the forms are, each within its kind, superlatively good and, as such, ideals and models, then the dropping of the doctrine of the Good would imply that Plato no longer thinks of the forms as ideals.[6] The silence of the hypotheses would thus be one way that he prepares for the introduction of a new or at least newly accented view of the forms. (We shall come back to this latter possibility by other paths below.) On the other hand, the silence may reflect some specificity or limita-tion in the hypotheses' mode of argument that prevents them from reaching as far as insight into the Good.[7] In this case, even while the *Parmenides* reappropriates some of the content of the *Republic*, it would fall short of its core. Thus construed, the silence would indicate the further ascent, beyond the reach of the hypotheses' mode of argument, still facing the aspiring

philosopher; Parmenides' very reticence would be a Platonic warning not to confuse the second beginning occasioned by the hypotheses for the ultimate goal of philosophical education.[8]

(3) Earlier we noted how the subsurface argument of the hypotheses serves to clarify and preserve the elder Socrates' contrast in *Republic* V between the form as "being purely" what it is and the participant thing as both "being" and "not being" what it is. If, however, we focus on Parmenides' introduction of the new sense of nonbeing in hypothesis V, this observation seems, at the very least, partial and incomplete. Parmenides argues that "the One which is not" both "is" and "is not" (161c-162b); since by "the One which is not" he refers back to the One of I, the atemporal form, he in effect extends to the form precisely the same formula that the elder Socrates restricts to the participant thing. Does this not mark a departure from, if not a reversal of, the *Republic*? In fact, the situation is ambiguous. The question requires at least two distinct and internally complex reflections. First of all, the subsurface argument of the hypotheses seems to suggest a way in which the two passages are in fact harmonious. In particular, we have seen how Parmenides' introduction of the new sense of "is not" helps to secure the basic point of hypothesis I: narrowly considered, the very intelligibility of the assertion that the One "*is not* existent" (in the sense of the temporally determinate existence proper to things) depends upon the intelligibility of nonbeing in the new sense of being-different; more broadly, the new sense of nonbeing is a precondition for the form's being subject to ἐπιστήμη and λόγος. In the same way, strikingly, the application to the form of the new sense of "is not" would seem to be a precondition for the intelligibility of the elder Socrates' notion of "being purely"—and, hence, also for his very *denial* of the application of nonbeing to the form!—in the *Republic*. Socrates' central point is that the form does not take on its contrary. Beauty, for instance, "is purely" (e.g., 477a, 478d) in the sense that it cannot be ugly; for it to be ugly would be for it to "not be" beautiful,[9] that is, for it to be what it is not, and this, Socrates holds, is possible only for the variable things of sense

(see especially 478d ff.). Doesn't the very intelligibility of Socrates' thesis, however, require that "is not" apply intelligibly to the form? Just as in the case of the recognition of the timeless being of the form at the close of hypothesis I, so here: to grasp the pure being of the form we must be able to say of it that it *cannot be* what it *is not*. On this account, Parmenides' introduction of the new sense of "is not" would be both a departure from and a return to the *Republic*. It is indeed a new sense, and Parmenides breaks new ground in introducing it. However, it is, it would seem, already implied by the elder Socrates' point. Far from overturning that point, Parmenides' innovation would serve to secure it.

This first reflection hardly exhausts the matter, however. Rather, it points to a nexus of further problems. Note that the new sense of "is not" pertains to what we can *say* about the forms. In first introducing it in hypothesis V, Parmenides pairs it with the corresponding sense of "is," and he treats both as belonging to the context of λόγος, of veridical *discourse* about the One. That the *Parmenides* secures the *Republic* with this new notion only after the fact, so to speak, makes conspicuous that the *Republic* itself is not primarily concerned with the forms as objects of discourse.[10] As many have noted, its dominant metaphors are visual; the goal of philosophical education is the noetic "*seeing*" of "what is" and "the truth" and "the Good" (note especially 518d5, 533a5, 540a8). There are a host of important issues to study here. How seriously should we take the metaphors of noetic "seeing" in the *Republic*? What precisely is the νόησις that they signify, and how does it interrelate with λόγος in dialectical inquiry? With regard, in turn, to the focus on λόγος in hypothesis V of the *Parmenides*, does this in fact mark or signal a break from the position of the *Republic*—in particular, a turn from the notion of knowledge that centers on the "visual model" of the forms prominent in the middle dialogues to a primarily "discursive account of knowledge"?[11] And if so, still, what sort of turn is this, with what implications for the systematic unity of the theory of forms? Ought we to understand the "discursive account" as grounding or, more dialectically, as complementing the notion of knowledge as noetic "seeing"—or, at the other extreme, does the new account simply eclipse and replace the latter?[12] Needless to say, these are intrinsically difficult questions. Moreover, they outstrip the textual reach of this essay on two fronts. Not only do they require the separate study of the *Republic* that I have deferred; also, since Parmenides' introduction of the eidetic senses of "is" and "is not" in hypothesis V anticipates and sets the stage for the *Sophist* and the *Statesman*, they require a separate study of these dialogues as well. On this account, it is now timely to turn to a consideration—necessarily, once again, preliminary and heuristic in character—of the connection of the *Parmenides* with the Eleatic dialogues. Interestingly, some of the issues we have noted here will reappear in a new form.

B. The *Parmenides* and the Eleatic Dialogues: The Forms as Wholes and Parts?

At the outset of the essay, I suggested that the *Parmenides* stands as a pivotal text between the *Republic* and the Eleatic dialogues, that it enables a transition from the imagistic grasp of the relation of the physical-sensible and forms to the conceptual grasp of the interrelations among the forms. Our analysis of the hypotheses has now brought into focus the place where this transition occurs. For the critical hearer who can penetrate Parmenides' apparent contradictions, hypothesis V anticipates with striking precision these central teachings of the *Sophist* and the *Statesman*: the strong association of the knowability of any form with its explicability by λόγος (160c-d); the grounding of this explicability in the "participation" (161c-e) of the forms in one another; the use of the process—or psychic "motion" (162c ff.)—of showing, alternately (162b-c), what a form "is" and "is not" (161e-162b) as the method of explication; the securing of this, the method of collection and division, by the construal of nonbeing as, in effect, being-different (162a-b and 162e-163b). On each of these points Parmenides elicits in an introductory way just what the

Eleatic stranger will spell out explicitly and in painstaking detail.

On one key matter, however, Plato's language in the *Sophist* and the *Statesman* contradicts the *Parmenides* and appears, at least initially, to undermine the harmony of the texts. Repeatedly, the Eleatic stranger characterizes forms[13] as "wholes" or as "parts." Sometimes he is referring to the way in which a form, as the object of division, is "cut" into other forms as, in their turns, its "parts." (For statements to this effect at the level of principle, see, perhaps, *Sophist* 253d1-e2[14] and, more surely, *Statesman* 263b7-8. For statements from within the actual practice of division, see, e.g., *Sophist* 219c2-7, 223c6-7, 266e3-267a1 or *Statesman* 261b10-11, 263e8, 265c2, 267a8-c3.) Other times he is referring to the way in which the "greatest kinds," tacitly understood as wholes, are instantiated by the other forms as, correlatively, their "parts." (See especially the stranger's remarks on difference and, perhaps,[15] being at *Sophist* 257c7-d5, 258a11-b3, and 258d5-e3.) In either case, however, the stranger's statements stand in jarring contrast with what is, on our reading, *the* central thesis of the *Parmenides*, that the forms are partless or simple. What are we to make of this?

On one level, the problem may be more apparent than real. Interestingly, the internal dynamic of hypothesis V seems to suggest how we might penetrate and dissolve the contradiction. Recall how in V Parmenides attributes to the One a number of the characters that he at first denied to it in hypothesis I. As we saw, however, by his arguments Parmenides forces us to reinterpret these characters, setting aside the spatio-temporally determinate senses they have in hypothesis I in favor of new senses proper to the forms. Thus, for example, when he attributes motion and rest to the One, Parmenides makes clear that the One prescinds from change of place (162c6 ff.), revolution in the same place (162d1 ff.), and change of character (162d5 ff.) and, again, that it is *as* prescinding from these types of physical motion that the One is at rest (162d8-e3); hence neither motion nor rest can be understood in a physical sense. We are provoked to turn instead to the eidetic senses—in short, the alteration of the predicate and the constancy of the sub-

ject—proper to the form as the object of discursive knowledge. Given this precedent, when the Eleatic stranger characterizes the forms as "wholes" and "parts," we should know
better than to think these notions in the spatial and temporal
sense they ordinarily have. Precisely because we have worked
through the argument of the *Parmenides*, we should be clear
that this sense must be restricted to the physical-sensible. And
the new positive sense? Though in its specific structure this is
intrinsically obscure and susceptible to different sorts of exe-
getic analysis,[16] it seems safe to say, at the least, that in the context of collection and division "part" and "whole" are used to
express the way forms participate in sameness and difference
with respect to one another: whereas collection discloses that
form in respect of which many particular forms are the same,
division discloses how, within this sameness, these particular
forms are different. Further, as we noted with regard to difference at *Sophist* 257c ff., the notion of "part" is invoked to express this very participation. In neither context, then, should
there be any question of physical relations; like "rest" and
"motion" in hypothesis V, "part" and "whole" should now
have clearly non-physical, eidetic senses. And if this is so, then
the contradiction between the denial of whole-part structure in
hypothesis I and the assertion of it in the *Sophist* is dissolved.
Indeed, in its analogousness to Parmenides' shift of senses in
passing from hypotheses I–II to V, Plato's shift of senses from
the *Parmenides* to the *Sophist* seems rather to underscore the
continuity of the two dialogues.

Even if this is so, however, we are still left with an important
difficulty. To see that the assertion of composite structure in
the *Sophist* and the *Statesman* is not incompatible with the assertion of simplicity in the *Parmenides* is not yet to understand
just how they fit together. As before, there are at least two general interpretive possibilities, each with its own potential basis
in the *Parmenides*.

The simpler of the two possibilities is that Plato *replaces* the
characterization of the forms as simple by the characterization
of them as subject to composite structure. That he does so in
the *Sophist* and the *Statesman*, moreover, would reflect the
depth and clarity that he has by then achieved in the gradual

process of coming to understand the forms in terms proper to them.[17] To flesh this out a bit, from early on it is evident that the forms must be immaterial. But as Plato comes to see, it is one thing to assert this, quite another to break the hold of the deep habits of thought that incline one to think the forms on the model of things. It is this inner split, as we have seen, that he means to dramatize by the *persona* of the youthful Socrates in the *Parmenides*, and it is the overcoming of it that he means to enable by the provocative power of the hypotheses. For one suffering this split, Plato sees, it is profoundly useful to center the conception of the forms on their incomposite unity; since having parts is a precondition for having spatial and temporal characters, to think through the implications of partlessness is to come to understand, extensively and in a mode free of sensible simile, the immateriality of the forms. At the same time, however—we may now go on to add—Plato also sees that once one has made this "conversion" and turns to the next major task in philosophical education, the practice of dialectic, the notion of partlessness will come to light as specific in sense and, on that account, no longer of central importance. As the *Sophist* and the *Statesman* make clear, the practice of dialectic implies a new characterization of the forms. Specifically, the method of collection and division requires that they both "combine" into self-same wholes and be "separate" as mutually different parts within these wholes; containing and being contained by one another in relations of inclusion and subsumption, the forms must therefore now be conceived as intrinsically composite or complex. Partlessness or simplicity thus drops into the background, revealed as a character proper only and specifically to the contrast of forms with physical-sensible things. Because it really means 'lacking *spatial or temporal* parts,' it is not strictly incompatible with the new notion of logical complexity; but for the same reason it is also no longer particularly relevant or useful to the practicing dialectician. Plato therefore lets it drop from view in the *Sophist* and the *Statesman*, replacing it with the latter notion.[18]

The second major interpretive possibility is that Plato, even while he introduces the characterization of the forms as wholes and parts in the *Sophist*, nonetheless *also retains* the characterization of them as simple natures. On this account, the forms would be both simple and composite.[19] This conjunction, at first sight paradoxical, begins to gain sense and coherence when we look back to the nexus of passages in the *Parmenides* that give it its initial motivation. Recall, first of all, that in hypothesis I Parmenides denies to the One not only all spatio-temporal characters but also sameness (and, so, likeness) and difference (and, so, unlikeness) (139b-e, 139e-140b). As we saw, however, by his pointed arguments Parmenides denies these characters only to the One as such, in its innermost being as a simple nature, and leaves invitingly open the possibility that the One be subject to these characters in some inessential or contingent context. Then in hypothesis V Parmenides takes up his own invitation: on the one hand, he attributes to the One difference (160c-d), likeness to itself (161b), and the veridical being and nonbeing (161e-162b) that allow for assertions of sameness and difference; on the other hand, by attributing these characters to the One as, specifically, the object of ἐπιστήμη and the λόγος associated with it, he appears to restrict them to the context of our discursive knowledge. Thus the form would have sameness and difference not as proper to itself in its innermost being but, rather, only in its posterior and inessential function of being the object for the psyche in the motions of discursive analysis. The possible implication of this for the status of the whole-part structure the Eleatic stranger attributes to the forms in the *Sophist* and the *Statesman* is striking: since whole-part structure in the new eidetic sense is a function of sameness and difference, it too would be secondary and inessential to each form as such. Is it plausible that Plato holds this position? On the one hand, there is striking evidence that he continues, in the *Sophist*, to distinguish between what is proper to the form as such and what characterizes it only secondarily and inessentially; in a passage that verbally echoes Parmenides' contrast between what the One "is" (hypothesis I) and what it "participates in" (hypothesis V), the Eleatic stranger says at 255e3-6,

> . . . we shall say that this nature [sc. difference] pervades all the forms, for each one is different from the others *not*

by virtue of its own nature but because it partakes of the form
of difference (οὐ διὰ τὴν αὑτοῦ φύσιν, ἀλλὰ διὰ τὸ μετέχειν τῆς ἰδέας τῆς θατέρου).

On the other hand, this passage does not itself reveal the underlying context and purpose of this distinction. Again, however, this may be suggested by the *Parmenides*. Earlier we noted
how Parmenides, in implicitly attributing sameness and difference to the One as the object of specifically discursive knowledge, leaves open the possibility of a nondiscursive knowledge. As nondiscursive, such knowledge would transcend the
analytic framework of sameness and difference; it would be
such insight alone, if any at all, that could reach to the form as
such, the form in its innermost being.[20] To these comments we
might now add the following reflection. In hypothesis V Parmenides indicates, by the subsurface content of his argument,
that as object of discursive knowing the form is subject to
"motion" and "rest"; as we have interpreted this, he is indicating how the form is the stable subject that is more and more
closely known *via* the changing predicates in the process of the
method of diairesis. At the end of this process the dialectician
collects these predicates in a synoptic list. The new notion of
whole and part would seem to have a precise application to this
list: the final collection, we should say, reveals the form under
investigation as a whole of the various predicates—that is, of
the forms they name—as its parts.[21] Now, granting all this, it
becomes interesting to ask: what, if anything, saves the dialectician's collections and divisions from lapsing into mere opinion or even outright deception? What enables him to cut "according to forms"? This is an especially pressing question for
the young mathematicians, Theaetetus and Socrates, to whom
the Eleatic stranger teaches the method for the first time, and
he provides them with two orienting techniques. First, he rec-
ommends and demonstrates the use of "lesser" beings like the
angler and the weaver, unproblematic and "in themselves easy
to understand," as "paradigms"—that is, as illuminating ana-
logues—in the study of "greater" and intrinsically difficult
beings like the sophist and the statesman (see especially *Statesman* 277d ff., 285d ff.). Second, until the last part of the *States-*

man (287b ff.), he restricts diairesis to the "safer," methodo-
logically rule-governed mode of "cutting down the middle"
(see especially *Statesman* 262b ff.); by holding back from cuts
that, however immediately compelling, do not pick out equal
halves, he guards against mistaking the content of customary
presumption for genuinely eidetic structure.[22] As he himself
appears to intimate, however, neither of these techniques is
self-sufficient. To be able to tell *which* "lesser" being is a true
analogue to *which* "greater" being would seem to presuppose
that one already has insight into the latter. How, if not by prior
insight into statesmanship, is the stranger able to see that shep-
herding is not, and weaving is, its proper "paradigm"? As for
"cutting down the middle," nothing guarantees that there are
not forms to which it is inappropriate, forms that such procedures may conceal more than reveal; indeed, when the stranger
suspends bifurcation at 287b-c, he indicates that statesmanship
is a case in point.[23] But again, how can one know when to set
aside the principle of halving, much less how to proceed in
one's cuts without it, unless one already has an insight into the
form in question? Only if the form is *already present and providing guidance*, can the dialectician know that he is cutting "according to forms." This has striking possible implications for
the question of simplicity and complexity. Insofar as diairesis
cannot first explicate what the form is unless the form is already present, there is a distinction to be drawn between the
form as it is explicated and the form in that prior presence.
And since the form *in that presence* is prior, it will not be subject
to the conditions that diairesis first imposes. These conditions
include, centrally, "rest" and "motion" and being a whole of
parts. The successful practice of diairesis thus appears to presuppose not only the characters asserted of the form in hypothesis V of the *Parmenides* and in the *Sophist*, respectively,
but *also* the very prescinsion from these characters that is asserted in hypothesis I. To be disclosed for what it truly is by
collection and division, the form must not only stand as the
stable subject of a series of predicates in order, finally, to be
spelled out as the whole of these, but it must *also* be present in
a way that precedes discourse and composite structure, pres-

ent, therefore, as a *simple* nature for a *pre-analytic insight* or intuition. The possible sense and coherence of the characterization of the forms as both simple and composite should now be
evident: in sum, it would be the form in its innermost being as
a simple nature that, present to a nondiscursive insight, first
orients and so enables its own discursive diairetic explication as
a composite. According to this second interpretive possibility,
even as Plato turns his attention to the procedures and precon-
ditions of λόγος, he preserves the notion of a noetic seeing; indeed, he situates such insight at the very heart of λόγος as itself
the fundamental precondition for the truth of λόγος.[24] The
double characterization of the forms as simple and composite
would express this. By providing a conceptual description of
the objective correlates, so to speak, for intuitive insight and
discursive analysis, respectively,[25] it would set the stage for a
nonmythic account of dialectical inquiry as a process of recol-
lection.[26]

Clearly, it would be out of place to try to decide between
these two interpretive possibilities here. Each requires, to begin with, much fuller explication, and this must be based not
on the *Parmenides* but on the *Sophist* and the *Statesman*. On the
one hand, the key passage in the *Parmenides*, hypothesis V, can
be taken as pivotal within each of the two interpretive
schemes. On the other hand, in the *Sophist* and the *Statesman*
themselves Plato neither explicitly drops nor explicitly affirms
the simplicity of the form. What is required, therefore, is a
probing examination of the Eleatic stranger's actual practice of
dialectic. We need to explore his deeds, testing the two possibilities by searching out the substantive implications of the
concrete ways he treats the forms as objects of inquiry. Such a
study, necessarily detailed and open to the possibility of subsurface meaning, must be reserved for another occasion.

APPENDIX A
STRUCTURAL OUTLINE OF
THE *PARMENIDES*

0. *Stage-setting* (126a-127d)

1. The *elicitation* of Socrates' theory of forms by Zeno's contradictions (127d-130a)

2. Parmenides' *refutations* of Socrates' theory (130a-134e)
   (1) Inquiry into the range of the forms (130b-130e)
   (2) The exposure of how participation appears to contradict the unity of the form (130e-133a)
      (i) Against the unity (to be understood as the integrity) of the participated form, the dilemma of participation by whole or by part of the form (130e-131e)
      (ii) Against the unity (to be understood as the singularity) of the participated form, the regress arguments (131e-133a)
   (3) The exposure of how, if the forms and their participants belong to separate domains, forms are unknowable (133a-134e)

3. Parmenides' *reorienting help*: the method of "gymnastic" (135a-137c)

4. Parmenides' *return* to Zenonian contradiction: the four pairs of apparently antithetical hypotheses (137d-166b)
   (1) If the One is, it *both* has none of the possible characters, including being and unity, (hypothesis I, 137d-142a) *and* has all of the possible characters (hypothesis II, 142b-155e) and transits between them (hypothesis IIa, 155e-157b).
   (2) If the One is, "the others" *both* participate in it and as a result have all the possible characters (hypothesis III, 157b-159b) *and* do not participate in it and as a result have no characters at all (hypothesis IV, 159b-160d).
   (3) If the One is not, it *both* is, as referent of speech and knowledge, different from "the others" and participates in greatness, equality, and smallness and participates in being in some sense, transiting between being and not-being, (hypothesis V, 160b-163b)

and—since it does not participate in being in any sense—cannot have any characters at all (hypothesis VI, 163b-164b).

(4) If the One is not, "the others" *both* will not "truly" have, but will "seem" and "appear" to have, all the possible characters (hypothesis VII, 164b-165e) *and*—since they cannot participate in anything that is not—cannot even "seem" and "appear" to have any of the possible characters (hypothesis VIII, 165e-166b).

APPENDIX B
STAGES IN THE PROCESS OF
CONVERSION FROM THINGS TO FORMS:
AN OUTLINE OF THE MOVEMENT
OF THE SUBSURFACE ARGUMENT
IN THE HYPOTHESES

1. The first turn toward the forms—the distinction and relation of form and thing (hypotheses I–IIa)

    (1) The One that is not in time and the One that is in time—how the form transcends the characters (hypothesis I) to which the spatio-temporally determinate thing is properly subject (hypothesis II)

    (2) "The instant"—how the thing, transiting between contradictory characters, depends upon the form for its abiding specific identity (hypothesis IIa)

2. Deepening and explicating the relativization of things to forms (hypotheses III–VIII)

    (1) How "participation" is the imposition of πέρας upon the mere πλῆθος that things would be just by themselves (hypothesis III)—and how this imposition is necessary to the very being and unity of things in the first place (hypothesis IV)

    (2) How the forms, just insofar as they do not have "being" in time, stand as different in kind from things, as capable of communing with one another, and as "being" and "not being" in the non-spatio-temporally determinate sense that is displayed in veridical discourse and inquiry (hypothesis V)—and how this distinction in the senses of "being" is necessary to the very intelligibility of the denial of "being" to the One in the first place, a denial that it thereby also undermines (hypothesis VI)

    (3) How spatio-temporally determinate things, reexamined in light of the discovery of the veridical sense of "being" proper to forms, only "seemingly" and "apparently" have all the char-

acters at first granted unconditionally in hypothesis II (hypothesis VII)—and how the participation of things in forms is necessary if there are to be things having this phenomenal status in the first place (hypothesis VIII)

NOTES

Preface:
Interpreting the *Parmenides*

1. For synoptic discussions see Cornford, 1939, and Brumbaugh, 1961. On the medieval history, see Klibansky, 1943. On the history of the text proper, see Brumbaugh, 1976 and 1982.
2. I will capitalize when referring to τὸ ἕν.
3. See Ch. III, n. 1, below.
4. Two exceptions are Friedländer's commentary, 1969, ch. XXIV, and Brumbaugh, 1961.
5. It is not, however, the argumentative monologue that, in Cornford's widely read English translation (1939) it appears to be. See Ch. III, n. 22 below.
6. Since the completion, in all essentials, of this study, two major contributions to the scholarly literature on the *Parmenides* have appeared, R. E. Allen's *Plato's Parmenides, Translation and Analysis* and Kenneth Sayre's *Plato's Late Ontology, A Riddle Resolved*. One major goal of Allen's rich and masterful exegesis is to show the unity of the *Parmenides*. It is especially impressive in its tightly woven analysis of the first part, the encounter between Socrates, Zeno, and Parmenides. In analyzing the hypotheses, Allen focuses exclusively on the way the arguments, interpreted as elements in an aporematic inquiry, constitute a whole that displays and universalizes the basic problem that has emerged in the first part (see pp. 178-180). As the reader will see, I agree with Allen's interpretation at many points. Above all, his exposition of the way Socrates undermines his own assertion of Ideas by construing participation as a real relation between sensibles and Ideas seems to me well oriented. Nonetheless, the interpretation I will offer differs fundamentally from Allen's. If my interpretation is correct, then Allen, by contrast, has misfocused the crucial error that leads Socrates to treat participation as a real relation (see esp. Ch. II, n. 11, below); has missed the central conceptual motif that binds the two parts of the dialogue together (see esp. Ch. II, n. 18, below); and has not seen the strikingly precise and extensive positive significance of the hypotheses, a significance that leads through and beyond the aporia generated by Parmenides' preceding criticisms (see below, esp. Ch. III, n. 17 and Ch. V, n. 2—and then, more particularly, Ch. III, n.

15; Ch. IV, nn. 23, 30, and 54; and Ch. V, nn. 21, 27, and 37.) The root of these differences, I think, is this: as powerful and illuminating as much of it is, Allen's study concentrates on the content of the arguments of the *Parmenides* at the expense of, rather than in conjunction with, their mimetic irony—but it is only by examining this irony, essential to dialogue as philosophical drama, that we can see the function Plato designed the arguments to have and, so, fix their true point. (For a systematic presentation of my disagreements with Allen's approach, one should see my review of his book in the forthcoming special Plato issue of *The Independent Journal of Philosophy*.)

Sayre's reading of the *Parmenides* is different in kind from Allen's. It constitutes only the first step within a much larger project. In the main, that project is fascinating: by bringing Aristotle's notoriously obscure testimony on Plato's doctrines concerning the One and the Great and Small to bear on the *Philebus* and vice versa, Sayre at once sheds new light on both and constructs an altogether new and yet common-sensical account of Plato's teaching in the Academy. Perhaps because he studies the *Parmenides* within the context of this project, however, his exegesis sometimes seems strained and sometimes thin. For specific objections, see, below, esp. Ch. II, n. 51, and Ch. III, n. 17—and then also Ch. III, nn. 4, 8, and 15; Ch. IV, nn. 3, 15, and 25; and Ch. V, n. 20. These particular differences, however, do not diminish my appreciation for what he has ventured; indeed, I shall have occasion to observe (in particular, Ch. V, n. 29) some key ways in which my own reading of the *Parmenides* appears to establish, perhaps more clearly than Sayre's own, certain key motifs that he wants to discern in Plato's thought.

7. *Meno* 82b ff. Note esp. 84b-c, with reference to 80b.

8. *Symposium* 201c ff. (note 201e), *Phaedo* 95e ff.

9. Consider, in the *Statesman*, 265a (with reference to 262a-264b) and 280b ff. (with reference to 267a and c, 277a).

10. If Ryle is right that the dialogues were written to be recited or read aloud at small gatherings (1966, p. 23 ff.), then the "audience" is just that, hearers rather than solitary, silent readers. Keeping this in mind helps to restore the sense of participation, of the constant invitation to active involvement, with which the dialogues need to be read and interpreted.

11. See Perelman, 1955.

12. Consider esp. *Meno* 86c-d.

13. Consider *Symposium* 223a in light, especially, of Socrates' challenge to the quest for praise and fame through Diotima's subordination of it, as "lower mysteries," to the "final revelation" (210a) of philosophy.

14. Consider especially *Statesman* 283b in light of 262a ff. (and 264a-b), 267a and c, 277a, and 280b and 281a.

15. Consider Cebes' failure—after Socrates' reflections on the need to get free of physicalistic thinking at *Phaedo* 96a ff.—to challenge the physicalistic treatment of forms and the situation in the body of the connection of soul with life (see 105c-d) during the final argument for immortality at 102b-107a.

16. For interesting and diversely relevant discussions of Socratic and Platonic irony, see, especially, Kierkegaard, 1971; Schaerer, 1941; Friedländer, 1958, Ch. VII; Rosen, 1968, Introduction; Griswold, 1985.

17. A major exception is Jonathan Ketchum, whose 1980 dissertation is part of a larger study, unfortunately not yet published, of the structure of all the dialogues. Although I have reservations about a number of particulars in this study—most notably, in the present context, I cannot accept his analysis of the *Parmenides* as structurally incomplete—his general approach to dialogue structure is an original and extremely valuable contribution to Plato scholarship. Other, well-known accounts of dialogue structure are offered by Festugière, 1936; Schaerer, 1938; Goldschmidt, 1947; and Gundert, 1971.

18. Of particular relevance to our project of interpreting the hypotheses in the *Parmenides*, these four moments organize the basic movement even in several of the dialogues in which dialogical drama gives way, in whole (e.g. *Apology, Menexenus*) or in part (e.g. *Crito*), to monologue. As J. Ketchum (1980) shows persuasively, *structure* runs deeper than *rhetorical form*.

19. A variation on this is the *Symposium*, in which nonphilosophers drive one another to deeper approaches. Note the shifts from cases to principles (180c ff.), part to whole (186a ff.), earnest pretence to comic self-knowledge (189a ff.).

20. By his philosophical unconcern for death (65d ff.), Socrates elicits the "*average person's*" fear that the soul is dissolved at death (70a); by focusing, in response, on the *pre*-existence of the soul, he elicits the counter-focus on the state of the soul *after* death (77b); and by pairing body with soul in his table of opposites, he elicits both the Pythagorean theory of soul as harmony (86b) and the distinction

between relative and absolute durability (87b). Thus the pointed inadequacy of his positions serves to provoke the deeper questions—culminating in the issue of physicalism—which he really wants to address from the beginning.

21. See Epilogue, n. 4.

22. Needless to say, this is a complex matter, requiring extensive discussion and interpretation. Here it must suffice to say that if Socratic elenchus is a part of the philosopher's art, then, by the standards of the stranger's own definition, to fail to distinguish it from sophistry would make the diairesis a "semblance" of what it pretends to be—and, so, sophistic rather than philosophical. For rich and mutually contrasting views of this, see Sayre, 1969, and Rosen, 1983.

23. This is explored in detail in Miller, 1980.

24. Missing the fundamental flaws in Socrates' last argument for immortality (see n. 15 above), Cebes is mistakenly content. By contrast, Simmias, who also misses the flaws and accepts the argument, is moved, as a result, to doubt argument generally (107a ff.). Neither, therefore, has yet achieved the mature appreciation for λόγος which Socrates aims to generate in them (see 89c ff.)

25. Neither Theaetetus nor Young Socrates recognizes the difficulties with the closing diaireses in each of these dialogues—in particular, the unclarities in the way sophist and statesman are and are not related to philosopher.

26. It might be better to say "in the Platonic sense of 'Socratic.' " It should be clear both here and throughout that my references to "Socrates" and to the "Socratic" are restricted to what Plato has fashioned in constructing the *persona* of Socrates in the dialogues. This restriction has a particular importance in the context of the *Parmenides*. Allen (1983, p. 63) is surely correct that the *Parmenides* is a *transparent* "fiction." I take it, therefore, that Plato, in putting the figure of the youthful Socrates before us, intends us to connect it not with the historical Socrates but with the *persona* so vividly developed in the earlier dialogues.

27. Allen nicely terms this "the reader . . . in first intention" (1983, p. 197).

28. A fourth check is, of course, critical attention to the extraordinary range of secondary scholarship on the *Parmenides*. I can hardly claim to have canvassed the whole of this literature in the notes that follow. Still, I have made a systematic effort to test my approach against—and to let myself be tempered by—the strengths of the major alternatives I have encountered.

Chapter I: The Dramatic Context

1. Though his interpretation is indeed "artificial" (as Friedländer writes, 1969, p. 192), Proclus comes closer to recognizing this structure than most modern commentators. See 1864, col. 662.

2. This is Parmenides' fragment B 1.22-23, 26.

3. See the metaphor of the ὁδός, "route" or "journey," as a line of in-quiry and thought in Parmenides' poem, both as exemplified by the action of the proem (fragment B 1) and as referred to explicitly at B 1.2, B 1.5, B 1.27, B 2.2, B 6.3, B 7.2, B 8.1.

4. Parmenides B 1.28-32, in which the goddess ordains a journey that will explore both truth and opinion.

5. It may be that in Parmenides' poem, too, the traveler knows his purpose in advance, for he begins by declaring that the inspired mares ". . . are bearing me as far as desire might reach" (B 1.1). It is a difficult point of interpretation whether the journey to and then under the guidance of the goddess fulfills the traveler's "desire" (θυμός) or transcends it or both.

6. Plato's words, καί μου λαβόμενος τῆς χειρὸς ὁ Ἀδείμαντος, χαῖρ', ἔφη (Parmenides 126a2-3), unmistakably recall Parmenides' de-scription of the goddess's greeting, B 1.22-23 and 26. This is also noted by Brumbaugh (1961, p. 27, n. 16).

7. The motif of ἀναγνώρισις, "recognition," occurs also at Statesman 257d ff. See Miller, 1980, pp. 6 ff.

8. This translation relies partly on Cornford's translation (1939).

9. Is Plato alluding to this contrast with playful subtlety when, after first presenting Antiphon in the act of designing or fixing a bit—that is, a restraining device—for his horses (127a), he then has Par-menides compare himself, in taking up the labor of the hypotheses, to a race-horse (137a)?

10. Plato elsewhere stresses that a good memory is an important pre-requisite to becoming philosophical. See Republic 486c ff., 535c, and Seventh Letter 341d, 344a1.

11. He has taken after his grandfather, we learn at 126c. It would be interesting to know more of his comrade Pythodorus (paired with him analogously as Glaucon and Adimantus and then Zeno and Parmenides are paired). The scanty information—that he studied with Zeno (Alcibiades I, 119a) and later was a minor general—leaves his philosophical development obscure.

12. Allen (1983, p. 65) dismisses the coincidence of the name "Ce-phalus"—and, too, the fact that the Cephalus of the Parmenides comes from Clazomenae, birthplace of Anaxagoras—as mere "ac-cident." But this is not fully consistent with his stress on the fic-

tional character of the *Parmenides*. Granting that Plato is writing transparent fiction, why would he have authored these coincidences if he did not intend them to call up the obvious associations?

13. Nothing in these observations about the way the *Parmenides* recalls the *Republic* should be taken to imply a denial that other dialogues—the *Timaeus* being only the most obvious case—also recall it. In general, there is nothing to prevent Plato from invoking one and the same dialogue as a background or subtext for several others; nor, when he does so, does this in itself imply that he intends any special interconnection between these latter dialogues. Consider, as a clear illustration of the point, the way both the *Gorgias* and the *Statesman* recall the portrayal of Socrates in court in the *Apology*.

14. The "Cephalus" of *Republic* I is a well-meaning but self-deceived hypocrite. He praises good conversation, freedom from the sexual passions, equanimity, justice, and religious practice, but his remarks to Socrates suggest that he has only recently acquired these values. Good conversation becomes more important only as age, not any act of will, dulls the "frenzied and savage master," sexual lust (329c); and religious practice is a hedge against punishment for earlier injustices—a prospect that apparently makes Cephalus "full of suspicion and terror" and causes him to "wake from his sleep in a fright" (330e). There is thus a sharp split between his appearance (even, it seems, to himself) and his reality.

15. See the acute remarks on the lack of distinction and the corruption in the new Athens in Voegelin's discussion (1957, pp. 52 ff).

16. Socrates describes Glaucon in particular as "most courageous" (perhaps, however, with the critical connotation of undue persistence, even stubbornness) at 357a3.

17. There are, of course, two other dialogues in which Socrates' youth is depicted: in the *Symposium* and the *Phaedo* Socrates himself, "now" an older man, tells of his youthful philosophical convictions and development. In fact, it would be of considerable substantive interest to compare both of these dialogues with the *Parmenides*. In the *Symposium*, there is a distinctly Parmenidean cast to Diotima's account of the Beautiful (see Solmsen, 1971b); at first look, however, there is also the tendency, in Diotima's ascent to the Beautiful, to treat beautiful things as if they have a "reality 'on their own' " (the phrase is Lee's, 1966, p. 353—see Ch. II, n. 49, below). In the *Phaedo*, likewise, one finds, on the one hand, a Parmenidean cast to the account of forms as incomposite and, on the other hand,

potentially problematic elements like the apparent grant of self-subsistence to a class of participant particulars (e.g. fire and snow, 103c ff.), the apparent designation of the form for equality as αὐτὰ τὰ ἴσα, see Ch. II, n. 6, below), treatment of the participant "equal sticks" at 74d-e as if they have a separate substantive status apart from the form (see, again, Lee, 1966, p. 361), and so forth. In both dialogues we thus find the same mix of achievement and defeçt that, as Chapters I and II will indicate, the *Parmenides* exposes in the *Republic*. Nonetheless, to extend our exegesis to the *Symposium* and the *Phaedo* would be a digression. This is because, in contrast to the *Parmenides'* subtle and pointed ways of invoking the *Republic*, there is nothing in its dramatic stage-setting that is specifically designed to provoke us to treat those dialogues as its proper background. This will turn out to be true even with regard to the reference to Clazomenae, birthplace of Anaxagoras; as we shall see (pp. 25-28), the way that Anaxagoras' thought figures in the background of the *Parmenides* is quite different from the way it figures in the *Phaedo*.

18. Two remarks, one by way of emphasis, the other a qualification, are important here. First, the implication of Plato's dramatic framing is not that he sets the stage for a simple restatement of what he has had Socrates say in the *Republic*. Rather, Plato appears, on the one hand, to acknowledge that, in giving the older Socrates non-philosophers as his interlocutors in the *Republic*, he did not provide himself with an occasion to articulate fully and rigorously what he most deeply thought and, on the other hand, to signal that the *Parmenides* will be (at least relatively speaking) such an occasion; he will now—the framing suggests—bring out what, in the *Republic*, he left implicit and opaque. Second, even with this qualification we still need to ask whether what Plato actually does in the *Parmenides* coincides with what he indicates, by his dramatic framing, he sets himself to do. It is of course quite possible that—indeed, either intentionally or unintentionally—he *both* projects a newly adequate articulation of the true substance of his own earlier position in the *Republic and yet*, in the course of this articulation, actually departs quite radically from that position. My interpretation of the dramatic framing should not be construed to beg this question; on the contrary, we must hold it open in order, at the close of our exegesis of the hypotheses, to raise it again. See the Epilogue, A.

19. Until recently, the point might have been considered hostage to the larger issue of what Cherniss has titled "the riddle of the early Academy" (1945). If the Tübingen "esotericists" were correct to as-

cribe to Plato an unwritten doctrine that he reserved for oral presentation to the inner circle of the Academy, then the dialogues would have to be relegated to the secondary status of exoteric work aimed at a more general public. On this view, even if some dialogues were subject for discussion within the Academy, they would not be of crucial importance, for they would surely be interpreted in the light of—and taken as, at best, preliminary to—the oral teaching. (For major statements of the esotericist position, see Krämer, 1959, and Gaiser, 1963 and 1980. For an illustration of the way esotericists and non-esotericists may disagree in their weighting of the dialogues, see Szlezák's review [1983] of Miller, 1980.) I take it as a major benefit of Sayre (1983), however, that he has freed the interpreter of the dialogues from the need to reckon with a separate esoteric unwritten doctrine. By showing that all the major elements of the notorious "lecture on the Good" and of the doctrine of the One and the dyad that Aristotle ascribes to Plato in, most notably, *Metaphysics* A, 6 can also be found in the *Philebus*, Sayre undercuts the importance of the distinction between oral and written, or esoteric and exoteric, teachings. This has the effect of restoring the dialogues to their important place in the intellectual life of the Academy.

20. Ryle (1968) writes, "For whose benefit did Plato compose the second part of the *Parmenides*? Explicitly for the benefit, not of Hoi Polloi, but of the young men who hoped to become philosophers, and therefore presumably for the young men in the Academy" (p. 77). Note, also, Allen, 1983, p. 197. Even if the intended audience of the dialogue extends to members of Pythagorean or Eleatic or Ionian schools, its focus on the forms orients it specifically to the interests of the Academy. It is therefore striking that so few—see Brumbaugh, 1961, and Ryle, 1966, above all—have tried to develop the specific implications of this.

21. This is Cherniss's thesis (1945). In fashioning a middle way between the esotericists (see n. 19, above) and Cherniss, Sayre (1983) contests much of the latter's position. Note, however, that he does not completely alter Cherniss's picture of the Academy on matters essential to my point. For Sayre as for Cherniss, mathematical studies are central; there is no separate unwritten doctrine to upstage what is written in the dialogues; and even if Plato did give the public "lecture on the Good" and "did talk philosophy at least occasionally with close associates" (p. 83), it was primarily the dialogues to which his students (taking Aristotle as exemplary on this

point) turned in studying Plato's thought. (On the possibility—suggested by Sayre's comments on Aristotle, pp. 82-83—of a substantive alienation between teacher and students in the Academy, see the suggestions in Miller, 1980, Ch. I and Epilogue.)

22. This may be the best moment to note two terminological difficulties that arise throughout this study. A central idea of my interpretation is that Plato intends us to take Parmenides' challenges to Socrates as a call for a non-imagistic treatment of forms, that is, for a thinking-through of the nature and function of forms that is primarily oriented not by instances and the imagistic understanding befitting them but rather by the forms themselves. This idea is not strange to the dialogues (cf., e.g., *Phaedo* 66a ff., *Republic* 518c ff., *Theaetetus* 185a ff.). But how should we refer to such thinking? To call it "abstract thinking" suggests, against the grain of the Platonic ontology that this thinking seeks to appropriate, that the instances of forms are, as "concrete," somehow prior. To call it "reflective thinking" or simply "thought" is, while not false, much too broad. To call it "contemplation" distracts from the aspect of active work that, as the hypotheses make quite vivid, such thinking requires. I have settled reluctantly on "conceptual thinking" as the least inadequate formulation. But I do not intend any assimilation of forms to concepts (on the problems of which, see *Parmenides* 132b-c and the discussion to come), nor do I intend the possible connotation of 'synthesis.' However much work such thinking requires, it is a mode not of construction but rather of response, recognition, and appreciation of that which stands prior to mind.

The second terminological difficulty concerns how one shall refer generally to the participants in the forms. Strikingly, Plato has no particular technical term. His protagonists often use examples or quasi-locative phrases; e.g., Socrates' citing of his body, 129c ff., and Parmenides' elenchtic introduction of the contrast between καθ'αὑτό and ἐν ἡμῖν, 133c4-5 ff. But if my interpretation is well oriented, the *Parmenides* seeks to liberate thought from the inevitable particularity of examples (see 135c-d) and from the notion of separate domains for forms and things. Again with some reluctance I have settled on the term "thing." It has the advantage over "singular" and "particular" of not connoting an Aristotelian logical context (even while it preserves the possibility for an ontological convergence of the participant with the "first substance" of the *Categories*), and it avoids the issue, as does the *Parmenides*, of the distinction between natural and artifactual. It is also not immediately too broad, as "entity" is. In fact, its connotation of physicality, place, and time is appropriate; Parmenides will focus on the spatio-temporal aspects of participants both in his refutations and, most notably, in the series of categories he selects in order to give his contrasting structural characterizations of form and participant in hypotheses I and II. But it is important to bear in mind that there is no particular term in Plato's Greek that my term "thing" trans-lates. I am referring, rather, to an idea that Plato is, astonishingly, articulating and delimiting categorially for the first time.

23. This is Shorey's translation, as published in *Plato: Collected Dialogues*, 1961.

24. See Miller, 1980, Ch. I.

25. No less than six times in the course of the dialogue, Theodorus resists Socrates' invitations to join the discussion. See *Theaetetus* 146b, 162b, 164e-165a, 168e-169a, 177c, 183c.

26. See the indirect references to his inability to distinguish appearance from reality and to recognize the distinctive value of philosophy at *Sophist* 216c and *Statesman* 257a-b.

27. See Ch. II, n. 55.

28. For a view comparable to this thesis of two beginnings, see Robinson's remark (1941, p. 265) that "The *Parmenides* does for the young philosopher what the Socratic elenchus did for the common man. It is the elenchus for the philosopher, who thought himself beyond the need for elenchus."

29. Indeed, it will still be premature to do so at the end of this study. Since, as shall gradually become clear, the reading I shall offer of the *Parmenides* illuminates alternative ways of approaching the *Republic*, on the one hand, and the Eleatic dialogues, on the other, its immediate effect will be to focus, not resolve, the question of the relation of the *Parmenides* to these other dialogues and to set the stage for fresh studies of the latter. Our closing stance will therefore have to be—though sharply focused—heuristic and problem-posing.

30. The classic example is Vlastos, 1954, especially pp. 254-255.

31. See, e.g., Cherniss, 1957, especially pp. 364-375; also 1944, pp. 296-299.

32. See, e.g., Owen, 1953, especially pp. 318-322. For recent examples, see Teloh, 1981, Ch. 4, and Sayre, 1983, esp. Ch. One, I. Note, also, Weingartner, 1973, Ch. 3. His interesting interpretation of the dramatic significance of Plato's use of the *persona* young Socrates—to wit, that since "no young Socrates ever made such a

distinction [between forms and participants] . . . ," Plato intends us to realize that "[t]he Socrates of this dialogue is pointedly made fictional: the young Socrates and the old Parmenides together are Plato himself in the process of being reborn . . ." (pp. 144-145)— seems to me one-sided and implausible. That Plato had thought through the way in which Socrates' youthfulness naturally calls to the reader's mind his maturity in the middle dialogues is clear from 130e, where he has Parmenides play on this motif.

33. See, e.g., Brumbaugh, 1961, esp. pp. 41-44 (and, on the way the dramatic framing prepares for this, pp. 28 ff.).

34. Allen (1983, esp. pp. 92-100) seems to present one version of the recognition of this. Parmenides' criticisms are "not meant to herald a rejection of the theory of Ideas or Forms found in the *Phaedo* and *Republic*" (p. 94), but they are nonetheless serious, "put as *aporiai*, perplexities, which must be faced and thought through if philosophy is to be pursued" (p. 96). The result of thinking them through, Allen holds, is neither a mere restatement of nor a simple departure from the middle period theory; rather it is the clarified *and* radicalized version offered not in the *Parmenides* proper (here, as will become evident, I part company with Allen) but, rather, in the *Timaeus*.

35. For cases in point, see the Epilogue.

36. See *Apology* 26d.

37. For discussion of Anaxagoras' effort to "save the phenomena," see Kerferd, 1969.

38. Of course, Plato affirms nonbeing in a new sense, not only in the *Sophist*, but also, strikingly, in the fifth hypothesis of the *Parmenides* itself. See V.B.2 and the Epilogue, B.

39. Both here and in the next sentence I use Kirk and Raven's translation (1964).

40. There is no sign that Anaxagoras intended what Leibniz, stressing the aspect of "*infinite* in smallness," later made of it, that the "seeds" must be immaterial; by retaining the notion of smallness, Anaxagoras shows that he is still thinking of extended being.

41. It is widely noted that for the Greeks "one" is not a number but rather the basis of number. Yet they did calculate (add, subtract) with "one." It is important to distinguish between "one" as 'singular,' by which we refer to what can be made plural, and "one" as 'unique,' by which we refer to what, since it cannot be made plural, is not subject to number or counting.

42. Allen (1964) notes this.

43. Socrates' phrase alludes to the report, passed on by Pythodorus, that Zeno "had been Parmenides' darling (παιδικά)," 127b.

44. διαλέγεσθαι is hard to translate here. It should not be taken too technically (as "dialectic" in a formal-philosophical sense) nor too loosely (as mere "conversation" or "discourse").

45. I want to acknowledge but postpone an open inquiry into whether Plato proposes a new interpretation of Parmenides and, if so, whether it is insightful and true. This would require an independent study, outside the scope of this essay, of Parmenides' poem. In the meantime, let me balance against the traditional view of the thrust of the *Parmenides* as anti-Parmenidean (see, e.g., Taylor, 1940, and Cornford, 1939) three considerations: First, there are some indications that Plato does not accept the dominant interpretation of Parmenides as a strict monist. These include his distinction between Parmenides and the eristic interpreters of his poem, at *Theaetetus* 183e ff. and again at *Sophist* 216a-b; his depiction of Parmenides as espousing the point, at least, of asserting a plurality of forms, at *Parmenides* 135b-c; and his indirect crediting to Parmenides of the position that being is one as a whole of parts, through the manner in which he cites Parmenides at *Sophist* 244e. In addition, there is the often overlooked point that Plato clears the way for his new interpretation of nonbeing as difference—already indicated by "Parmenides" in the fifth hypothesis of the *Parmenides*, as noted—by first radicalizing Parmenides' own denial of the intelligibility of not-being as the contrary or "opposite of being" (τοὐναντίον τοῦ ὄντος, *Sophist* 258e).

Second, close attention to the substance of the proem and the Doxa-part of Parmenides' poem make the dominant interpretation problematic. For the moment, I must rely for this point on arguments I have made earlier in "Parmenides and the Disclosure of Being." Parmenides' monism is dialectical, founded on the disclosure of the internal reference of the contraries of Ionian cosmology to "nothing" (μηδέν) and, in turn, of "nothing" to being-as-such. Since, within this context, being emerges as the being, as such, of the contraries, the contraries emerge *as beings*. The precise irony and pointed language of a number of passages in B4, B7, and B8 indicate that Parmenides recognized the implication of this—that the unity of being includes plurality even while it precludes heterogeneity—and began to wrestle with the consequent problem of the ontological status of difference.

Third, if my reading of Parmenides is well-taken, then Plato's distinction of the two senses of nonbeing not only radicalizes but also completes Parmenides' own insight, for it permits the inclusion of difference within being. This might well be the clue to interpreting why Plato has "Parmenides" introduce and the Eleatic stranger develop the new notion of not-being in the *Parmenides* and the *Sophist*: the traditional construal of "father Parmenides" notwithstanding, the new notion is an internal implication or, at least, a proper development, of Parmenides' true thought.

46. For discussion of Plato's appropriation of Eleatic concepts in *Republic* V and VI, see especially, Solmsen, 1971b; Nehamas, 1979; and Teloh, 1981, pp. 89-96.

47. On Plato's appropriation of Parmenides' notion of unity, see especially Teloh, 1976 and 1981.

48. Patterson (1985, p. 87) appears to note this problem when, in the course of objecting to a recent line of interpretation of this and similar passages, he observes that "one may be led to believe that sensible opposites, considered precisely in that respect in which they are *F*, do exactly resemble the Form of *F*. . . ."

49. Solmsen (1971a) raises the possibility that there is more dramatic fiction than historical fact in the portrayal of Zeno in the *Parmenides*. This is quite possible, but see n. 52 below, in the context of the whole argument of I.C.3.

50. Remaining outside and arriving too late for the main speech are dramatic symbols of distance and disagreement elsewhere in Plato. Recall the opening action of *Symposium* and of *Gorgias*.

51. Is the story of the "theft" fact or fiction? Why, in either case, does Plato make a point of telling it? His desire to distinguish a mature Zenonian dialectic from the eristic monism of the treatise would answer the second question, at least.

52. It is unclear how this "Zeno" fits together with the reports about "Palamedes" at *Phaedrus* 261b and d. When Plato credits Palamedes with "an art of speaking, such that he can make the same things appear like and unlike, or one and many, or again at rest and in motion," is he simply referring to the dialectical strategy of Zeno's treatise? Or might his words indicate that Zeno sees that his dialectic, equally capable of proving that things are "one" (and "like," "at rest," etc.) or that they are "many" (and "unlike," "in motion," etc.), serves as a formal procedure of argument rather than a means of securing ontological monism in particular? If the latter, then the *Phaedrus* gives a sketch of the older Zeno consistent with that, on my reading, of the *Parmenides*.

53. There is a difficulty in the translation of 135e1-4. Parmenides, having recommended the method of Zeno's arguments to Socrates, nonetheless sustains Socrates' objection to their limited range; he says that he admired Socrates' earlier point, ὅτι οὐκ εἴας ἐν τοῖς ὁρωμένοις οὐδὲ περὶ ταῦτα τὴν πλάνην ἐπισκοπεῖν, ἀλλὰ περὶ ἐκεῖνα ἃ μάλιστά τις ἂν λόγῳ λάβοι καὶ εἴδη ἂν ἡγήσαιτο. Cornford (1939) translates: "you would not allow the survey to be confined to visible things or to range only over that field; it was to extend to those objects which are specially apprehended by discourse and can be regarded as forms." Schleiermacher (1966) takes the same tack in his translation. Allen (1983) however, objects, arguing that the notion of restriction rendered by "confined to" and "only" is not in the Greek (1983, pp. 183-184). He offers the following alternative: "you would not allow inquiry to wander among the things we see, nor even within their domain, but rather in the field of those things there, which one could most especially grasp by rational account and believe to be characters." Diès (1956) takes the same tack as Allen in his translation.

If we distinguish between a literal translation of the line by itself from a translation that takes its specific context into account, Allen and Diès offer better literal translations than Cornford and Schleiermacher. The specific context, however, appears to require a decision in favor of Cornford and Schleiermacher. Parmenides is referring back to Socrates' objection to Zeno. Zeno, having made no distinction between visibles and forms in the first place, had produced a host of seemingly contradictory characterizations of visible things; Socrates' objection took essentially the following form: So long as you do not distinguish forms from visibles, your contradictions will seem genuine; but forms should be distinguished from visibles, and once you make this distinction, your contradictions will dissolve. But this is to say that Socrates objects *not* to the fact that Zeno fails to restrict his examination to forms; rather, he objects to the fact that Zeno restricts his examination to visibles. It follows that the change Socrates seeks (cf. Parmenides' ἀλλά, "but rather") should be not that forms be made the subject of inquiry in place of visibles but rather that the unwitting restriction to visibles be lifted, that is, that the inquiry be extended to forms as well. Cornford and Schleiermacher, putting Parmenides' words into the context to which they refer, therefore quite properly 'translate in' the notions of "confining" and "extending." At another level, the conflict may be more apparent than real. As we shall see, in the hypotheses themselves visible things are considered (thus supporting Cornford and Schleiermacher)—but they are considered in their general categorial structure, hence *as* objects of "rational account" (thus supporting Allen and Diès, in a way that, however, undercuts the sheer disjunction between visibles and objects of "rational account" that their translations imply). Thus the conflict dissolves.

54. These reflections have a bearing on the question of the relative date of composition of the *Parmenides*. My reading of the dramatic framing of the *Parmenides* supports the long-standing consensus that places it after the *Republic* (for, as I have been suggesting, the *Parmenides* refers to the *Republic* in setting out its own project) and prior to the *Sophist*. The latter point is confirmed not only by the fact that the *Sophist* refers back to the *Parmenides* at 217c but also, as I shall argue in V.B.2.c, by the way in which the *Parmenides* provides substantive preparation for the *Sophist*'s method of division and interpretation of nonbeing. For statements of the consensus position, see, e.g., Cornford, 1939, p. 63, and Guthrie, 1975, pp. 41-59, and 1978, pp. 32-34. Beyond this, I intend to leave open the more particular question—first made controversial by Owen (1953) and recently renewed by Sayre (1983)—of the relative dating of the *Parmenides* and the *Timaeus*. At the risk of begging questions about the interpretation of the *Timaeus*, let me just indicate two points of agreement I have with Sayre. First, he does a masterful job exposing difficulties in the stylometric evidence that was once presumed to settle the question in favor of the relative lateness of the *Timaeus*; as he says (p. 257), this evidence is too ambiguous to serve as the basis for a decision one way or the other. Second, I also agree with Sayre (p. 239), though for quite different reasons, that the substantive content of the *Parmenides* does not settle the question. Owen originally argued that the *Parmenides* discredits the interpretation of participation by the simile, key to the *Timaeus*, of model/ likeness. In Chapter II, however, I shall argue that Parmenides objects not to the simile as such but rather to an excessively literal understanding of it; in Chapters IV and V, in turn, I shall try to work out the conceptual account of participation that Parmenides suggests in the hypotheses (see especially the discussion of hypothesis III in V.A.2). Since this account serves to bring out the nonliteral content of the simile, the *Parmenides*, in both of its main parts, and the *Timaeus* prove to be compatible. On this view, we need neither place the *Parmenides* "in the shadow of the *Timaeus*" (Owen, 1953,

p. 338) nor reject the *Timaeus* as expressing an essentially defective teaching that Plato, in and after the *Parmenides*, abandoned. I also intend to leave open, for two reasons, the larger question that is often at issue in discussions of relative dating, the question whether Plato's thought is best understood by a developmental or a unitarian approach. First, to prejudge this question here, at the beginning of my exegesis, would limit in advance my interpretation of the content of the *Parmenides*, and this would be wrong-headed; the judgment about whether Plato's thought develops in major ways should follow, not precede, the interpretation of particular dialogues. Second, once the interpretation is accomplished and we are in position to summarize and assess its results, we shall see that the content of the *Parmenides* in fact provides possible support for both approaches and so does not, taken by itself alone, help to decide the case between them. (See the Epilogue.)

Chapter II: Parmenides' Challenge
to Socrates

1. Thus *Hippias Minor, Gorgias, Protagoras* (in which Socrates himself has elicited the "performance," Protagoras' myth). And cf. *Symposium*, in which Socrates follows Agathon's speech with his characteristic questioning.
2. See the general analysis of dialogue structure in the Preface.
3. My italics. Cherniss (1957, p. 372) paraphrases this Platonic formula, ὃ ἔστι X, as "what is identical with x" and thus distinguishes it from an attributive statement meaning "what has x [as an attribute]." He cites *Republic* 597b5-7 (and some other comparable passages, see p. 372, n. 4) as evidence. An alternative reading, taking the x as the grammatical subject, would yield the paraphrase "what x *is*." (For a recent discussion of the possible construals of the Platonic formula, see Kahn, 1981, pp. 127-129.) In any case, this is *not* one of the instances of phrasing that shows young Socrates' difficulty maintaining his distinction between form and its participant thing.
4. αὐτὸ καθ᾽ αὐτό is a key Platonic phrase. Here its thrust is to separate the form—to set it off "by itself"—apart from its instances. But κατά also has the sense, "in accord with," and this lets αὐτὸ καθ᾽ αὐτό, applied to the form, suggest the appearance of the form in its own distinctive terms, as it were, or in accord with itself and nothing else. Thus we can also translate the phrase as "in and for itself."

5. It is noteworthy that Socrates does not distinguish the respects or senses in which things are "like" and "unlike." Plato of course knows this sort of distinction (see, e.g., *Republic* 454b ff., *Sophist* 259c-d) and will invite its employment later on (see IV.B.2). But it would not be timely here. If he had Socrates invoke it against Zeno, then there would be no immediate need or occasion for introducing the theory of forms. Cf. Allen, 1983, pp. 74-77.

6. Geach (1956) warns against taking only the general noun (e.g. F-ness) as the proper expression for the form. He holds that since the form is, as a standard, also an individual, the substantive adjective (the F) is just as appropriate. And he argues that, given the specific character of some forms like equality or plurality, we should not be jarred when Plato uses the substantive plural, as in the cases of "the equals themselves" (αὐτὰ τὰ ἴσα) in the *Phaedo* or αὐτὰ τὰ ὅμοια or τὰ πολλά in the *Parmenides*, to refer to forms. Geach may rightly identify the reason why Socrates slips into the plural: Socrates shows later that he does regard the form as being, and not merely being like, a model or paradigm, and a model is indeed an individual. As Parmenides' objections reveal, however, such a reduction of form to the status of an individual brings participation and the unity of the form into contradiction; moreover, Parmenides' hypotheses will purge this reduction (see IV.B.1). If, therefore, we read this passage in light of the dialogue as a whole, Socrates' use of the plural form seems to signal the difficulties in his understanding of the form rather than the form's own nature. For different responses to Geach, see Vlastos, 1956, pp. 286-291, and Owen, 1968, pp. 114-115. Whether Owen's interesting justification of αὐτὰ τὰ ἴσα in the *Phaedo* can be extended to our passage in the *Parmenides* is problematic. Although Owen assimilates young Socrates' αὐτὰ τὰ ὅμοια and τὰ ἀνόμοια to the αὐτὰ τὰ ἴσα of the *Phaedo*, he makes no reference to τὰ πολλά. In any event, his way of accounting for αὐτὰ τὰ ὅμοια in the *Parmenides* is not in principle in conflict with mine. That the young Socrates merely intends to set the predicate, as it has just appeared, apart from its referent in that appearance is not incompatible with the thesis that Plato wants to signal the dangers of doing so in such a direct fashion, as if one were setting one thing apart from another.

7. On the "reification" of the forms as the central theme of the first part (up to c. 135c) of the *Parmenides*, see the analyses in Cornford, 1939; Friedländer, 1969; and Sinaiko, 1965.

8. We shall see later how Parmenides' hypotheses respond to Socrates'

tacit challenge by showing how the forms are isolate (IV.C.1 on hypothesis I) *and* related in several sorts of "sharing" or "communion" (V.B.2. on hypothesis V).

9. For a comparable characterization of the youthful Socrates' state of mind, see Lee, 1973, esp. p. 106 and nn. 3, 9, and 29. Although Lee discusses only the second regress argument at 132d ff., the account he offers both of Socrates' unwitting equivocation between "everyday" and philosophically radical understandings of his own theory and of the way Parmenides' response is designed to force a distinction and reflective choice between these can be fruitfully extended, as we shall see, to cover the whole series of exchanges between the two.

10. This is the sense of the particle γε at 135c7.

11. It is, I think, at this point that Allen (1983) misfocuses Socrates' error. In (1) refusing to grant forms for "the things which we see," Socrates, Allen holds, is forced (2) to grant these latter a nature and reality of their own, independent from the forms; this, however, commits Socrates (3) to interpreting the participation of sensibles in forms as a real relation, and this, in turn, leads him (4) into the grip of the dilemma of participation with its devastating consequences for the theory of forms. (See Allen, 1983, esp. pp. 105, 108-113, 122, 168, 178-180.) I quite agree that Socrates is guilty of (3). But the reason for (3) and (4) is that, in spite of his explicit and intentional assertion of forms as causally prior to their participants, he is still under the sway of δόξα and takes his orientation in thinking from things. Because he therefore thinks of the form as if it were a thing, he cannot help but think of it as composite (this, I shall argue, is why he must submit to—and is what Parmenides means to expose by—the dilemma of participation) and he cannot help but think of participation as if it were a relation between things, that is, a real relation (this is revealed both by the dilemma of participation and the following regress arguments). This orientedness by things—which is the way I would refocus (2)—is, moreover, the ground, not the consequence, for (1), as I go on to argue in the main text immediately following.

12. Allen (1983) rightly observes that "the first set of Ideas Socrates accepts" is not "purely mathematical." Insofar as this set includes not only likeness, unity, and plurality (which themselves "have application beyond mathematics as well as in it") but also "all the terms in Zeno's argument" (130b), it represents distinctively "general" forms (Allen, 1983, pp. 106-107). By singling out likeness,

unity, and plurality, however, Parmenides focuses Socrates' attention—and Plato focuses the Academic hearer's attention—on forms that play a key role in the mathematical training prescribed in *Republic* VII. With regard to the second set, note that justice is the form sought in *Republic* II-IV; beauty (τὸ καλόν) is Socrates' exemplary focus in introducing the conception of the forms in *Republic* V (see 474d ff., 475e, 476b ff.); and the good is revealed as the highest form in *Republic* VI (505a ff., especially 506a and the following simile of the sun). Thus Plato strongly evokes the *Republic* as background and point of departure.

13. Unless he is simply self-contradictory, however, Heraclitus' notion of "everliving fire" is metaphorical. Consider fragments 30 (number 220 in Kirk and Raven, 1964), 31 (number 221, ibid.), and 93 (247, ibid.).

14. See Parmenides B4, as discussed in Miller, 1979.

15. This distinction in senses is not altogether new to Socrates. As we noted in Ch. I, he displays an incipient sense of it by his examples at 129c ff. Parmenides will not bring it out directly, however, until his pointedly twofold argumentation in hypothesis II, 142d ff., which will be discussed in IV.A.3. Teloh (in 1976 and in 1981, esp. pp. 151, 158, 160), notes this distinction in Parmenides' refutations (but see n.16, below).

16. It is important not to miss the fact that Parmenides does not actually infer the plurality of the form from either its self-separateness (Teloh, in particular in 1981, p. 155, fails to observe this) or from its divisibility. Though plurality is entailed, to make this inference would leave the distinction between integrity and singularity as senses of unity less sharp.

17. See his references to the form as "one" at 131a9, b1, b7, b9, c9, c10, 132a1, a2, a3, a7, b2, b7, c3, c4, c6, d9, 133b1, 135c9. Socrates refers to the form as "one" at 131a10, b3, b5, 132b5. These references do not stand out as fully as they should in Cornford's translation (1939), unfortunately, since he shifts between "one," "single," and "unity" in rendering ἕν (or the feminine μία); furthermore, Cornford's variations tend to take out of the reader's hands—and even prevent him from recognizing that Plato presents him with—the *task* of discriminating between the different senses of the selfsame word (ἕν).

18. There is, strikingly, very little discussion of the theme of the unity of the form in the voluminous literature on the first main part of the *Parmenides*. Partial exceptions are Teloh, 1976 and 1981, and

H. Rochol, 1971. But Teloh fails to go on to explore the hypotheses and so fails to have occasion to see how the theme of the unity of the form binds the two parts of the dialogue together; and Rochol fails to see the positive significance of the conception of unity as simplicity. In efforts to save the third-man argument from the inconsistency seen by Vlastos (1954), both Sellars (1955) and Strang (1963) focus on the sense of "one" in the argument's opening steps at 132a1-4, and Vlastos refines and articulates this focus further in responding to them (1969a). Interestingly, Allen—both in 1974 and in 1983—finds the properly mathematical distinction between "two kinds of infinity: a dense infinite allied to that of continuity, typical of extensive magnitudes, and the infinitude of succession, typical of number" (1983, p. 219) centrally present in the opening deductions of Parmenides' second hypothesis. This is a mathematical parallel, with regard to infinity, to the more general distinction between integrity and singularity, with regard to unity. But neither Allen nor any other modern interpreter has shown just how this latter distinction is thematic and central in 130e-133b. Nor, therefore, has any commentator gone on to make the further distinctions—which, as we shall see, are called for by 130e-131e and 131e-133b, respectively, but not worked out until the first two hypotheses—between integrity and simplicity and between singularity and uniqueness, nor has anyone pointed out the tight connection between the negative treatment of the unity of the form at 130e-133b and the positive explication of this unity in the opening deductions of the first two hypotheses. See IV.A.3 and IV.B.3.

19. Allen (1983, pp. 121-122) connects this moment with Parmenides' declaration at 146b that anything that is related to anything else is related by being either the same or different or whole to part or part to whole. This connection will become all the more compelling once we are in position to see (but here we depart from Allen) that 146b is focused specifically on relations between physical-sensible things (see IV.B.1 and IV.B.2).

20. Cf. Ross, 1951, p. 86. Admittedly, whole-part structure need not itself imply materiality, as Allen observes (1974, p. 724; 1983, pp. 124-125). But by his spatializing vocabulary and the illustrative conundrums treating the forms of size as physical things with size in their own right (131c-e), Parmenides leaves no doubt that here whole-part structure does connote materiality. For some of the difficulties Allen's effort to sustain this distinction involves, see Chap. IV, n. 30.

21. My italics.

22. It is the spatial aspect of "day" as the environing expanse of daylight sky that Socrates has in mind, not the temporal aspect of daytime. Socrates' willingness to accept Parmenides' supposed equivalent, the sail, shows this.

23. Of course, to show that material partition is an untenable interpretation of participation is not to show what alternative notion is correct. Socrates will shortly try another simile, that of model and likeness, but this, even while it intends the form as one over its many participants, has other difficulties which destroy its unity. As we shall argue below, Socrates needs to conceptualize the transcendence of the form with respect to spatiotemporal categories, then grasp the immanence which this sense of transcendence makes possible.

24. Ross (1951, pp. 87-88) makes roughly the same point but in terms of language, holding that Parmenides' objection is "fatal, not to the theory of Ideas, but to the language in which Plato had formulated it. The expressions 'share' and 'imitate,' against which the arguments [here and at 132d ff. below] are directed, are alike metaphors inadequate to express the relation of particulars to an Idea." But because he does not go on to disclose or discuss the non-metaphorical meaning and the conceptual formulation of it which Plato knew to overcome Parmenides' objections, Ross's distinction seems vacuous and open to the sort of criticism that Sellars (1955, pp. 422 ff.) and Vlastos (1955, pp. 445-446) offer. But it is not vacuous. Properly grasping the subsurface function of the hypotheses (as Ross himself did not) saves Ross's point, as we shall see.

25. Against Vlastos's view that the conundrums represent the effort to identify and expose the problematic assumption that the forms are self-predicative (1954, pp. 256 ff.), Teloh makes the interesting objection that the conundrums have their absurdity only as violations of self-predication (1981, pp. 156 ff.). That what partakes of largeness, for example, be large by virtue of something smaller than largeness seems absurd, Teloh observes, only if one presumes that it *should* be by virtue of something itself large that the participant is large. Thus the conundrums would serve to reinforce rather than critically probe into self-predication. If, however, Nehamas's analysis of self-predication (1979) is correct, the dispute itself is misfocused (see n. 35 below). It is not self-predication but materialization that is at issue.

26. We come now to the two versions of the "third-man" argument.

The horizon-setting treatment of the TMA in contemporary scholarship is still Vlastos, "The Third Man Argument in the *Parmenides*," 1954. It has provoked an astonishing volume of major philosophical scholarship, with notable contributions by Sellars (1955), Geach (1956), Cherniss (1957), Strang (1963), Allen (1960), and Moravcsik (1963); closely associated, although preceding Vlastos's essay, is Owen, 1953. While I have learned a great deal from this literature, I find some pervasive problems in its interpretive reach. Since the work of identifying and articulating these problems has been integral to the formation of my own interpretive orientation, it seems timely to give a brief accounting of them here. There are two distinct orders of problem to be noted.

In a general *methodological* vein, much of the foregoing discussion is not well attuned to the extent and character of the context within which the TMA is presented. Most strikingly, although Vlastos (1954) considers Parmenides' objections at 130e ff. and 133c ff., neither he nor any of the others just cited considers the hypotheses as part of the relevant background for interpreting the TMA. To do so, it would not be necessary to interject discussion of the hypotheses explicitly into the analysis of the TMA. Since, however, the hypotheses are presented in response to the basic problem that Parmenides reveals in Socrates' thought by means of the TMA and his other arguments, interpretive analysis of these should be oriented by the anticipation of the hypotheses. In addition, none of the commentators cited takes the dramatic setting, established in the opening pages of the *Parmenides*, and the pedagogical interchange between Parmenides and Socrates as substantively relevant in interpreting the presentation of the TMA. This is an important oversight. Because the dramatic form of the dialogue embeds argumentation in interpersonal interplay, argumentation always has not only its properly logical content but, too, a function in the dramatically presented context of communication; moreover, this function is itself subordinate to the function of the presented drama in the encompassing context of communication between author and audience. (See the Preface, A.) Therefore, that Parmenides presents the TMA *to the youthful Socrates* who, in turn, stands in *a determinate representative relation to Plato's projected audience* should inform and orient analysis of the TMA. (For a discussion which makes a similar point, see Barford, 1978.) Finally, the formalization of the TMA, itself a persistent project in the literature, makes various crucial details disappear from view altogether. These include the sorts of examples Parmenides invokes, the shadings in Socrates' accepting replies, and a number of possibly significant phrasings and shifts in phrasing in Parmenides' argumentation (including, for instance, the uses of ἰδεῖν at 132a3 and 7 and the elimination of ἐοικέναι in favor of ὅμοιον ὁμοίῳ at 132d5-7). (A partial exception is Cherniss, 1957; see esp. pp. 365 ff.) Since, however, Parmenides' examples and phrasings show the focus of his argument and since Socrates' moments of resistance reflect the points of difficulty Parmenides means to expose, these are important sources of orientation for the interpreter and need to be highlighted rather than obscured.

In a general but *substantive* vein, Vlastos's decisions to concentrate on "the logical structure of the argument" of the TMA, "to treat it as a formal structure of inference from premises," and to focus the emergent issues in terms of "predication" (Vlastos, 1954, pp. 232 ff.) have been determining for all the subsequent discussion. While his findings and the debate they have stimulated have been of great intrinsic interest, it is not so clear that they have been basically well-oriented to the *kind* of problematic Parmenides raises by his arguments. From the beginning of the TMA, Parmenides focuses on the basic *cognitive situation* within which Socrates is first motivated to assert the forms. "Whenever many things *appear* (or *seem*, δόξῃ) to you to be large, then, perhaps, a certain one character *appears* (δοκεῖ) to you, as you *look* (ἰδόντι) at them all, to be the same" (132a2-3). "But, then, what about the large itself and the others, the large things, if, with the soul, you *look* (ἴδῃς) at them all in just the same way? Does not large *appear* (φανεῖται), once again, as a certain one, through which all of these *appear* (φαίνεσθαι) large?" (132a6-8) Vlastos himself calls attention to the phrasings just stressed, first in 1955 (pp. 442 ff.) and later in a 1963 "Addendum" to his 1954 essay, and notes that they provide "the materials for . . . an epistemological [version]" of the TMA (1954, p. 262). But I think my disagreement runs deeper. The issue is not so much whether the "formal structure of inference" addresses ontological or epistemological issues as whether it really is a "formal structure of inference" that Parmenides means to present in the first place; to put it anachronistically, the question is whether Parmenides invites Socrates—and Plato invites us—to undertake a logical-linguistic or an intentional analysis. By the phrasings I have stressed, his opening remarks to Socrates refer to the many large things as *an object field* or field of appearances given in correlation with the *cognitive act* of looking or sight. Note, too, that later, when Socrates tries to forestall the regress by distinguishing the form as a νόημα ("thought") which arises only in the soul or mind (cf. ἐν ψυχαῖς) (132b3-6), Parmenides counters by distinguishing a νόημα ("thought") from its referent or intentional object, the νοούμενον ("what is thought of") (132b7-c7); thus Parmenides, even while challenging Socrates' particular point, accepts the cognitive or intentional-analytic context to which Socrates, guided there by Parmenides' own preceding phrasings, appeals. Nor, further, is Socrates' ensuing turn to the analogy of model and likeness (132c12 ff.) a departure from this context; rather, model/likeness points back (in real historical order) or ahead (in the dramatically projected history) to the elder Socrates' figure of the divided line, and there the analysis—consisting in a distinction of object-types together with their correlative cognitive powers—is pointedly cognitive or intentional rather than logical-linguistic. Although I will develop this interpretation in the text, it should be generally clear just from these remarks that this sense for the basic context within which the TMA unfolds gives rise to a *cast* of interpretation different from that which dominates the literature cited above.

27. This turn, a characteristically Platonic return to the beginning, is generally missed. Like Cornford in his translation (1939), most commentators miss the predicative role of ἕν at 132a1 and take Parmenides to be addressing why Socrates "believes a single form to *exist* (εἶναι) in each case."

28. Cf. Moravcsik, 1963, p. 57.

29. See n. 26 above. The pointed play on ἰδεῖν, "to look," in this and the next passage is crucial but rarely noticed. Even in his later essay (1969a), in which he offers detailed translation of the passage, Vlastos's rendering of ἰδόντι by the vague "in your view" downplays Parmenides' punning comparison of the form, ἰδέα, to the objects "for [the one] looking," ἰδόντι, in a sense-perceptual sense. He also fails to call attention to the pointed ambiguity of Parmenides' phrase in the next passage, τῇ ψυχῇ . . . ἴδῃς (literally, "you look at . . . with the soul").

30. Note how—as with his fourth question regarding the range of the forms at 130c5-7 and as with his pointed conundrums regarding the forms of size-characters—Parmenides directs the argument to "the things we see." See n. 26 above. This focus is missed by those who, rightly noting that Parmenides introduces his argument as universal in scope (132a1), pay no attention to the specificity of his example. They thereby miss the way Parmenides is repeatedly

leading Socrates back to the edge of the "abyss of nonsense" (τινα βυθὸν φλυαρίας, 130d7).

31. I follow Cornford's translation here and take ἕν as predicative. It is grammatically possible (following Vlastos, 1969a, p. 290) to treat ἕν as part of the subject of an existential εἶναι, thus: "hence you believe that the one thing, Largeness, exists." But see n. 27; the Vlastos reading appears to miss the characteristic Platonic turn back to the beginning, from the challenge to the unity of the form at 130e ff. to the reflection, here, into the basis for supposing it in the first place. Note, too, the numerous comparable passages which, otherwise strained, make very good sense if ἕν is taken predicatively, e.g. 132a1, b2, b5, b7, c6, and cf. 133b1.

32. Vlastos (1954) begins his analysis by remarking that formalization makes conspicuous what otherwise remains inconspicuous, namely, the extreme *non sequitur* of reasoning from the claim that a host of items are F by virtue of F-ness (at 132a2-4) to the claim that a host of items are F by virtue of F_1-ness. Formalization may, however, be misleading here. The symbolic notation makes it easy to overlook what Parmenides' words make clear, namely, that F_1-ness (the second "[the] large," 132a7) differs only numerically from F-ness (the first "large," 132a3). If F_1-ness differed intensionally from F-ness, then it would indeed be astounding that they are held to be responsible for imparting the self-same "immanent character," F, to the participant items. Since, however, they are not intensionally different, they *should* be responsible for imparting the same immanent character, as Parmenides makes them to be. The paradox therefore really does lie in what Parmenides stresses, the fact that there are two (and more) such forms rather than just one.

33. A crucial point in Vlastos, 1954, is that the "Nonidentity Assumption" (i.e. "If anything has a certain character, it cannot be identical with the Form in virtue of which we apprehend that character," p. 237) is an unspoken premise. But this may be more a function of the way Vlastos has reformulated Parmenides' description of the cognitive situation as if it were, instead, primarily a series of inferences. Though not explicitly spoken, NI is immediately manifest—and so is neither an assumption nor a premise—insofar as the form is present as one distinct object, definite and different from "the others," within the whole object field. As such, it cannot be the same as the character common to them all, that is, as the form newly emergent in each "looking." For another version of this point, see Pickering, 1981, pp. 267-268.

34. There is a question whether ἄπειρα here should be rendered "in-

finitely" or "indefinitely." If every set of particulars is united by a character common to all, and if this character, just insofar as it appears, becomes a member of this set and so provokes the emergence of a new character common to all, then the regress will be "infinite." But Parmenides' formulation is not clearly so formal and tight as this recapitulation suggests; if each new set is formed only as a result of a free act of comparison, then "indefinitely" is the better translation.

35. Since Vlastos, 1954, the central notion in the discussion of the regress arguments has been self-predication. Against Vlastos's view, in 1954, and Owen, 1953, that the forms are self-predicative, Cherniss (1957) and Allen (1960 and 1983) have argued that the numerous statements in the dialogues that instantiate the pattern, "F-ness is F," ought to be read as statements of identity, not attribution. The distinct merits of these opposed positions seem to me to be insightfully captured in one account by Nehamas (1979): he holds that the forms are self-predicative but that the proper sense of self-predication, that is, of "F-ness is F," is that F-ness "is what it is to be F." "So construed, self-predications describe the Forms, but what they describe is the Forms' very nature" (pp. 95-96). (Vlastos, 1981, appears not to take note of this point. He reduces Nehamas's construal of "F-ness is F" to a tautology by means of a series of substitutions; but to proceed by substitution implies that "is" functions as an equals sign and that the movement from subject to predicate involves no shift in level. On Nehamas' reading, as I understand it, Plato's sentences of the form, "F-ness is F," are abstract formulae for what, in another context, Mourelatos first called "speculative predication" [1970, pp. 55-60]. Since "F"—that is, "what it is to be F"—describes the "very nature" of "F-ness," the "is" leads thought not between interchangeable terms but from surface to depth, from what is as yet undefined to what defines and reveals it for what it really is. [Needless to say, the formulae must in each case be filled in by concrete inquiry into what "what it is to be F" is, if this movement is to be actually made.]) On my interpretation of the regress arguments and, more generally, of all of Parmenides' criticisms of Socrates, Plato's focal concern is not self-predication but, rather, the reduction of the forms to the status of their physical-sensible participants.

Nehamas's discussion, though not itself addressed to the *Parmenides*, is particularly helpful for seeing the ways these issues are and are not related. On Nehamas's view of self-predication, it applies generally to all the forms. That is, it holds for each form as a form that it (say, F-ness) "is F." (For convenience, call self-predication taken in Nehamas's way self-predication "proper.") As Nehamas would interpret it, the self-predication "Largeness is large" involves no logical or metaphysical absurdity; specifically, that Largeness is "what it is to be large" does not imply that it is a large thing. In his conundrums at 131c ff. and again in his regress arguments, however, Parmenides does treat Largeness as a large thing. And this would, if put in the form of an assertion, be expressed by the statement, "Largeness is large." *This* statement, however, will have a distinct sense from that of a self-predication "proper," for now "is large" means "has largeness as an attribute." (Call self-predication taken in this way "accidental" self-predication.) In this latter sense, "Largeness is large" is untrue. (Parmenides will show this, I shall argue, in hypothesis II. See IV.C.3.) There are, however, some "accidental" self-predications that are not untrue. Some forms, for instance, unity (note *Parmenides* 144c8-d1, as cited on p. 97) and being, would seem to have to possess themselves as attributes in order to be forms in the first place. (Vlastos himself, arguing on the basis of the *Sophist* and also citing Moravcsik [1963, p. 52], makes this point against Cherniss in 1969b, pp. 75-76.) That this is so and that Parmenides himself argues for it make improbable that "accidental" self-predication *in general* is the target of his regress arguments. (For a comparable reply to Vlastos, 1954, and to Owen, that is, however, based on the *Timaeus*, see Prior, 1983. Note also Patterson's argument [1985, pp. 74-76] that Plato's distinction in the *Timaeus* between two kinds—one for forms, another for sensibles—of being, sameness, and difference implies that the forms Being, Sameness, and Difference, even while they are "self-exemplifying," are not subject to the regress arguments of the *Parmenides*.) In sum, neither self-predication "proper" nor "accidental" self-predication *in general* are at issue in Parmenides' criticisms of Socrates. It is only a certain species of "accidental" self-predication—in particular, "accidental" self-predications that express what is the core error, the reduction of the forms to the status of physical-sensible things—that is objectionable.

36. There are of course other ways that would not be subject to just these difficulties. Socrates might have distinguished soul or mind as such from particular "souls" and—inventing something like the ontology of mind that (according to Plato's fiction in the *Phaedo*) he had hoped to find in Anaxagoras—made the forms in some

sense products or functions of the former. Or he might have tried to keep his incipient conceptualism from collapsing into subjectivism by making the forms, precisely as "thoughts," directly reflective of the common and repeated structures of things. These would be, very roughly, the neo-Platonic and Aristotelian alternatives to the Platonic position developed in the hypotheses.

37. On two central points, Allen's innovative reading (1983) of 132b3-c12 is problematic. First, his philological support for treating the argument up to 132c9 as leading to 132c9-11 as its single conclusion—namely, his interpretation of τί δὲ δή at 132c9—is arguable. As a "surprised question," τί δὲ δή serves both to announce something new and yet to connect this with the preceding as what comes next after it. By his Ἀλλ᾽ οὐδὲ τοῦτο . . . ἔχει λόγον ("Nor, again, is that reasonable") at 132c12, Socrates acknowledges that Parmenides has now shown two problems, in succession, in his position; this serves to confirm my interpretation of τί δὲ δή. For analysis of the usual functions of these particles, see Denniston, 1959, pp. 21-22 and 259. Second, Allen's interpretation of νόημα as the "act of thinking" and of νοούμενον as its "result" (p. 154) is strained. As he himself observes (p. 149), the verbal noun ending -μα most typically has a passive sense; -μα nouns generally refer to the result or product of the action named by their verbal stems. See Smyth, 1963, sections 841.2, 861.1(2). Hence it is natural to take νόημα to mean 'thought' in the sense of the result or product of the act of thinking. And if we do so, then it is also natural—since Parmenides distinguishes νοούμενον from νόημα—to take νοούμενον to refer not to the product of thinking but to what that product, as a thought or concept, is about, its object or content. Is there any reason to presume that this object or content is *also* a product of the act of thinking? Such idealism is hardly to be expected in general, and there is no supporting argument by Socrates or Parmenides to indicate it. Moreover, to conceive the νοούμενον as a product of thinking would drain the contrast between νόημα and νοούμενον of its force and point. But if the νοούμενον is not a product of thinking, then it will have whatever being it has independently of being thought. What Allen calls "the received wisdom, almost universally accepted" (p. 153) is, therefore, hardly as capricious or unwarranted as he suggests.

38. Thus, many likenesses can be made from one original or model without implying that the latter is divisible. But as we shall see, Parmenides' next argument shows that it is crucial to bear in mind

that the model-likeness relation is only a simile: if forms *are* models (not just "like" them, in their relations to participants), then the regress argument holds, and the unity of the form—now, however, in the sense of its uniqueness—is negated after all. In short, to save the form from divisibility by making it a model is, in turn, to subject it to plurality.

39. It is striking that, to put the point in terms of Lee's (1966, p. 353, note n. 24) valuable distinction between "substantial" and "insubstantial" images, the images cited by Socrates at *Republic* 510a1-2 are of the "insubstantial" sort. By staging matters so that the youthful Socrates misses the focus that, "later" in the *Republic*, the mature Socrates achieves in that particular passage, Plato appears to give his alert hearer an occasion to rethink the *Republic*, retrieving and preserving that focus as—in distinction from, e.g., the sort of image represented, for example, by the artworks discussed in Book X—particularly appropriate for the ontological analogy of imaging.

40. My phrase, "is in the image of," translates ἔοικεν with an eye to expressing the kind of resemblance or likeness which it connotes; the connotation is underscored by τῷ εἰκασθέντι.

41. There is a long-standing polemic over the question of whether the asymmetrical model-likeness relation genuinely entails, or is fallaciously supplanted by, the symmetrical relation of like-to-like. Some of the major antagonists are Taylor, 1926, p. 358, who cites Proclus; Hardie, 1936, pp. 94-97; Cornford, 1939, pp. 93-95; Cherniss, 1944, pp. 297-299; Ross, 1951, p. 89; Owen, 1953, pp. 318-320; Vlastos, 1954, p. 242; Cherniss, 1957, pp. 365-366; and Lee, 1973, p. 115. Plato knows full well that the difference in kind between model and likeness is situated within their likeness as sensible things; this is why, in the divided line passage in the *Republic*, the relation between a thing and its shadow or reflection can only be—and is put forth pointedly (see *Republic* 510a8-10) as—a simile for the relation between a form and its participant thing. With this in mind, we can say *both* that Owen is right to assert that the model-likeness relation "includes" the like-to-like relation (1953, p. 319, n. 3) *and* that the point made by, e.g., Taylor and Cherniss (1944)—that the like-to-like relation reduces the form to the level of its participants and so deforms the genuine insight captured by the model-likeness simile—is true to Plato's intent.

42. Addressing Allen, 1960, Weingartner (1973, pp. 173 ff.) is right to object, seizing on Allen's own example, that model (original) and

likeness (image) do stand in a relation of like-to-like in respect of some insubstantial sensory qualities; in particular, a red scarf and its image in a mirror are similar in respect of redness. That this is so, however, presupposes the fact that, in their own being, both the scarf and its image are singular objects of sense (sight) and, *as such*, reciprocally like. And that, again, is why the model-likeness relation can be only a simile for the asymmetrical, or nonreciprocal, relation between forms and things. For extended and helpful discussions of the analogy of model/likeness for form/participant, see, in addition to Allen, 1960, also Lee, 1966, and Patterson, 1985.

43. To transcend simile by giving a conceptual account is, however, not to destroy or dismiss it so much as to secure its real point, preserving it from the misunderstandings that a literalizing interpretation would give rise to. It may be that this is why Plato feels able to return to the simile of model and likeness in the *Timaeus*; see Cherniss, 1957, pp. 360 ff., 375 ff., and, very recently, Patterson, 1985, esp. pp. 51 ff., for versions of this position. On the other hand, the introduction of the notion of the receptacle makes it arguable whether the *Timaeus* is really a "return." See, for instance, Lee (1966), who takes the *Timaeus* to be Plato's response to the difficulties exposed in the youthful Socrates' insufficiently developed use of the simile, and Sayre (1983), who takes the *Timaeus* to expose the irremediable incoherence of the notion of participation (pp. 246-255) and, partly on this account, inclines toward dating it before (at least the first part of) the *Parmenides* (Appendix B). For extensive reflections on the complexities and *aporiai* associated with the use of the simile in the *Sophist*, see Rosen's major new study (1983).

44. Cornford (1939) calls the argument "grossly fallacious." Against him, Forrester (1974) asks why, if the argument is so poor, Parmenides should declare that its refutation requires such an "able" man and such "a host of remote arguments" (133b7-9, cited in the text below); Peterson (1981) makes the same general point in stressing "Plato's claims that unravelling this argument requires experience, talent, and patience" (p. 10). But these objections are not well focused. It is not the dissection and identification of problems in the reasoning at 133b-134e but, rather, the larger, more positive task made urgent by these arguments—namely, the task of seeing how it is that the forms, granted that "they are of such a sort as we say they must be" (133b5-6), can be known—that is so difficult. As Parmenides' restatement of the point at 135a-b implies, the thinker

who attempts to meet this difficulty must examine the very mode of being proper to each form as an essence in and for itself (135a8-b1). By the "host of very remote arguments," in turn, that he mentions as providing the necessary means for this examination, Parmenides refers not to any reconstruction or analysis of the particular arguments at 133b-134e but, rather (as I shall try to confirm in Chs. III-V), to the intricate and, at first sight, extraordinarily abstract argument of the eight hypotheses on the One.

45. It is worth nothing that, if Parmenides is to be taken as serious when he declares these closing arguments to pose even greater difficulty than the TMA (133b), then, since he holds that one of "wide experience and natural ability" *can* overcome them, he must also hold that such a one can overcome the TMA. Moreover, he seems to point to the hypotheses—surely "a host of very remote arguments"—as the needed means. This tells against the views of Vlastos (1954), that Plato was "puzzled" by the TMA, and of Owen (1953), that Plato had no answer to the TMA.

46. Plato may be referring ahead, between the lines, to hypothesis V, in which (on my interpretation) the forms are characterized as truth or "what truly is." See V.B.2.

47. Forrester (1974) follows up the implicit analogy of mastery/slavery with knowledge/the-object-of-knowledge by proposing a form, Object-of-Knowledge. He then finds the whole argument subtly (rather than flagrantly, see n. 44, above) fallacious: it does not follow from anything in the argument that our knowledge (not the form) may not have "other Forms, . . . not identical to Object-of-Knowledge," as its objects. If we isolate the two arguments, this would be so. But note the absurd consequence that arises if we look to step (2)(i) in Parmenides' argument. If our knowledge, which is much less "perfect" or "precise" than knowledge itself, knew other forms, then, since the forms are "truth itself" (134a4), we would have a knowledge that both was imperfect and grasped the truth itself. More significantly, however, it is not clear at all that there is much to be learned from such a subtle fallacy as Forrester identifies, whereas the flagrant errors we see instead seem quite instructive.

48. For very different analyses of Parmenides' arguments, see Lewis, 1979, and Peterson, 1981. Though I have learned from both, my disagreement with the general approach their essays represent is fundamental. Not only do they fail to try to orient their interpretations of the passage by any extended consideration of its place within the dialogue as a whole; they also aim their reconstructions

of the arguments so exclusively at the goal of achieving the maximum possible logical soundness that they fail to attend to—and even risk inadvertently dissolving—just the sort of striking obscurity in Parmenides' rhetoric that, on my view, is designed to provoke the critical hearer. Hence they tend to correct the particulars of Parmenides' reasoning in a way that, because it fails to first acknowledge and respond to the elicitative force of his language, conceals more than reveals the function Plato intends the arguments to fulfill. For instance, in Lewis' reading of (what I have just designated as) step (1) (iii), he must ignore both the reversal of the order of (a) and (b) from step (ii) and the repetition of the genitive. He must also argue that the passive construction (". . . is known by . . .") at 134b6-7 does not reduce the form to an agent and, so, a particular. Lewis' reasoning—that the passive ". . . is known by . . ." is equivalent to the active ". . . knows . . . ," which, in turn, Plato elsewhere treats as equivalent to the unproblematic ". . . is (a) knowledge of . . ."—raises the question, however, of why, granting that Plato could have chosen one of two less problematic active constructions, he in fact chose the passive, the most problematic of all; no phrasing could better suggest the reduction of form to thinghood than the one Parmenides is made to use. In Peterson's reconstruction, similarly, she barely mentions the master/slave analogue, and she dissolves away the problem of the reduction of the form implied in the phrase ". . . is known by . . ." by simply presuming, where Plato gives us an exact repetition of phrasing (see 134b6 and 11), a distinction in senses (see her p. 4).

49. This is roughly the converse of the point made by both Allen (1960, esp. pp. 48-51) and Lee (1966, esp. pp. 360-362), namely, that it is misleading to think of particulars as entities that "resemble" forms, as if this were a function distinct from their being proper; rather, particulars are "wholly dependent" (Allen, p. 50), "hav[ing] no reality 'on their own' " (Lee, p. 353) but being first constituted in their relation to what they resemble. To speak, therefore, of a "relation between" form and participant risks obscuring the radical asymmetry in play. Whereas a form may *be* whether or not there are participants participating in it, a participant thing is first constituted, first has its being, by its participation in its proper form. (Note, however, that this is not yet the full story of the dependent nature of the being of particulars. Lee goes on to explicate—and criticizes Allen for failing to explicate—the way in which, as images, particulars also depend on their medium. See pp.

364-366. This difference between Allen and Lee reflects in part Allen's concentration on the *Parmenides*, Lee's on the *Timaeus*. As we will see, except for a brief hint at 145d, the *Parmenides* leaves unexplored what the *Timaeus* makes central, the status of "space" as the medium essential to the being of things as images of forms.)

50. In setting up transcendence and immanence as polar possibilities for the relation of forms and things, Ross (1951, pp. 228 ff.) obscures this crucial point.

51. If this is well focused, then Sayre (1983) goes too far in holding that Plato intends the first part of the *Parmenides* to call into question the "separateness" of the forms (see, e.g., pp. 22, 26-27, 36). It is rather a *specific misunderstanding* of "separateness" that Plato exposes and challenges. Sayre's error is one of omission. It is, moreover, rather surprising since he makes a point of criticizing the "mistake of assuming that every thesis affirmed by Socrates is espoused by Plato himself" (p. 18); since he characterizes Parmenides' objections to Socrates as Plato's way of "drawing attention to certain difficulties involved in the theory [of forms]—but . . . dramatically rather than dialectically" (p. 25); and since he suggests, interestingly, that the "*very* young (σφόδρα νέον: 127c5-6) Socrates" (p. 20) is made to "present . . . for dismemberment . . . [a] version of the theory [that] is a thing of the past" and that "Plato no longer considers worth defending" (p. 36). These are all good reasons to raise, not to beg, the question of whether the immaturity of Socrates' "version of the theory" consists in the unqualified fact that it treats the forms as "separate" or, rather, consists in *the specific way* in which it interprets this "separateness." There is another reason as well: even while claiming to find in the *Philebus* clear evidence against the "separateness" of the forms and concluding that the "respective modes of being [of Forms and sensible things] can no longer be conceived as radically distinct" (p. 184), he also argues that "Forms might exist independently of sensible things" and not vice versa, and from this he draws the implication that "Forms have a mode of existence distinct from that of sensible objects" (p. 180). Unless there is a distinction to be drawn between the "radical" separateness denied on p. 184 and the unqualified distinctness affirmed on p. 180, Sayre will have contradicted his own basic thesis in the course of arriving at it.

52. Does this line of reflection imply that Plato thought of freedom from simile as a real and desirable possibility for philosophical discourse? This is a question that we would only beg if we tried to an-

swer it on the basis of the *Parmenides* alone. Quite apart from the question whether Plato's position on this was constant or changing, we need to bear in mind the limited topical range of the *Parmenides*. It does not (on the reading I shall offer) treat either the soul or the cosmos as a whole, and (for whatever reason—see the Epilogue, A) it barely mentions the Good; these, however, are all primary occasions in other dialogues for the fashioning of mythic simile.

53. Not least of the formulations to be rethought is that of the "conversion," περιαγωγή of the soul. If we treat this too literally and take it as the turning of the mind's eye from one real region, namely, that of becoming or what is sense-perceptible, to another, namely, that of being or what is intelligible, we will make just the mistake young Socrates makes repeatedly in the *Parmenides*: we will treat the forms as a second set of objects, occupying their own separate 'place' and standing as a correlative (or "like") system to that of physical-sensible things. In truth, the metaphor of "conversion" refers to the overcoming of just this excessively literal construal of the "conversion" itself.

54. But see n. 49, above. On account of the absolute asymmetry of the relation of forms and things, the very notions, "relation" and "relativity," though indispensable as conveniences of discourse, are finally misleading.

55. That Eudoxus could have proposed the doctrine of μίξις suggests how real this distinction is. Moreover, Cherniss (1944, Appendix VII) provides the elements for the view that Plato is attacking Eudoxus' doctrine *via* Parmenides' refutation of Socrates at 130e-131e. According to Cherniss's reconstruction from Aristotle and Alexander, the doctrine implies the physical presence of forms in things; things have their immanent characters because forms are "mixed" into and with them. Two notes are in order here. First, Aristotle calls attention to the kinship of Eudoxus' doctrine with Anaxagoras' doctrine of the mixture of seeds, at *Metaphysics* 991a14 ff.; this is particularly interesting in light of the Anaxagorean interest, which we analyzed in I.C.1, in the theory of forms. Brumbaugh (1961, esp. Chs. I and III) offers interesting speculations on this kinship and the possible positive presence of an Eudoxan Anaxagoreanism in the *Parmenides*. Second, that a great mathematician should offer a materializing interpretation of participation to which Plato, through Parmenides' refutation at 130e ff., finds it necessary to object ties in well with our more general view of the

mimetic irony of the *Parmenides*. But it should be evident that the latter view provides a framework for, and does not depend upon, such a reconstruction of the history of the Academy.

56. As we noted in I.B., Plato's depiction of Theodorus in *Theaetetus-Sophist-Statesman* may be designed to present this sort of evasion. It is remarkable that Theodorus could both be a great geometer and sympathize with the quasi-Protagorean definition of knowledge in terms of sense perception. However valuable Plato regards mathematics to be as propaideutic to philosophy, by his dramatic characterization of Theodorus he reminds his hearers of the fundamental distinction between them.

57. Implied by the thesis that Plato presents Parmenides' objections to Socrates as a pointed provocation is the distinct thesis that he regarded these objections not as ultimate but, rather, as subject to solution, or dissolution, when properly met. To this some have objected by citing *Philebus* 15b-c—note, e.g., Vlastos, 1954, p. 256. On the difficulties of interpreting that passage, see Hahn, 1978. But even if one resolves the basic ambiguities (see, e.g., Gosling, 1975, pp. 143-153) by reading it as a reiteration of the difficulties asserted at *Parmenides* 131a-b, this does not in itself entail that Plato is perplexed by these difficulties. If, first of all, he regarded thinking through these difficulties as a valuable task for one seeking to understand the notion of forms, then it would not be surprising that he have the elder Socrates set them as problems for the young Protarchus. More directly, note Socrates' remark about them at 15b8-c3: "These are the questions about these sorts of one and many . . . that are the cause of all the difficulties in this area if wrongly, *and of all progress if rightly settled.*" (Gosling's translation, 1975; my italics.) Does this not suggest that Plato saw a "right settlement"—and, indeed, one of great pedagogical value—to Parmenides' objections?

Chapter III: Parmenides' Help

1. Ryle has gone so far, indeed, to assert that "Plato cannot have composed either Part with the intention that it should be the complement, inside one dialogue, of the other Part" (Afterword, 1963, to "Plato's 'Parmenides,' " p. 145). See also Ryle, 1966, pp. 286 ff. This conclusion, however, is based largely on his observation that the first part is written in indirect discourse, the second in direct discourse. In his "Notice" to his translation (1956), Diès had already observed that there are several places *in the first part* where

"indirect discourse disappears completely . . . in favor of immediate narration" (p. 7). He cites 134a, also 131b, 135e, 136a–b; he also notes that there is a comparable simplification in the *Symposium*. Allen (1983, p. 61) in effect extends this observation to cover the second part of the dialogue in its entirety, asserting that its direct discourse is "governed by" the indirect discourse at 137c4. In any case, the basic point is that Plato, whatever his process of composition, did present the *Parmenides* as a whole. This alone secures the interpretive problem, as such, of how the two parts go together.

2. This sequence occurs, with variations, in many dialogues. Consider *Protagoras* (in which, however, Protagoras' deference and acceptance of help is grudging); *Symposium* (in which the audience's intervention occurs before, not after, Socrates' refutation); *Phaedo* and *Republic* (in which the refutations *seem* to be given by the interlocutors, though really Socrates elicits them from the interlocutors and thus brings the latter into aporia and need of his help); and *Euthyphro, Lysis, Meno, Phaedrus, Gorgias, Sophist*, and *Statesman* (in all of which, however, there is no explicit intervention by the audience). This sequence fits into, and is a transparent expression of, the dialogue structure outlined in the Preface.

3. In fact, the *Sophist* and the *Statesman* pursue the forms of important (whether dangerous or invaluable) types and stress the exemplary value of the search over the particular substantive results. See esp. *Statesman* 285c ff.

4. In all three of his discussions of the interlude (135a–137c) in the *Parmenides*, Sayre singles out as of special importance Parmenides' instruction to study the consequences of positing the not being of the subject in question. (See 1969, esp. pp. 103–104; 1978, esp. pp. 142–143; and 1983, esp. pp. 38–39.) On Sayre's account, Parmenides' method of hypothesis is the second of three attempts by Plato (the first being the method of hypothesis in the *Phaedo*, the third being the method of collection and division in the *Sophist*) to work out a method for discovering necessary and sufficient conditions. Sayre points out that if not-P→Q, then not-Q→P, and argues on this basis that Plato intends the study of the consequences of negative hypotheses (e.g. Q) as a means of yielding, by a further negation (e.g. not-Q), sufficient conditions. Although ingenious and, for those seeking to reconstruct a continuous line of development in Plato's thinking about method, attractive, this proposal is not supported by a close reading of the *Parmenides*. If it captured Plato's intent, we should expect to find Parmenides, in hypotheses V–VIII, deriving

from the not being of the One consequences whose negation would be sufficient conditions for the being of the One. In hypothesis V, however, Parmenides derives from the not being of the One the consequence that "it must somehow participate in being" (161e3). Can the negation of this latter participation be a condition sufficient for the being of the One? (For other problems in Sayre's reading of hypothesis V, see Ch. V, n. 20.) Evidently, and as I shall try to show in detail in V.B and V.C, when he has Parmenides insist on the examination of negative hypotheses, Plato intends something different from what Sayre proposes.

5. Indeed, there is a reverse Berkeleyan touch here: by affirming apparent contradictories of the One within hypothesis II, Parmenides makes it impossible to imagine or picture the One as a definite physical-sensible thing.

6. Note the kinship of this transcendence of the senses to that discussed at *Theaetetus* 184b ff. Here it is mutual exclusiveness of the characters themselves, as contradictories, that forces the mind to conceive rather than perceive; in the *Theaetetus* it is the mutual exclusiveness of the senses themselves and their various proper objects (185a) that requires the mind, if it will think features common to the several senses (e.g., existence, sameness, difference, number, etc., 185a ff.), to conceive rather than perceive. For discussion of *Theaetetus* 184b ff., see Holland, 1973.

7. On the pedagogical irony of this, see IV.B.2: as we shall observe, Parmenides' synopses present contraries as if they were mutually contradictory whereas in the arguments themselves, he lets their senses shift in such a way that, really, they are mutually complementary.

8. This is a key question for the interpretation of the hypotheses. Robinson (1941) holds both that the contradictions strengthen the function of the hypotheses as inciting and even humbling exercise (pp. 264-265) and that the fact that Plato makes dialectic serve this role of exercise, γυμνασία, suggests that he is beginning to give it less importance, as Aristotle also did later, within philosophy as a whole (p. 279). Brumbaugh (1961) and Runciman (1959) both regard the contradictions as giving the hypotheses the basic function of a *reductio* or indirect proof, but they differ radically on just what it is that Plato means to establish. Brumbaugh regards the implications of the *reductio* as substantive: as a dianoetic display of the contradictions that befall the major possible positions within a merely formal, value-neutral ontology, the hypotheses provide in-

direct proof of the need to root ontology in a noetic grasp of the Good. Runciman, by contrast, regards the implications as methodological: the contradictions show the fruitlessness of the method of hypothesis commended in the *Phaedo* and so set the stage for the introduction, in place of that method, of the new procedure of collection and division. Schofield (1977) in effect charts a mean between these positions: he tries to argue that Plato is exploiting the "idea of antinomy" as a methodological principle for "conceptual exploration"; and he tries (with considerable strain, however, as he seems to acknowledge, p. 159) to show that the *Parmenides*, thus interpreted, comes to "fruitful" results. A dissenter from all these positions is Sayre (1978 and 1983, Ch. One, 2; he argues for a new grouping of the hypotheses (I and VI, II and V, III and VII, and IV and VIII) which renders them consistent, not contradictory. The key to his interesting reconstruction is the way he parses out the respects—i.e. "with reference to itself" and "with reference to the others"—in which the One and "the others" are to be studied, according to Parmenides' instructions at 135c-136c. Parmenides' "distinction between things considered with reference to themselves alone and things considered with reference to other things" (1983, p. 40), Sayre argues, produces, in principle, eight, not four, distinct lines of deduction; he then attempts to show that these eight are what Parmenides actually presents in his display of the method regarding the One and "the others."

There are, however, several serious difficulties with Sayre's position. First, the phrase just quoted from 1983, not to mention Sayre's charts in 1978, p. 140, and in 1983, p. 44, make it explicit that on his reading each hypothesis is supposed to treat its subject only in one of the two respects, that is, only with reference to itself or with reference to what is other than it. The text, however, contradicts this in many places; numerous passages indicate that the subject is under consideration in *both* respects within each single hypothesis. For instance, in hypothesis I, which Sayre takes as considering the One only with reference to itself, the One is also, and explicitly, considered with reference to "the others" at 139b-c, 140a-b, 140b-d, and 140e-141a. In hypothesis II, which Sayre takes as considering the One only with reference to "the others," the One is also, again explicitly, considered with reference to itself at 145b-c, 146a, 146b-c, 146c, 148d, 148e, 148e-149a, 150e, 151b-d, 152a-b, 152b-e, and 152e. In hypothesis III, which Sayre takes as considering "the others" only with reference to what is other than

themselves, namely, with reference to the One, they are also examined "in their own nature in and for themselves" (ή έαυτῶν φύ-
σις καθ᾽ έαυτὰ, 158d5-6). And so on. For further examples in the
remaining hypotheses, see 159b, 159e, 161b-c, 164a, 164b-c, 165a,
165d, and 166a. Second, it may be that Sayre allows himself to dis-
count these passages because he thinks he can find, in "the way
Unity is characterized at the initial statement of each hypothesis"
(1983, p. 42), decisive indications that the subject is going to be
considered in just one of the two respects in the argument of that
hypothesis. For instance, when Parmenides begins hypothesis I by
asserting that the One "is one itself" (ἓν αὐτὸ εἶναι, 137d2), Sayre
reasons that since this characterization, as he interprets it, makes it
"entirely predictable" that the One in hypothesis I "admits no relationships to other things," "the conclusions following from hypothesizing such a Unity must be drawn for that Unity with reference to itself alone" (1983, p. 42). Likewise with regard to
hypothesis II, since the initial presentation of Unity as having a
being that is not identical with it makes it clear "from the beginning
. . . that the argument . . . is about a Unity admitting relationships
to other things," it is also clear, Sayre holds, that the argument has
as its subject "Unity with reference to the others" (1983, pp. 42-
43). And so on. Sayre's reasoning, however, is problematic on several scores. To begin with, he seems to fail to distinguish the programmatic range of our consideration of a subject from the range
of the being of that subject that our consideration actually discloses. That the One of hypothesis I has no relations to "the others"
is only first disclosed because we consider it with reference to "the
others." If, moreover, we take the non-relatedness of the One of I
to "the others" as a clue to the range of our consideration of it, we
shall also have to do so with regard to its non-relatedness to itself;
but if we say that since the deductions of hypothesis I (to hold, with
Sayre, to their explicit content) yield the "entirely predictable" result that the One has no characters or being in relation to itself, we
are therefore not considering it in that respect, then we shall be reduced to the absurdity of having to say that we have been considering it *neither* with reference to itself *nor* with reference to "the
others." Likewise for the second hypothesis: since it does have
characters in relation to itself as well as in relation to "the others,"
and since our consideration of it discloses these (see the list of passages above), we shall have to say that we are considering the One
both with reference to itself *and* with reference to "the others." Such

problems and paradoxes will beset Sayre's reading of the following hypotheses as well. Third, Sayre does not address, nor can his account explain, the fact that Parmenides, in his summation of the results of hypotheses I-IV at 160b, explicitly focuses attention on a number of basic contradictions that (as I shall show in IV.A) set hypotheses I and II, and then III and IV, into opposition. Nor does Sayre explain the extraordinary web of contradictions Parmenides weaves in his closing speech of the dialogue, at 166b. Finally, Sayre fails to explain why Plato projects the *appearance* of contradiction between I and II, III and IV, V and VI, and VII and VIII. Surely this must be fully acknowledged and interpreted; Parmenides' crediting of the method to Zeno (135d), shortly after Zeno has presented a series of hypotheses *with intentionally contradictory consequences*, gives all the more impetus to this last objection.

9. For the sense in which the dialogues are all, essentially, tests of this sort, see the Preface. Plato finds a particularly marvelous image for this at *Symposium* 215c. The λόγοι of Socrates, Alcibiades claims, are like the songs of Marsyas: they sort out—by their erotic effect—those who are fit to receive their divine content from those who are not. See, too, the characterization of the function of preliminary education in philosophy as a way of putting the depth of the hearer's interest and capacities to the test, *Seventh Letter* 340b ff.

10. Recall I.C.3.

11. For a cogent discussion of this provocation, see J. Klein, 1965, Ch. V, sections 2 and 3.

12. This is Cornford's translation, 1935.

13. I disagree with Cornford's translation here. He takes ταύτῃ, 135e5, to mean "in that other field," i.e., in the domain of visible things. I take it to mean "in that way" and to refer to the extension of the discourse to include forms as well as things. Diès' "par la première voie" seems to accord with Cornford, whereas Schleiermacher's "auf jene Art" takes the position I would prefer. In any case, the interpretation of the passage as a whole does not hang on this point.

14. Recall the references to the form as ἕν, cited in Ch. II, n. 17. Note, too, the references to the participants in forms as τὰ ἄλλα at 130e6, 131e4, 132a6, c9, d2, d3, and 133a5.

15. Neither Allen nor Sayre offers adequate discussion of the possibility that τὸ ἕν is systematically ambiguous. In discussing Parmenides' refutations of Socrates, Allen (1960) introduces the notion of systematic ambiguity as a principle for distinguishing

between a term as it expresses what a form *is* and as it expresses what a participant *has*. In both 1974 and 1983, however, he objects to the construal of τὸ ἕν as intentionally ambiguous. His argument in 1983 is in part positive, focusing on 137b3-4 (pp. 183-184), and in part negative, proceeding by a refutation of the particular versions of "the ambiguity theory" offered by Proclus and by Cornford (1939). On neither count, however, is his reasoning sufficient. With regard, first, to 137b3-4, when Parmenides declares that he will speak περὶ τοῦ ἑνὸς αὐτοῦ ὑποθέμενος εἴτε ἕν ἔστιν εἴτε μὴ ἕν ("concerning the one itself, hypothesizing either that one is or that one is not"), it is an open question, not addressed by Allen, whether by "one" he refers directly back to "the one itself" or, instead, intends "*a* one." In the former case, he would be naming the form Unity as the subject, as Allen holds; but in the latter case, he would be shifting attention from Unity to what instantiates it— that is, to those entities that (however variously) have unity and so are, in each case, a one. (For linguistic evidence for the second reading, see Ch. IV, n. 16, below.) With regard, second, to the negative part of Allen's argument, its insufficiency should become clear when we explicate, in Chs. IV and V, an interpretation of the systematic ambiguity of τὸ ἕν that neither Proclus nor Cornford— nor, consequently, Allen—discusses.

Oddly, Sayre (1983) never raises the question of the specificity of the sense of τὸ ἕν. For several reasons, this question is crucial to his interpretation of the *Parmenides*. Since he argues that the hypotheses show the unintelligibility of separate forms, he seems to equivocate between reading τὸ ἕν to refer to the form Unity (the reading that his constant translation of τὸ ἕν as "Unity" suggests) and reading it as to refer to any of the forms "conceived as unities" (p. 46). He also asserts, however, that hypotheses I and II "posit the existence of different Unities" (p. 45)—and leaves it unclear whether the Unity posited in hypothesis II is to be thought as (in whichever of the two senses just noted) a non-separate form, as his account of the hypotheses as breaking with the middle period notion of separateness would suggest, or a sensible thing, as his account of hypothesis II as deriving the existence of sensibles would suggest. Most intriguing of all, however, even as he argues that the hypotheses show the emergence for Plato of Unity as one of the elements of which each form is composed (e.g., p. 67), he doesn't stop to ask whether, if Unity itself is a form in the *Parmenides*, we are to think of it itself as somehow composed, in part, of itself—or, if not, whether we have in this incomposite Unity, once again, a separate form.

Of the most important and interesting modern explorations of the possibility of ambiguity, see especially the major studies by Wahl (1951) and Brumbaugh (1961). There is also the narrower study, linking the two main parts of the dialogue, by Rochol, 1971. The recognition of ambiguity in the meaning of ἕν in the *Parmenides* may go back to the early Academy, if Ryle's reading of *Sophistic Refutations* 182b22–27 is correct. See Ryle, 1968, p. 72, and note, in connection with it, Allen, 1983, p. 271.

16. These remarks in my text are intended to indicate the senses of "one"—and, so, of "the One"—that Parmenides' refutations of Socrates should prepare the reader of the dialogue to hear in the hypotheses. The full and genuine substantiation of the point, however, requires the detailed analyses in Ch. IV (esp. A.3 and B) and in Ch. V (especially A.1, B.1, and C.1). At this point, it is instructive to supplement my text, oriented as it is by the specificity of the *Parmenides* as a dramatic whole, with an abstract survey of the possible meanings of the expression [τὸ] ἕν, "[the] One." The major possibilities are (1) that it refer to the whole of reality (τὸ πᾶν, 128b) in accord with the young Socrates' interpretation of Parmenides at 128ab; (2) that it refer to the number One or, in stricter accord with Greek thought about number, to One as the ἀρχή or principle of number; (3) that it refer to the Platonic form Unity, mentioned as τὸ ἕν by Socrates at 129e and as ἕν by Parmenides at 130b; (4) that it serve as a general formula referring to forms as forms, under the aspect of their essential simplicity and uniqueness, and perhaps as a linguistic abbreviation of τὸ ἓν εἶδος, "the unitary form," at 131c; and (5) that it serve as a general formula referring to spatio-temporal things, under the aspect of their unity as individuals. (Note 135b8.)

Of these interpretations, (1) seems most unlikely, since Parmenides both implicitly rejects Socrates' interpretation by entertaining the possibility of the existence of τὰ ἄλλα, "the others" (than the One), in hypotheses II–VIII and, too, asserts that the One is many in number in hypothesis II. Whereas there are certain passages in hypothesis II where interpretation (2) could be argued (see Allen, 1974), it too is unlikely; if the One were the basis of number, it would not be necessary, as it is in II, to show the existence of number on the basis of its distinction from being and difference. Moreover, a number of other issues would be extremely unclear, e.g., just how (since hypothesis II places the One in space and time) the basis of number could be a spatio-temporal thing—a most unlikely position for Plato to take, given the discussion of the mathematicals in the *Republic*; just how (since II makes the One many in number) the basis of number could be many in number; just what "the others" would then be, etc. There are two sorts of questions regarding (3): first, whether it can be preferred to (4), and second, whether either is to be accepted. With respect to the first question, it is linguistically possible that Plato uses τὸ ἕν to name the form Unity, as the citations of 129e and 130b show; but a host of references in the following refutations, where the question is whether the form generally—i.e., any and every form, considered simply *qua* form and not with regard to the particular character which it is—is "one" (ἕν), show (4) to be just as, if not even more likely. Also, in the single passage in which Parmenides clearly *does* have the form Unity in mind, 143a-144e in hypothesis II, he speaks of it distinctively as αὐτὸ τὸ ἕν, in contrast to τὸ ἕν. Note, in particular, 144e5-7, and see Ch. IV, n. 16, below. Finally, nothing in the hypotheses warrants preferring (3) to (4); all the characterizations of the One, insofar as they can be made of the form Unity, can just as well apply to form as such. (The converse is also true, of course—and predictably, since the form Unity is an instance of form as such.) However, is it justifiable to accept either (3) or (4), in the first place? In a number of passages, primarily in II and also arguably in V, the One is characterized as a spatio-temporal whole, and this makes (5) seem preferable. What is striking, however, is that (5), considered in its own right, has the converse liability to (4): there are a number of passages, primarily but not solely in I and V, where spatiality and temporal being are denied to the One, and this makes (4) preferable. On the basis of these reflections, therefore, this would seem to be the proper heuristic conclusion for the analyses ahead: sometimes τὸ ἕν seems to refer to form as form (or, more narrowly, the form Unity), and other times, to spatio-temporal individuals, as such. Of course, the context of the whole dialogue shows how to take these shifts in meaning. First, since Parmenides is interested not in any particular form but in whether and how they might *be*, in the first place, (4) seems clearly preferable over (3). Second, since the core error in the refutations is the conceiving of forms, with regard to their being simple and unique, after the model of things, the shifts from (4) to (5) and (5) to (4) seems to suggest that Parmenides is exploring the unity-characters of forms and of things in an effort to show whether and how forms might be properly conceived.

17. Thus the hypotheses will prove to have a rich, positive significance. Here again I depart fundamentally both from Allen (1983) and from Sayre (1983). Allen argues that the hypotheses have only an aporematic and dialectical significance, serving both to universalize the dilemma of participation (because their subject, the form Unity, is "an Idea of the utmost generality") and to show that rejecting the existence of forms is no escape (for absurdities follow from the nonbeing as well as from the being of Unity) (pp. 178-180). What Allen takes as the positive implication of the hypotheses, that we should withdraw Socrates' initial assertion of the separate existence of sensibles, is, he insists, made explicit only "outside the *Parmenides*" (see, e.g., pp. 180, 275, 288-290), most pointedly in the *Timaeus*. For specific objections to Allen's reading, see esp. Ch. V, n. 2, below, and also Ch. III, n. 15, above, and Ch. IV, nn. 23, 30, 54, and Ch. V, nn. 21, 27, 37, below.

On Sayre's reading, the hypotheses fulfill a plurality of projects: Plato makes a complex deductive argument against the separateness of the forms (pp. 46-47), exposes the many inappropriate positive attributions and the fundamental self-contradiction in the historical Parmenides' way of Truth (pp. 49-52), and gives a sustained argument for the Pythagorean theses that "Unity generates number" and that "number is constitutive of sensible things" (p. 52 and, for the argument, pp. 52-60). These projects fit together as aspects of Plato's underlying plan to "mark off the boundaries of a new ontology" (p. 37). For Sayre, too, however, the fulfillment of the *Parmenides* comes only in another dialogue; it is in the *Philebus* that Plato first shows explicit systematic control of the concepts, just emerging in the *Parmenides*, of the One and the Unlimited (or, later, the Great and Small) and builds an alternative to the earlier theory of separate forms around them. For specific problems in Sayre's exegesis of the hypotheses, see Ch. III, nn. 4, 8, 15, above, and Ch. IV, nn. 3, 15, 23, and Ch. V, n. 20, below. In spite of these problems, however, the general outline of Sayre's vision is tenable (indeed, in some ways more so than his reading of the hypotheses suggests) and important—see Ch. V, n. 29, below.

In my own view, Allen and Sayre must look outside the *Parmenides* for its positive fulfillment because, or largely because, they have missed the basic project of the hypotheses and, with this, the remarkably tight unity of the dialogue as a whole. According to the reading I shall present in Chs. IV and V, the hypotheses not only regenerate, in a more conceptual mode than Parmenides' refutations of Socrates, the basic problems these refutations have revealed, but they also chart a precise path through those problems, in this way enabling, for whoever can take up the provocations they offer, a conceptual and self-consistent reappropriation of the theory of forms.

18. Ryle's suggestion (in 1966, p. 109) that Plato had the young philosopher Aristotle in mind is interesting in the context of his reconstruction of Plato's authorship and life story; but Plato's reference, *via* Antiphon, to Aristotle's future status as one of the Thirty Tyrants (127d), not to mention Aristotle's passive, very often thoughtless performance in the course of the hypotheses, makes it highly implausible.

19. Socrates' silent presence is an important dramatic motif in the *Sophist* and *Statesman*, too. See Miller, 1980, ch. I.

20. τὸν τῶν τριάκοντα γενόμενον. From the little we know of him, he was bright but ruthless. Brumbaugh (1961, p. 31, n. 35) cites *Republic* 491b-494a and 550b, passages in which Socrates describes the seduction and corruption of the best natures to the worst evils. In the *Parmenides*, however, not much of Aristotle's brightness comes through.

21. Although the interpretation to come differs fundamentally from those of Cornford and Friedländer, my conception of the general project is akin to theirs in important particular respects. Note Cornford's comment on Parmenides' final synopsis at 166c as "a challenge to the student" (1939, pp. 244 ff.), and compare with the Preface, section A.3, Cornford's remarks on the way in which, in the hypotheses as in a number of other dialogues, "the conclusion that is meant to be accepted is skillfully masked, so that the reader may be forced to discover it by careful study" (p. 245). Friedländer, in turn, sees the replacement of Socrates by Aristotle as a provocation and writes, "should not the reader put himself in the place of Socrates standing by in silence? . . . above all, the entire dialectic of the second part acquires new meaning when it is viewed from the Socratic perspective" (1969, p. 200).

22. It is a great misfortune for English-language readers that Cornford, intending to make the coherence and flow of Parmenides' argumentation more accessible and finding no particular value in Aristotle's responses, chose to omit the latter from his translation and, in those places where Aristotle was responding to Parmenides'

questions, to reformulate these as positive statements. In fact, as we shall see, there are a number of crucial points at which Parmenides asks Aristotle significant questions and builds his argument upon Aristotle's conspicuously problematic replies; the critical Academic hearer would have been alert to these moments as he studied and reflected upon the hypotheses. Brumbaugh, too, insists on the importance of Aristotle's replies but for quite different reasons: he takes the variations from simple affirmation through hesitation and qualification in the replies as Platonic signals, as it were, of points in the argument where its logical form, "horizontal," tends to do injustice to its metaphysical substance, "vertical" in character. See Brumbaugh, 1961, pp. 47-52, esp. p. 52. Some of Aristotle's replies, however, are such clear errors, sourced in such uncritical presumption, that I find him and his own inclinations and judgments a very unlikely means for *Plato*'s self-expression.

23. Recall, however, Ch. I, n. 18, and see the Epilogue, section A.

Chapter IV: Hypotheses I, II, and IIa

1. See V.A.1.

2. Parmenides makes this explicit by his use of the intensive conjunction τε . . . καὶ (roughly rendered by "both . . . and") in his summative sentence at 160b2-3.

3. Sayre (1983), on the one hand, takes the hypotheses as a coordinated demonstration of the incoherence of the earlier Platonic thesis that the forms are "separate" and, on the other hand, resumes the position of Cornford (1939) that Plato is "taking sides" against the historical Parmenides' One Being and for the Pythagorean doctrines of the generation of number from Unity and of sensibles from number. There are three different sorts of problem with Sayre's position. To begin with, he never really tells us how these two functions interrelate. This is a particularly intractable problem in regard to hypothesis I. Can it *both* combine with VI to form one of the several lines of argument rejecting the separateness of forms *and* serve by itself as an attack on Parmenides' One Being? What would be the meaning of τὸ ἕν within these two lines of argument? (Recall Ch. III, n. 15, above.) If it is different, there is the danger that the functions fall out of relation, leaving the hypothesis equivocal and unintegrated. If it is the same, however, it is not clear that the hypothesis can perform both functions. For just what would the meaning be? If the "One Being" of Parmenides, then it cannot

serve as the subject in an argument against separate forms, for they are many. If the meaning is "each one of the many forms," however, then Plato will be begging the question against Parmenidean monism.

More serious for Sayre's larger interpretation of the late Platonic ontology is the apparent one-sidedness that afflicts his account of the argumentation by which hypothesis I, together with VI and with various other pairs (II/V, III/VII, IV/VIII), serves to undercut the separateness of the forms. If we grant for the sake of argument (but recall Ch. III, n. 8, above) that Sayre's pairings and interpretations of them are correct, how is he able to take them as argument against separateness any more than, as well, against relatedness? True, on his reading, I and VI show that whether Unity does (I) or does not (VI) exist, if it has "no relationships with other things," it "has no characters" (p. 46); and IV and VIII, in turn, show that whether Unity does (IV) or does not (VIII) exist, if it is "entirely separate from other things" (p. 47), the others too "have no characters at all" (p. 47). What, however, of II and V and of III and VII? Do not II and V show that whether Unity exists (II) or not (V), if it is related to the others, it has all the characters they have? And do not III and VII show that whether Unity exists (III) or not (VII), if the others are related to it, they have all the characters it does? And is not the implication that so long as there is relationship between the One and the others, they will be "indistinguishable" (p. 47)? Significantly, Sayre would seem to agree; by a related reasoning involving a combination of II, III, V, and VII, he comes to the conclusion that "These difficulties posed by conceiving the Forms as entirely separate unities . . . cannot be resolved by opening the Forms up to relationships with other things indiscriminately" (p. 47). But this seems an unfairly pre-emptive way to put the matter. As we shall see, hypotheses III and VII in particular do not suppose "indiscriminate" relationship—they propose "participation" (see V.A.2 and V.C.1) as, explicitly, a mean between total separateness and total identity. To accept Sayre's interpretation in an even-handed way, therefore, is to find an argument that rejects both "separateness" *and participation*, not separateness alone. Can *this* be the substantive point of the hypotheses?

Sayre does not appear to notice the provocative fallacy at 141e, nor does he anywhere apply to the hypotheses the hermeneutic principles for entering into Plato's philosophical drama that he declares at pp. 18-19. I will try to show how bringing such principles

to bear on 141e (see IV.B.1)—and, shortly, on other similarly provocative passages as well (see IV.C)—is the key to discovering the
substantive argument of the hypotheses.

4. With important specific differences, of course, this has been the
dominant general course of modern interpretation. Most see the
first hypothesis as a sort of *reductio* aimed against Eleatic strict monism and/or Socrates' view (representative of Plato's thought in his
middle period) of the simple unity of each form. Taylor, for example, writes, "The argument is that *all* affirmation implies plurality. . . . If there is anything which is such a mere undifferentiated
unity that there are no distinctions within it, you cannot even affirm of it that it is one" (1926, p. 363). Cornford agrees, writing
that the results of the first hypothesis are "as unacceptable to Parmenides and Zeno as . . . to Socrates" (1939, p. 134) and finding
the indirect message that "no such Form [as the One or Unity] can
exist at all or be an object of Knowledge, unless the contraries, one
and many, are in some sense combined in it" (p. 135). Lynch (1959)
stresses this second point in his interpretation. So do Chen (1944)
and Liebrucks (1949), who see hypothesis I as an indirect denial of
the isolateness or essential nonrelatedness of any form. Liebrucks
writes, "Erst das negative Resultat der ersten Position des Parmenides zeigt endgültig die Unverbrüchlichkeit der Relationalität alles
bestimmten Wirklichen nicht nur in der Welt des Sichtbaren, sondern genau so in der Welt der Ideen. Damit ist das Hindurchgehen
des Genus des Anderen quer durch die Welt des Denkbaren und
Sichtbaren endgültig bestätigt, indem die Unmöglichkeit auch nur
einer einzigen Ausnahme durch die Absurdität der Konsequenzen
aufgewiesen ist" (p. 194). Though he takes hypothesis I as an examination of the categorial status of Unity—part of his general approach (in 1939) to the *Parmenides* as an early effort at a theory of
types—Ryle, too, regards it as a *reductio ad absurdum*, and Owen,
connecting the One of hypothesis I with the quasi-mathematical
interpretation suggested for it in *Republic* 525e, concurs (1970, pp.
343-344). Perhaps the strongest statement is Rochol's (1971, p.
503): "the One that is non-existent, therefore not capable of being
One, not knowable, and not thinkable, cannot be anything positive. . . . Rather it is . . . a mere negation." And he writes (pp. 498-
499), "neither Parmenides himself nor his interlocutor, young Aristotle, is willing to accept this result. Thus they resort to the only
remaining alternative, i.e., to the introduction of the existent
One." All of these views are of course mutually exclusive with the

neo-Platonic interpretation of the nonexistent One as a One *beyond* existence. For appreciative accounts that, nonetheless, rightly reject the neo-Platonic reading, see Cornford, 1939, pp. 131-134, and Allen, 1983, pp. 189-195; or, for a modern representation, Speiser, 1937. For a discussion that attempts to incorporate both the positive reading of the neo-Platonic orientation and the negative reading of the prevalent modern view, cited above, that hypothesis I prepares the way for the assertion of the relatedness (κοινωνία) of forms, see Wahl, 1951, esp. pp. 128 ff. Another extremely interesting variation on the neo-Platonic reading, one that draws provocatively on strains in Heidegger and Wittgenstein, is Wyller, 1962, esp. pp. 628 ff.

5. The major noteworthy exceptions are discussed in IV.C.2 and IV.C.3.

6. The shift in word order—from εἰ ἕν ἐστιν in hypothesis I, 137c4— seems intended to call attention to the new consideration, in II, of unity and being, ἕν and ὄν, as distinct substantive complements.

7. Cornford finds confirmation in this passage for his view that "the term 'part' is to be understood in the widest sense. It covers not only the parts into which a whole thing might be divided . . . , but any and every diversity of aspect or character" (1939, p. 116). His distinction between the *divisa* of a thing and a mere "aspect" appears to be founded on the view that a *divisum* would be a "thing" in its own right, that is, a "one being," whereas at 142c-d "one" and "being," ἕν and ὄν, are distinguished and then each called "parts." Plato's argument, however, seems to subvert Cornford's notion of a broad sense of the term "part." So soon as Parmenides distinguishes "one" (ἕν) as a part, he points out that it must therefore *be* and, so, be a "one *being*" unto itself; and likewise, so soon as he distinguishes "being" (ὄν) as a part, he points out that it must therefore be *one* and, so, be a "*one* being" unto itself. The point seems to be that though we can indeed distinguish the mere aspects under which a being presents itself, so soon as we distinguish these *as parts*, they cease to be mere aspects and take on the status of "whole things" in their own right. The notion of a part, therefore, remains narrow; parts are those real beings, each a "one" that "is," into which any real being can be divided. (For confirmation that parts are analogous in structure in this way to the wholes of which they are parts, see 157e5 ff.)

8. There is just one exception, the addition, late in hypothesis II, of the characters having-/not-having-contacts (148d-149d). These

characters would not have made sense in I since there the One was denied spatiality.

9. Thus being a whole and having parts are mutually implicative; to be a whole *is* to have parts, and to be a part *is* to be part of a whole, by definition.

10. Except for 143a4-144e3, where Parmenides speaks of αὐτὸ τὸ ἕν, this is the phrase that Parmenides uses throughout hypothesis II to designate its subject.

11. This is Cornford's well-focused and supple translation (1939).

12. Allen (1974, pp. 712 ff., and 1983, pp. 227 ff.) points out that Parmenides does not so much generate as give an existence proof for number. Note, too, his counter to Aristotle's objection that Parmenides does not generate the primes (as well as his correction of Cornford's counter, 1939, p. 141), in 1974, p. 713, n. 44, and 1983, n. 158, and his observations on the non-exclusive relation of Parmenides' four classes of number (1983, n. 159).

13. As the parenthesis indicates, I do not mean to suggest that infinity is itself to be thought as a number. On the mathematical senses of infinity in play in these arguments, see Allen, 1974.

14. Parmenides' terms—κατακεκερμάτισται, "is broken down into small pieces" (144b5, see also e4), and μεμέρισται, "is parted, divided into parts" (144b6, also d2, d4)—suggest or connote physical divisibility and so recall the materializing dilemma of participation by whole or part at 130e-131e. See the discussion in IV.B.3.

15. On Sayre's analysis, these two arguments function together to execute the first of the two Pythagorean theses that Plato wants to establish in hypothesis II, that "Unity generates number." (Note his qualification of the notion of "generation," pp. 58 ff., in response to Allen, 1974.) Sayre's reading is stimulating, and the larger picture of which it is part is intriguing (see Ch. V, n. 29). But there are two serious problems with it. First, in the first argument, at 142d-143a, Parmenides starts from "the One which is" and reasons that it is ἄπειρον πλῆθος. Sayre discovers in this the notion that will later become the Unlimited of the *Philebus*. It is, he argues, "a numberless multitude," for "the constituents within the ἄπειρον πλῆθος fail to be integral, hence are numberless in the sense of lacking identity" (p. 55). Now, the strange nature that Sayre describes does in fact play a crucial role in the *Parmenides*; we shall encounter it first in hypothesis IIa (see IV.D) and then more clearly in the "reduction" of hypothesis III (see V.A.2.b). But it does not really appear—or it appears only in a specifically indirect way—in 142d-

143a of hypothesis II. The best way to begin to see this is to observe that Sayre's account of "the One which is" in this passage is essentially one-sided. True, the One is here ἄπειρον πλῆθος, possessed of uncountably many parts. True, each of these parts "is always necessarily becoming two, and never is one at any time" (142e7-143a1, Sayre's translation). But if this were the whole story, then, since each of its parts is also a "one which is" and, as such, is analogous to *the* "One which is" of which it is a part, this latter One would not be "integral"; but it *is*—it is "one" (142d4) and a "whole" (142d4). The situation is therefore obscure. On the one hand, the numberless and non-integral multitude that Sayre describes cannot be one and a whole; so, it follows, the "One which is" that Parmenides studies is not the numberless and non-integral multitude that Sayre describes. On the other hand, there is no doubt that that strange nature is, as it were, half the story, one 'side,' so to speak, of the "One which is." How are we to think through this problem? In fact, hypothesis II will not help. We have to wait until the "reduction" in hypothesis III, where we will discover that the non-integral multitude is present in the "One which is" (to be understood as an exemplary physical-sensible thing) as the intrinsically unstructured material element that is first given structure, or "limit," by the imposition of form. In hypothesis II, 142d-143a, we only glimpse that non-integral multitude as, under the imposition of form, structured as the parts of a one whole. A second problem with Sayre's reading is that, in making the two arguments collaborate, he appears to miss the shift from τὸ ὂν ἕν, in 142d-143a, to αὐτὸ τὸ ἕν, in 143a-144e. See n. 16 below and recall Ch. III, n. 15.

16. The many commentators who take τὸ ἕν to refer to the form Unity ought to have been given pause by the phrasing at 144c5-7. Plato has Parmenides explicitly distinguish and pair τὸ ὂν ἕν and αὐτὸ τὸ ἕν by the conjunction οὐ μόνον . . . ἀλλὰ καὶ . . . , "not only . . . but also. . . ." He thus makes clear that τὸ ἕν and αὐτὸ τὸ ἕν are different subjects. But if this is so, then, since standard Platonic usage and the specific sense of 143a-144e (as I interpret it, pp. 89-94) both require that the expression, αὐτὸ τὸ ἕν, refer to the form Unity, the expression, τὸ ἕν, must refer to something else. The qualifying ὂν, in turn, gives a first clue what this latter might be. τὸ ὂν ἕν, as a one that is and as a being that is one, *has*—rather than *is*—unity; it is (at some level) an instance of Unity.

17. Note the contrast between the singular ἄπειρον τὸ πλῆθος at

143a1, concluding the first argument, and the plural ἄπειρα τὸ πλῆθος at 144e4-5, concluding the second. My distinction between what is being considered in each argument—each One-being, with respect to its parts, in the first, and the many instances of Oneness *qua* singularity, in the second—accounts for this.

18. The term "the One" becomes more densely ambiguous here than anywhere in the dialogue. To understand Parmenides we must bear in mind, at once, the distinctions between unity as integrity (wholeness) and as singularity and between the existent one and the aspect of 'one' taken by itself. Whereas the first argument takes the existent one and centers on its integrity (whole-part structure), the second abstracts the character 'one,' thereby isolating the form Oneness, and then counts those beings which, as ones, thereby instantiate it in its sense as singularity. It is important to underscore that the second argument asserts plurality *of the instances* of Oneness, not of the form Oneness itself. Parmenides makes this clear by the phrases κεκερματισμένον ὑπὸ τῆς οὐσίας (144e4) and ὑπὸ τοῦ ὄντος διανενεμημένον (144e6) in his summative remarks: it is Oneness *as distributed to beings, not in and for itself or* καθ' αὐτό, which is many.

19. For two other efforts to account for the twofold argumentation for the plurality of the One, see Brumbaugh, 1961, esp. p. 102, and Allen, 1974 and 1983 (esp. pp. 219-220, noted above in Ch. II, n. 18).

20. This is the language of the comparable (not identical) process of dialectic described at *Republic* 533c. In both cases, the mind moves by reflexive questioning from an essentially formal reasoning based on given assumptions to a substantive insight into what *is*.

21. All the italics are mine. One sees here the first of a number of passages in which Cornford's omission of Aristotle's replies is crucial and unfortunate. Since he does not include the replies, Cornford makes it impossible for himself to render the distinction between Parmenides' questions and assertions; thus he gives the impression that Parmenides is always assertive and, so, always himself endorses the content of his own proposals. As the present passage, fully rendered, shows, this is highly problematic. Presumably, Plato wanted his hearer to face the question, for himself, of what to accept and why. By putting the authoritative Parmenides into the genuinely ambiguous role of questioner and by giving certain key assertions to the (as dramatically projected) quite *un*authoritative Aristotle, Plato gives the hearer an interpretive burden and philosophical task which Cornford's translation simply conceals.

22. Insofar as "tense" refers to aspect, my formulation is not sufficiently precise. By associating "is" with "is becoming" and treating this present as counterpart to past and future being and becoming, Parmenides implies that the "is" which does *not* apply to the
One is that which, associated with change, involves a history.
Thus, for instance, it would be relevant for our understanding of
whatever "is" in this sense to know what it was before and what it
is in the process of becoming; indeed, even if it had not changed
over time, that itself would be relevant information. The forms, by
contrast, have no possibility of such change; thus we would never
discover actual change in them, nor—even more to the point—
would it be meaningful to say of them that they had not changed,
as if this were an historical fact. This ahistoricity, however,
amounts to a sort of *presence*, and this is why the "is" which is per-
tinent to the forms is *both* distinct from the "is" of ordinary time
present (the "is" associated with becoming and properly distinguished from past and future) *and* is not, in a strict sense, "tenseless." For Plato's own recognition of this problem, see *Timaeus*,
38a-b. In 1984 (too recently, unfortunately, for me to incorporate it
more thoroughly), Mohr has offered a particularly incisive exposition of the *Timaeus* passage and the sense in which the forms are
timeless. See also the illuminating discussions in Owen, 1966, and
Mourelatos, 1970.

23. Recent works that have recognized this include Whittaker, 1968,
pp. 136-137; Forrester, 1972, p. 6; and Allen, 1983. Whittaker
makes no attempt to interpret. Forrester's account, to the effect
that Plato uses a bad argument because, for "structural" reasons, he
needs an ostensibly negative conclusion for hypothesis I, is highly
artificial; it is also flawed by his mistaken ascription of the conflation of "all being" with "being subject to time" (p. 6) to Parmenides. Allen's interpretation requires extended discussion. He
rightly points out that the conflation is "unusual" and "wholly unacceptable to Platonism" (p. 215). But he argues that it follows
from the dilemma of participation: "Parmenides' criticisms [in the
first part of the dialogue] proceeded on the premise that sensibles
exist, and exist separately from Ideas. . . . [Therefore] they must
participate . . . in Being. . . . [S]ince participation implies participation in parts of Ideas, it implies participation in parts of Being—
that is, Being is a whole, some of whose parts are in sensible participants, since those participants are. . . . But sensibles are in time.
. . . Therefore, some parts of Being must come to be and pass away
with the sensibles they are in, for each sensible has its own part of

Being. Given that a whole is that from which no part is absent, generation or destruction of parts of Being implies change in Being itself, since Being is a whole consisting of parts. But Being, if it changes in this way, admits a before, an after, and a now, and therefore is in time. Therefore, to be is to be in time, since to be is to partake of Being, and Being is in time" (p. 215). Although elegantly assembled, this is an implausible interpretation of 141e. First, Allen overlooks the fact that Parmenides *asks Aristotle* whether, in effect, to be is to be in time. Parmenides relies on Aristotle's answer here. Can we credit Allen's position to Aristotle? Is it plausible that, with no explicit guidance from Parmenides, he has thought through the implications of the dilemma of participation (under "the locative reading"—Allen, 1983, p. 124) in preparing his reply? If so, he could be well beyond Socrates in his grasp of the problems of Socrates' own new theory of forms. This is highly improbable, given the dramatic projections of his character (127d) and age and inexperience in argumentation (137b). Moreover, it is effectively ruled out by 144c-d: there, when Parmenides wants Aristotle simply to consider each of the horns of the dilemma of participation, he finds it necessary to formulate them explicitly and, pausing, to instruct Aristotle to "reflect upon this" (144d1); had Aristotle so fully mastered the dilemma and its implications that, as Allen's reading of 141e must have it, he could work out, quite by himself, the position that Allen reconstructs, Parmenides' explicit and step-by-step manner at 144c-d would be unnecessary and out of place. An analogous objection holds at the level of *Plato*'s intent. If, as Allen must hold, Plato wants his readers to see that an implication of the dilemma of participation (in its "locative reading") is the collapse of being with being in time, then why isn't he more explicit in suggesting it? When he wants to call the dilemma back to mind at 144b-e, his language—not only in Parmenides' explicit instructions to Aristotle at 144c-d but also in his use of the verbs κατακερματίζειν and μερίζειν at 144b4-6, d2, d4, and e4 (see IV.B.3)—is quite pointed. The contrast between these passages is striking. For these reasons, a more plausible interpretation of 141e is required. We must be able to show why *Aristotle* would be likely to answer Parmenides as he does and what the point of this is in *Plato*'s larger plan.

24. Note 145e3-5, where Parmenides first gives, then conspicuously drops these qualifications. "In that respect in which the One is a whole," he says, "it is in another; but in that respect in which it

happens to be all the parts, it is itself in itself; and so the One necessarily is both in itself and in another." The qualifications are
dropped from here on in all the conclusions, with the partial exception of 148c-d.

25. That "limit" is here intended in a spatial sense can be seen from
the context. Parmenides establishes that the One is limited by ar-
guing that the parts "are contained" ($\pi\epsilon\rho\iota\acute{\epsilon}\chi\epsilon\tau\alpha\iota$) by the whole
(144e-145a). (On the paradoxical play with the notion of "contain-
ment" later in hypothesis II, see IV.C.3.) On the basis of such limitedness, Parmenides argues that the One has extremities (beginning, middle, end) and, therefore, shape (145b). Now, it will
follow that the One has shape only if the "extremities" are spatial,
and if they are, then the limitedness that is constituted by them
must also be spatial. Note that this puts into doubt Sayre's interpretation (1983), following Cornford (1939), that Plato in hypothesis II proves the Pythagorean thesis that "number is constitutive of
sensible things" (p. 52). In a re-statement of that thesis, Sayre asserts that "Parmenides shows that if there is number, *and the limit
typical of number*, then there might be things characterizable by
shape, place, motion and rest" (p. 60, my italics). Sayre needs the
italicized qualification, for to take "limit" in a *spatial* sense (as I
think we must) does mean—since it, in turn, is derived from
whole-part structure—that we have been granting the existence of
spatial wholes, that is, sensible things, from the beginning of the
argument at 142c. But if this is so, then we can hardly be said now
to be *proving* their possible existence (see n. 30 below). On the later
use of "limit," in Ch. III, in a sense not fundamentally spatial or
temporal, see V.A.2.

26. Thus the *Parmenides* refers, albeit very tersely, to space. Whether
Plato is here building on or anticipating the notion of the "receptacle" in the *Timaeus* is, however, a complex question. See Ch. V,
n. 15.

27. One of the surprising by-products of this interpretation of the hypotheses is its disclosure of some very central points on which Plato
converges (even if, in some cases, only potentially) with Aristotle.
At the close of our discussion of IIa we will be in position to observe how II and IIa implicitly contain key elements in the Aristotelian doctrine of categories (see n. 64, below), and our analysis of
III will show that Plato has already worked out the rudiments of
what, in Aristotle, will be the hylomorphic analysis of the concrete
individual (see Ch. V, n. 16). These disclosures would make an in-

teresting starting-point for a fresh study of Aristotle's break with Platonism.

28. My italics.

29. By "the One," again, I am translating Parmenides' phrase τὸ ἕν, *not* the briefly interposed discussion of the essentially distinct αὐτὸ τὸ ἕν. See nn. 10 and 16, above.

30. My interpretation of the *Parmenides* parts company with the great majority of interpretations on this point. Most take τὸ ἕν to refer to a form, not a physical-sensible thing, in the opening arguments at 142b–143a and 143a–144e, whether this form be Unity, in particular, or any form considered in its unity. For different readings that agree on this point, see, e.g., Cornford 1939; Lynch, 1959; Rochol, 1971; Teloh, 1976; Allen, 1983. This majority reading gains its plausibility from the abstract character of the opening arguments of hypothesis II. The "parts" of τὸ ἕν in the argument at 142c–143a are ἕν, "one," and ὄν, "being." And the argument at 143a–144c introduces, in addition, οὐσία, "beingness" or (the form) being; αὐτὸ τὸ ἕν, (the form) Unity; τὸ ἕτερον, (the form) difference; and number. There is no explicit reference to specifically physical-sensible characters. How, then, can my claim that the subject of these arguments, τὸ ἕν, refers to a physical-sensible one be justified?

The question requires several different lines of reply. To begin with, I would argue that at three points the coherence of the *Parmenides* as a whole requires my interpretation. First, and as we have already observed in another context (see n. 25), the arguments immediately following at 144e ff. show that "whole" and "part" are intended as spatial (or, more fully, as spatio-temporal). At 144e8–145a3 Parmenides derives the characterization of the One as "limited" from the initial characterization of it as a "whole," and at 145a4–b1 he specifies its parts as beginning, middle, and end; then at 145b2–5 he cites the equidistance of the middle from the extremities as the ground for characterizing the One as having shape. These arguments follow only if Parmenides intends "whole" and "part" in a sense applicable to spatial being from the beginning; Parmenides cannot derive a spatial sense of limitedness from a nonspatial sense of wholeness. The majority reading, however, must somehow ignore this. It must assume, instead, a sharp discontinuity between the opening arguments, in which a nonspatial sense of "whole" and "part" applicable to forms is supposedly in play, and the attributions after 144e, in which, now for the first time in hypothesis II, "whole" and "part" supposedly have a spatial significance. Often this is not argued explicitly; the text is simply treated as if it were two discontinuous passages. To his credit, Allen (1983) tackles the problem directly. His discussion shows, however, the considerable strain the majority reading must put on the text. Allen takes the One as the form Unity. He holds that "there is nothing in 142b–145a to directly justify the claim [that the One has shape]. . . . The fact is that Parmenides is here [i.e., 145a–b] assuming a proposition that will later be made explicit: that to be is to be somewhere (145e), that is, in a place." (1983, p. 239; note: This last text citation reads 143e in Allen's book. This must be a typographical error, and I have therefore corrected it.) This reasoning seems *ad hoc*. If Parmenides is assuming this spatialization of being without any explicit comment at 145a–b, why not also at 142b–145a? As we have observed, the attributions at 145a–b are derived directly from those preceding, and this requires that the terms have a constant sense. Or again: if, as Allen holds here (though, curiously, he is not so clear about this earlier on—see p. 126), Parmenides wants to assume a spatial sense of "whole" and "part" for the first time at 145a–b, why does he wait until 145e to introduce the proposition upon which the assumption is based? Surely there must be some reason for this delay, something that might explain why Parmenides is willing to tolerate the confusion it should cause for a careful hearer. Note, finally, how implausible an interpretation of the dramatic situation Allen's reconstruction requires. If we suppose that Aristotle follows the surface logic of Parmenides' argumentation, it seems highly improbable that after having just unhesitatingly identified being as such with being in time at 141e, he should now be able, throughout the argument at 142b–145a, to keep the notion of whole-part structure free of any spatial connotation; and even if we accept this, it then becomes all the more improbable that at 145a–b, again with not a word of explicit instruction from Parmenides, he should suddenly see an appropriateness, much less truth, in now treating whole and part as essentially spatial. Such nimble thinking is much more than we have interpretive warrant for imputing to the passive and philosophically inexperienced young Aristotle. (Indeed, his response to Parmenides at 145e3 shows that the first possibility is already beyond credibility. On the comparable implausibility of the insightfulness Allen must impute to Aristotle at 141e, see n. 23, above.) Second, a primary reason why many seek to read "whole" and "part" at 142b–143a, especially, as nonspatial is that they see in the passage a Platonic anticipation of the implications of the method of diairesis. On this interpretation (as noted in n. 4, above), hypothesis I serves as a *reductio* in which Plato rejects his own earlier conception of the forms as simple unities and prepares the way for the introduction, in hypothesis II at 142b-143a, of a new conception of the forms as complex and subject to division in a purely intellectual or cognitive sense. As I shall argue in the Epilogue, section B, the general point made by such a reading has much to recommend it; but it does not require, and a later part of the *Parmenides* militates against, the majority interpretation of 142b-143a. It is true that in the *Sophist* and the *Statesman* a nonphysical notion of whole-part structure will be applied to the forms as the subject matter of (or, in their roles as enabling) the method of diairesis. And significantly, in hypothesis V Parmenides introduces the conceptions prerequisite to the application of this new notion, namely, the conceptions of the communion of forms and of nonbeing as difference (see V.B.2.c). This makes it very striking, however, that in V Parmenides does not interpret these conceptions in terms of—or, indeed, ever refer at all to—"whole" and "part." If he had already introduced the nonphysical notion in II, this would be a natural connection to make. Third, as we have observed (Ch. II, n. 20), Parmenides' explication of the dilemma of participation at 131a-c by his conundrums at 131c-e makes clear that he there intends "whole" and "part" to connote spatial being. Only if he continues to take "whole" and "part" in this sense in the opening arguments of II, do these arguments have a bearing on Socrates' difficulties in the first part. On the majority reading, the two passages focus on unrelated problems—the participation of things in forms and the communion of forms, respectively—and the connection of the two parts of the dialogue is significantly diminished.

Positively, the abstract character of the opening arguments of II reflects their mode, not the subject to which they finally refer. As our analysis in IV.A.3 holds, the function of these arguments is to provide a conceptual statement of the two sorts of unity—being a whole of parts and a one amongst many—that apply distinctively to the physical-sensible thing and so set it into contrast with the form. Thus the first argument serves, by conceptual analysis, to lay out the whole-part structure, including the structural analogy of part with whole, that properly applies to any physical-sensible thing. And the second argument, again by conceptual analysis, serves to lay out the structure of plurality—that is, of being a one amongst unlimitedly many other similar ones—that applies to any thing.

These points call to mind one further bit of evidence against taking τὸ ἕν in the opening arguments of II to refer to forms: even when understood according to the eidetic sense of whole/part structure introduced by the *Sophist*, the form is not to be thought as made up of *unlimitedly* many other *forms* as its parts. Yet this would be implied by the argument at 142d-143a, if τὸ ἕν is taken to refer to a form. Since, according to that argument, the whole is no more and no less a "one being" than each of its parts, these latter would be no less forms than the whole. But the whole has unlimitedly many parts. Therefore, the form would be made up of unlimitedly many other forms. For the contrast between the definite or limited number of forms that any one form can be shown to consist in and the unlimited number of its phenomenal instances, see *Philebus* 16d and ff. (For the possible connection of this passage with the *Sophist* and the *Parmenides*, see the Epilogue, n. 18.)

31. Parmenides will return to this point in hypothesis V, showing the distinctive way in which the One (form) is subject to speech and knowledge. But he does not take up the issue of naming again. If Nehamas' striking suggestion, that for Plato a name in the proper sense "expresses the nature or essence of its referent" (1979, p. 101) and so is the name of a form, primarily, and of its participants only "derivatively" (p. 100), is correct, Parmenides' silence may reflect the formal and indirect nature of his approach to the forms; this notion of what a name does is peculiarly hard to explicate without concrete examples of "natures" or "essences," that is, of "forms." In any case, see both Nehamas, 1979, and Allen, 1960, on the general issue of names for forms and their participants.

32. This was established by the opening argument at 137c4-5 and ff.

33. Parmenides will begin to bring out the point of these subtle maneuverings when, in hypothesis V, he observes that so far as "the One that is not" (that is, the form) can be made the referent of discourse (λόγος), it must be understood also as "different" from what is other than it (160c-e) and as "like" itself (161b); here in I he is establishing the priority of the being of the form to its being known discursively even while preparing the way for the securing, in V, of this latter possibility. See V.B.2. For a statement of the distinction between a form's having a character by inner necessity and contingently, see *Sophist* 255e: "each [form] is different from the others not by virtue of its own nature but because it partakes of the form

of difference." Of course, at this stage in the hypotheses, Parmenides has not yet introduced the notion of the forms' partaking of each other. He will do so, as we shall see, in hypothesis V.

34. The argument for this, itself suspect, runs as follows: sameness and difference are contraries; from this it follows that difference will never "be in" what is the same; and this means (since the One and "what are not one" are presumably each self-same) that neither can participate in difference. The parenthesized step is not explicit in Parmenides' argumentation, yet it is both necessary and troublesome. It is necessary because only the presence, in the One and in "what are not One," of sameness would preclude the presence of difference, and that is Parmenides' immediate goal; moreover, it must be *self*-sameness since, obviously, sameness-with-the-other is the goal of the whole argument and so can hardly be presumed here. But the step is troublesome on just this last count. If the One and "what are not one" are each only *self*-same, nothing prevents them from being different from one another, that is, from participating in difference-with-respect-to-the-other. To permit this, of course, would defeat the elimination process towards sameness-with-the-other; moreover, it would suggest of "what are not one" that they are, as "different," simply other Ones, on par with the One as reciprocal "others" (ἕτερα) are on par. Thus Parmenides' twofold goal—to establish sameness between the One and "what are not one" and, as we shall consider shortly, to raise the possibility of *another sense* than other Ones for "what are not one"—would be defeated. Does he, to preserve this goal, take the parenthesized step yet conceal it by his inexplicitness?

35. Parmenides here takes this "not" in the most radical sense. "What are *not* one" cannot have any number (for number presupposes singular units which may be counted) nor be parts (for parts are ones, unitary beings—recall the discussion in n. 7 above, which the present passage appears to confirm). Thus Parmenides requires that, if we are to think "what are not one," we not think the sense 'other Ones.'

36. It is odd-sounding but not really troublesome that Parmenides takes the One and "what are not one" as, in their mutual difference, like; we need only keep the different levels or orders of these predicates distinct in our thinking. But it is by no means clear how he is able to reason that as the same (as was 'established' at 146d5-147b8), the One and "what are not one" are "unlike." His argument—that being the same is the contrary to difference and that,

since their difference made the One and "what are not one" like, then their sameness should make them the contrary, namely, unlike—seems almost algebraic in its abstractly calculative character; what is the sense of the operator "make" (or, in my text proper, "lead to," translating the force of the verbal forms ὡμοίου, 148b5, and ἀνομοιώσει, b5-6)?

37. Compare his responses at 148c2-3 and d4. His assent to the first set of arguments—"[The One] does stand in these relations, it seems, according to this sort of argument" (Ἔχει γὰρ οὖν δή, ὡς ἔοικεν, κατὰ τοιοῦτον λόγον, 148c2-3)—has the ring of perplexity and hesitation. (Interestingly, Cornford translates this reply. He suggests that it may be a Platonic acknowledgment that the argument is problematic, 1939, p. 166.) Aristotle gives unhesitating endorsement to the next set of arguments, by contrast.

38. "Constitute an identity" is deliberately open as a characterization. We shall have to see, from the dialogue itself (see hypothesis III, discussed in V.A.2.c), just what sort of identity or sameness the One and "what are not one" may constitute. Suffice it to say here that notions like merging or combining are dangerous, for they connote an identity between commensurates or likes.

39. Our interpretation of this whole passage, 146a-148d, should be compared to Cornford's (1939, pp. 154-167). He deliberately anticipates the characterization of the One *qua* "limiting factor" for "the Others" *qua* "the Unlimited" in hypothesis III and introduces it to interpret some of the ambiguities in the present passage. Though there is much valuable insight in his commentary here, Cornford loses the pointed pedagogical structure of the hypotheses by using III, which gets its specific sense *from* II and IIa, to resolve difficulties in II; wins his clarity about II at the high price of failing to distinguish the One of II (which is the composite of limit and unlimited, as we shall later argue, V.A.2) from that of I (which is the limit-providing term, itself incomposite); and moves almost chaotically, without heeding the inner order of Parmenides' process of argumentation, from "numerical difference" through "conceptual sameness" to the integrity of limited and unlimited as his key interpretive notions in 146d, 146d-147a, and 147a-b, respectively.

40. Cornford (1939, p. 171) calls it "the hardest [section] in the whole dialogue" and regards his own "interpretations here offered"—which draw imaginatively and yet improbably on Pythagorean geometry, Zeno's paradoxes, and a Gorgian fragment—"as specially doubtful."

41. To underscore their mutual relativity, "largeness" and "small-ness" are paired by οὔτε/οὔτε (149e2-3), μὲν/δὲ (e5-6, e6-7, e7-8), τε καὶ (e9), and the dual person and case endings (e8-150a1).

42. See ἄλλα τοῦ ἑνὸς, 149e2. The phrase confirms what we just ar-gued, that Parmenides here refers to other Ones, not non-ones.

43. The point seems restricted to equality *with others*, however. Can the size relation of a thing to itself—insofar as the distinction can be made in the first place—be anything else than equality? As we shall see, the subsurface implication of the next phase of argument, 150e-151a, is that the One *qua* whole is equal to itself *qua* all the parts.

44. Parmenides will return to this conjunction of forms again in hy-pothesis V. See V.B.2.b.

45. Recall 130d, which we discussed in II.B.1.

46. Note the specific difference, too, between the dilemma of partic-ipation at 130e ff., where it is the *form* that is participated in whole or in part, and the alternatives at 150a-b, where the form is in the whole or in just part of the One, i.e., of the *participant thing*.

47. Cornford (1939) searches for the meaningfulness of this difference in the dialectics of the geometric continuum. Perhaps some back-ground context of higher mathematics in the Academy is in play, unbeknownst to the modern reader. But Cornford's solution—to distinguish the actual parts of a whole from the whole itself as hav-ing potentially more parts—is unsatisfactory, for it explains how the whole would be greater in number (multitude), not in extent (magnitude). The distinction between these senses is Plato's—note the next section of argument, 151b-e, as discussed on p. 111, above—and the present passage treats extent (magnitude), not number. For a different objection, cf. Allen, 1983, p. 253, n. 196.

48. Compare 145c1-2: "the One is all the parts of itself, and neither more nor less than all." Here Parmenides makes the same point, al-beit in terms of number rather than extent. This supports our read-ing both of 150e-151a and of the analogous subphase within 151b-e.

49. See IV.D and then V.A.2.a.

50. It is no objection that on this view the One would be larger than some, and smaller than some others, of "the others," rather than being larger and smaller than all of them. Parmenides nowhere makes the latter claim.

51. The Greek ἐκτὸς is conspicuously spatial in its connotation and, so, serves as a provocative signal of the basic problem.

52. Again, the term "relation," however convenient, should not mis-

lead. As noted earlier (ch. II, n. 49), there can be no *real* relation between form and thing, for while a form has its being independently of its participant things, these latter are first constituted by participation in their essential forms.

53. Some commentators, e.g., Liebrucks, 1949, Speiser, 1937, and Wahl, 1951, treat 155e-157b as hypothesis III and count nine hypotheses in all. This is tempting in that Parmenides begins by proposing to "take up the argument a third time (τὸ τρίτον)" at 155e. In substance, however, this passage is part of hypothesis II, if only in the sense of a corollary, for it treats the One which, as one and many and in time, has all the contrary characters. Thus we will call it IIa. Plato's reference to the "third time" announces not a new, third hypothesis, but rather, as the Greek proverb has it, a "third time for the saviour," that is, an insight which will rescue the inquiry by getting beyond the seeming manifold absurdity of hypotheses I and II.

54. This is a difficult passage to translate on several counts. In the last part I follow Cornford in interpolating "[one]"; though it is not explicit in the Greek, its elliptical presence is suggested by the strictly parallel syntax (ὅτι μὲν . . . , ὅτι δ᾽ . . . , "insofar as . . . , insofar as . . ."). (Allen, 1983, chooses instead to drop the ἕν from 155e6 in his translation, without explanation.) More importantly, I take the καὶ of καὶ μήτε ἓν μήτε πολλὰ to have the force of "namely," "and so" (see Smyth, 1963, section 2869a). Apart from the intrinsic propriety of such a reading for any καί, it also prevents this καὶ from becoming redundant in combination with -τε . . . -τε . . . , and it shows the sense of the whole conjunction. The One is, as one, not many, and as many, not one. Thus, this passage does not announce a "synthesis" of hypothesis II (in which the One is both one and many) and hypothesis I (in which the One is neither one nor many), Friedländer, 1969, pp. 206 ff., Sinaiko, 1965, pp. 249 ff., Allen, 1983, p. 261, *et al.* to the contrary.

55. Thus "not being" here refers to a state *in time*, either to the (retrospectively recognized) condition of something before its coming-into-existence or to its condition after passing out of existence.

56. For crucial and (in varying senses) saving "thirds," cf. *Charmides* 167a, *Philebus* 66d and 67a, *Symposium* 213b, *Gorgias* 500a, *Republic* 583b, *Sophist* 242a (note, also, 252d), *Laws*, 692a, and *Seventh Letter* 340a (and 334d).

57. This translates τότε, the usual temporal sense of which—"then," "at that time"—is obviously improper here.

58. For the critical hearer who earlier saw that the contraries asserted

of the One in II were asserted of it in different senses or respects, to now see them as mutually exclusive pairs involves a new interpretation of them.

59. See pp. 131 ff. The notion of such a "*mere* many," a non-differentiated and non-integrated plurality is, of course, not unique to Plato. It goes back at least to the archaic Greek notion of the body as μέλη, the plurality of "limbs," and in a stricter form to Hesiod. See the discussion of Τάρταρα in Miller, 1977.

60. In an illuminating expansion on Cornford's use (1939, pp. 201-202) of the analogy of the relation of point to line, Sinaiko (1965, pp. 250-251) integrates these two perspectives as follows: "It should be noted that according to the terms of the argument 'the one' [in this context, of hypothesis II] is constantly passing through 'the moment' [i.e. the "instant"], for since 'the moment' itself is of no duration, it is, so to speak, *always present to* 'the one.' There is, as Cornford notes, a tight analogy between a point in relation to a line and 'the moment' in relation to the passage of time. A point has no linear extension and so is not a quantitative part of a line, although there is no place on a line where there is no point. Similarly, 'the moment' has no temporal duration, although there can be no period 'during which' there is no 'moment.' Thus 'the moment' is *always present, actual and necessary to* 'the one that is' " (my italics).

61. Note that the form's saturation of the temporal stretch, its presence in each of the "instants" in that stretch, implies only that its instances, not it itself, will be plural. Suppose we try to distinguish its "instants" of presence from one another, sorting them in the only way possible, namely, by reference to the different times at the centers of which, so to speak, each occurs. Since what we will have distinguished will be, in each case, the occupant of a stretch of time, we will have isolated only the instances, not the form itself. If, on the other hand, we focus on the form itself, it will present itself as indifferent to the temporality, and hence also to the plurality, of its instances.

62. In choosing examples, it is hard not to be struck by an important potential convergence of Plato and Aristotle. To use an oak tree as an example is to consider a form that falls into Aristotle's category of substance. This is misleading in one respect, well attuned in another. Nothing prevents Platonic forms that belong to other categories from serving as examples. If, however, we are considering the changes from not being to being (or *vice versa*) or from mere plurality to composite unity (or *vice versa*), then it becomes appro-

priate to look to essential forms, that is, to characters that a thing has (at least in principle) throughout the course of its existence, and among these, what Aristotle designates as genus and species come most readily to mind. For discussion of this in the context of the striking array of parallels between Aristotle in the *Categories* and Plato in the hypotheses, see n. 64, below; for extension of the parallels into the *Metaphysics*, see Ch. V, n. 16, below.

63. It is worth explicit stress—both for its intrinsic importance and because, as a qualification that other Platonic texts of different periods also make, it helps to confirm that this interpretation is on the right track—that the form plays the role of a principle of temporal integration here, not that of a principle of individuation. That is, the form does not serve as a positive criterion for differentiating particulars within the same species. On Plato's view, articulated, for instance, in the *Theaetetus* and the *Timaeus*, the instability and indefiniteness that its physical-sensible nature gives the particular thing makes any such criterion impossible; in the *Parmenides* he will have occasion to make this point in hypothesis VII, in which—to anticipate his argument—he qualifies the unity and identity attributed to the thing in II, IIa, and III as phenomenal and relative (see V.C.2). Note, moreover, that for the form to serve as such a criterion would seem to require a distinct form for each particular; this would violate the distinction—secured by the subsurface argument that contrasts the sorts of unity proper to form and to thing in the opening passages of I and II—between the uniqueness of the form and the plurality of its participants.

64. If these reflections are well oriented, they suggest a number of points on which Plato anticipates—if, in some cases, only potentially—Aristotle's *Categories*. Consider these five: (1) The One of II, the composite singular, is just that being, "one in number" (1b6, 3b12), that Aristotle designates as "first substance" in the *Categories*. (On Aristotle's meaning in pairing "one in number" with ἄτομον, "indivisible," see Frede, 1979.) (2) Hypothesis II provides the materials for a genuinely categorial analysis. As we have observed, by pairing contrary characters, opposing similar pairs, and contraposing dissimilar appositions, Plato guides the hearer's attention from isolate particular characters to the general kinds to which they belong. (3) The structure of Parmenides' analysis, moreover, anticipates Aristotle's central distinction between character and substratum. Plato does not have Parmenides explore the various characters for their own sake, nor does he in any sense ap-

ply the One to them, asking, for instance, into their unity; rather, Parmenides is made to explore, in case after case, whether and how a character *applies to* the One. Thus the One plays the structural role of substratum or subject. (4) The interplay between II and IIa suggests as well Aristotle's contrast—expressed in the distinction of what is present in a thing from what is said of it—between accidental and essential characters. By treating as contradictories what are, in II, merely contraries and by showing how the thing transits between them, IIa establishes the contingency of each of these characters; the thing no more needs have than not have any one such character. By contrast, the nontemporal One that the thing must *be* in the instant is indispensable to its very being as the singular, selfsame thing that it is. (5) Taken together, these observations point to the way Plato's treatment of the composite singular anticipates (again, if only potentially) Aristotle's isolation of substance—and, within it, the εἶδος in its special sense as species form—from all the other categories. This becomes most compelling if we set II and IIa into comparison with *Categories* 5: 3b24-4b18. Here Aristotle establishes three features proper to substance: (1) it has no contrary (3b24-32); (2) it does not itself admit of "the more and the less" (3b33-4a9), and (3) it does admit attributes contrary to one another (4a10-b18). Of these three, Aristotle is most qualified about the first, observing that "it is not peculiar to substance but [holds] of many other [categories] as well, for instance quantity" (3b27-28)— "unless," he adds in a formulation that should remind us of Plato's language in naming and distinguishing magnitude and multitude in 149d-151b and 151b-d, "someone should say that the much (τὸ πολὺ) is contrary to the little (τῷ ὀλίγῳ), or the great (τὸ μέγα) to the small (τῷ μικρῷ)" (3b30-31). In context, the primary value of (1) seems to be that it helps differentiate substance characters from quality (see 3b10-24). In hypothesis II of the *Parmenides*, neither (1) nor this differentiation are argued in any explicit way; they are, however, strongly suggested by the recurrent structure of Parmenides' analysis. Again and again, Parmenides shows the One to be subject to characters that stand as contraries to one another; it thus becomes conspicuous that while each of these characters has a proper contrary, the One (the thing), at least in its role as substratum, does not. This reflection already indicates that Plato also in effect anticipates Aristotle on (3); what is still more striking, however, is the close coincidence of Plato's account in IIa with Aristotle's on *just how* the One admits attributes contrary to one another. Like Plato, Aristotle gives a temporal analysis of "transformation" (μεταβολή, 4a33): "a particular man, for instance, being one and the same, becomes at one time (ὁτὲ μὲν) pale, at another (ὁτὲ δὲ) dark" (4a18-20). And as with Plato, this raises the question: what assures that the particular really is "one and the same," if its states are mutually exclusive? The answer lies in Aristotle's feature (2). Earlier, after describing how qualities vary over time, he concludes that substances do not; for "a man is not said to be a man more now than before, nor are any of the things that are substance" (4a6-8). Thus Aristotle appeals to the invariance of the εἶδος; because, e.g., "man"—that is, the species form of the particular man—is not subject to increase or diminution but remains unchanging, all the qualities of the particular may undergo transformation without depriving it of its unity and identity. This, however, is just the solution to which Plato's subsurface argument in IIa leads the hearer: that the form is not in time guarantees the basic identity of its participant through its temporal transformations.

In itemizing these various points, I speak of "potential" anticipations or convergences in order to acknowledge that although the substance implied by the structure of Plato's approach to the One in II and IIa *could be* thematized in Aristotle's way, it is not at all clear either that Plato ever intended this or that Aristotle had the *Parmenides* in mind in working out the *Categories*. If (1) to (5) do point to a shared seminal insight, they also throw into relief how differently Plato and Aristotle articulate and develop it. Thus, to cite a conspicuous illustration, Plato, intent on the project of enabling the "conversion" of mind, sees in the categorial study of the One of II (the thing) a means of clarifying the transcendence of the One of I (the form); Aristotle, by contrast, sees it as the first step toward a replacement of the vertical relation of each one form with its many derivatively named participants by the horizontal relation of πρὸς ἕν order. (On the presence of the latter in the *Categories*, see Aubenque, 1962, pp. 190 ff.) Again, whereas for Plato the distinction, in effect, of accidental from essential provides occasion for showing the dependence of the One of II, the thing, on the One of I, the form, for Aristotle it is a way of sorting characters, all of which are dependent *qua* characters on the concrete individual as their substratum. An adequate exposition of these moments of simultaneous coincidence and departure and of the contrast of philosophical motives that they signal would require a separate study. For an analogous case of potential convergence, equally complex and substantively close to this one, see Turnbull, 1958.

65. For a distinction between two such stages of reflection in Plato, see Lee, 1976, esp. pp. 90-93.

Chapter V: Hypotheses III-VIII

1. Parmenides' word στέρεται (159e1, echoing 157c1) brings to mind Aristotle's doctrine of στέρησις (privation). See n. 16, below.

2. Allen (1983) holds that the real point of the hypotheses is to display the implications of the dilemma of participation; he also argues that in the *Parmenides* Plato presents the dilemma as insuperable (recall Ch. III, n. 17). A close reading of hypothesis III, however, provides decisive testimony against these positions. Consider, first, Allen's account of how the dilemma and its implications unfold: once one grants (at least some) sensibles separate existence, then one is committed to interpreting participation as a relation in which the participant takes *either* the whole *or* a part of the participated form into itself; the first of these possibilities is absurd, with the resulting implication that if there is participation, the participant must take into itself a part of the participated form, which, therefore, must be divisible into parts; if this last consequence is unacceptable, then, since participation can only be by means of parts of the form, there can be no participation, with the resulting implication that forms will contribute nothing to the existence of sensibles, will be unknowable, and so forth—essentially the consequences that Parmenides suggests at 133b-134e. Now, in hypothesis III Parmenides establishes that "the others" neither "are" the One nor are utterly "deprived" of it; rather, they "participate" in it (157b-c). And he establishes that "the others" are other both by virtue of "having parts" (157c) and by virtue of being "many" (158b); but if these are the ways in which the others differ from the One, then the One must be both partless and not many, that is, simple and unique. This, however, yields a conjunction of conditions that is impossible within the context of the dilemma of participation as Allen interprets it: the One does *not* have parts and *is* participated. (Likewise, the One excludes plurality and yet is participated, in direct contradiction of the consequence Allen derives from the dilemma of participation, that "if Unity excludes plurality, it cannot be participated in," p. 273.) The threefold implication, against Allen's

reading of the hypotheses, is, first, that Parmenides does not accept, as the thrust of the dilemma, that if there is participation, it can only be by means of parts of the form; second, that the hypotheses as a whole cannot be construed to be governed by, much less to be a display of the implications of, the dilemma of participation; and third, that (given, additionally, that hypothesis III is not to be interpreted as absurd or self-defeating) there *is* an overcoming of the dilemma of participation within the *Parmenides*. (Of course, it is a central purpose of my Chs. IV and V as a whole to attempt to explicate the full sense of this last point.)

3. My italics.

4. For the specific sense of this otherness as ἑτεροιότης, see hypothesis V and my discussion in V.B.2.a, esp. n. 22, below.

5. I mean this not in the sense of a leveling and not in the logical sense of a *reductio* but, rather, in its genuine etymological sense of a leading back, in thought, to the elementary.

6. The widely accepted view of this passage is rather that "the others" all together make up one all-comprehensive whole. See, e.g., Cornford, 1939, Brumbaugh, 1961, Sinaiko, 1965, Schofield, 1977. (Note, however, that the first three want to argue that each of "the others," as a part of this whole, itself possesses whole-part structure too.) My disagreement is based on three points but is, finally, a matter of interpretive judgment. First, when Parmenides characterizes "the others" as "having parts," ἔχοντα μόρια (157c3), he chooses the plural ἔχοντα rather than the singular ἔχον; yet the latter would have been a precise and grammatically standard way to indicate that he takes τὰ ἄλλα as a collective whole. Doesn't his choice *not* to use the singular suggest that he thinks of τὰ ἄλλα as many which have parts, and isn't the likely sense of this, if this many is not a collective, that *each* of them has *its own* plurality of parts? Second, Parmenides calls "the others" ἓν ἐκ πολλῶν, "one out of many" in the sense of a composite whole, at 157c6. He then goes on to argue that they are "many," πολλά, at 158b1-4. How could *one* composite whole be "many"? Through the many "out of" which it is composed? If this were Parmenides' meaning, then his characterization at 158b1-4 (which, note, does *not* take the plurality of parts as its basis) would be redundant, simply reasserting, as it were, the characterization of "the others" as ἓν ἐκ πολλῶν at 157c6. Isn't it a likelier alternative that, intending his earlier argument to establish whole-part structure for *each* of the others considered alone, Parmenides now turns from whole-part structure to singu-

larity/plurality—just as he did in the double argumentation in II at 142d9-143a3 and 143a4-144e3—and makes explicit that there are *many* such particular wholes or composite ones? Finally, in the summative sentence for the next phase of argument, the so-called "reduction" at 158b-d, he says, "Thus the others than the One, both as wholes and in [their] parts (καὶ ὅλα καὶ κατὰ μόρια, 158d7), both are unlimited and partake of limit." If "the others" make up just *one* whole, how can Parmenides refer to them as "wholes" (ὅλα)? If they both make up one whole and yet are each, as a part of this whole, also a whole of parts in its own right, then doesn't Parmenides, by referring to them only in the latter respect, speak one-sidedly, at best, and omit the primary and most important aspect of their being, at worst? On the other hand, if Parmenides *only takes each of them to be a whole*, and does not argue for an all-comprehending whole, then these problems dissolve. The alternative reading, of course, stresses 157e4-5, where Parmenides declares it "necessary that the others than the One, having parts (μόρια ἔχον), be one complete whole (ἓν . . . ὅλον τέλειον)." Here Parmenides does use the singular ἔχον, to be sure, but on my reading this is precisely because—given that his use of the plural ἔχοντα at 157c3 above has attuned his hearer to think of *each* of the others as having parts—he is now thinking of *each* of the others, not of their collective unity.

7. Thus αὐτός, "same," refers us back to the λόγος applied to "the others" as such. As not being the One yet not being deprived totally of it, hence as being one in some intermediate sense, whole and part alike must be neither simple nor unintegrated (a "mere many") but, rather, composite, a whole-of-parts.

8. Brumbaugh (1961) regards the reconstructions of this argument by Cornford and Taylor as woefully inadequate ("an affront to the reader," p. 153). I am not certain whether or not my reconstruction overcomes the simplicism he criticizes. But in any case, I find Parmenides' argument both simple at its surface and profound in its implications. Merely by pointing out the mutual exclusiveness of parts, he is able to show that, if they really are *parts*, they must be organized or gathered into a whole through the presence of a 'part' of a different and higher order. This reasoning will be crucial to Aristotle's two-level analysis of the physical individual into a plurality of material parts unified by an immaterial 'part,' the form. See n. 16, below.

9. Parmenides says that the part is part μιᾶς τινὸς ἰδέας καὶ ἑνός τινος ὃ καλοῦμεν ὅλον. Two questions, interrelated, arise: How shall

we interpret the genitive (μιᾶς τινὸς ἰδέας, "*of* a certain one character")? And how shall we understand the connective force of καὶ,
as that of simple conjunction ("and") or as that of the explicative
"namely," "and so"? It is hard to understand the sense the phrase
would have if we opted for the partitive genitive, in response to the
first question, and the simple conjunction, in response to the second. How could an ἰδέα, a unitary (μιᾶς) character, have parts?
And what would the collection of such an ἰδέα "*and*" a "one" in the
sense of a "whole" amount to? If, however, we let καὶ serve the explicative role (again, see Smyth, 1963, section 2869a), then we
might interpret the whole construction in a somewhat dialectical
way. The καὶ would shift the reference of the partitive genitive from
the ἰδέα to the ἕν τι (or ὅλον) in which it, the ἰδέα, is present and
which, indeed, it first constitutes as a ἕν (and ὅλον) by its presence.

10. It is basic to the later hylomorphism of Aristotle and, indeed, of
Kant. To recognize the *concretum* as such, in its experiential primacy, yet imaginatively to seek its constituents, is in a way *the* fundamental act of metaphysical thinking.

11. It is important to note how, in his next sentence, Parmenides suggests there is no absolute limit to such smallness, hence no intrinsically minimal unit. "*Each time* we consider (or *for as long as* we go
on considering, ἀεὶ σκοποῦντες), itself in and for itself, the nature
other than the form, whatever of it we see will *always* (ἀεὶ) be without limit in quantity" (158c5-7).

12. Of course, this double aspect—multitude and magnitude—belongs to the very notion of quantity, πλῆθος. As we saw earlier
(IV.B.2 and IV.C.3), Parmenides treats these as kindred aspects of
the notion of size.

13. With this language at 158c2-4, cf. 155e5-6, discussed in Ch. IV,
n. 54.

14. I am trying to express the force of γε in the opening καὶ μὴν ἐπει-
δάν γε, 158c7.

15. Parmenides' reduction cannot help but bring two other Platonic passages to mind: the account of the "receptacle," described
as ἄμορφον (50d), in the *Timaeus* and the account of the four kinds,
including πέρας and τὸ ἄπειρον, at *Philebus* 23c-27b. The relation
between these three texts requires and merits a separate study. On
the one hand, there are striking convergences: like the *Philebus*, the
Parmenides characterizes all physical-sensible individuals as in some
sense "mixtures" of what limits with what is intrinsically without
limit; and like the *Timaeus*, the *Parmenides* characterizes the latter as

something not qualitatively specific. On the other hand, there are equally obvious divergences: in contrast with the *Timaeus*, the *Parmenides* appears to distinguish between the "other" that all physical-sensible individuals are "in" (recall 145d, as discussed on p. 94, above)—this, presumably, would be place or space—and the unlimited factor within each such individual; and in contrast with the *Parmenides*, the *Philebus* presents a host of distinct species of the unlimited and offers a specifically mathematical characterization of πέρας. The different perspectives from which we might try to grasp the coherence of the three dialogues are striking. Shall we, for instance, regard the *Timaeus* and the *Philebus* as complementary explorations of the medium and the substrata, respectively, of physical-sensible things (see, e.g., Sinnige, 1968, Ch. VIII B)? In this case the *Parmenides*, since it alone distinguishes the two, represents a sort of bridge. When we come across the great and the small as a plurality of phenomenal fields in the *Philebus*, shall we insist with the *Parmenides*, 149d-151d of hypothesis II (see IV.C.3), that the great and the small themselves are forms, so that the fields in the *Philebus* must be participants? If so (to extend the argument of Lee, 1966), we shall need to turn to the *Timaeus* with its account of the receptacle for help in understanding how those participants can first exist. Or shall we acknowledge the fundamental obscurity of the very idea of the receptacle (see Lee, 1966, pp. 366-368, and Sayre, 1983, pp. 246-255—and see Ch. II, n. 41, above) and interpret Plato as intending to dissolve the problem in the *Philebus* by making the great and the small (whether forms or not) immediately phenomenal (Sayre, 1983, Ch. 3, sections 2 and 3)? Note that for each of the latter two possibilities, the *Parmenides* is, again, a kind of bridge—but the route leads in opposite directions.

16. On a number of central points, hypothesis III suggests a second area of potential convergence with Aristotle. (For the first, recall Ch. IV, n. 64.) Plato appears to provide the rudiments of what in Aristotle will be the hylomorphic analysis of the concrete individual. Let me, again, itemize a number of particulars:

(1)(i) In focusing on τὰ ἄλλα "then, at the moment when they participate" (158b9) and bringing 'them' to light as, at that point, "the nature other than the form" (158c6), Plato's Parmenides discloses (what Aristotle will explicitly call) matter. (ii) Plato's technique of reduction resembles Aristotle's speculative exercise of "stripping away" (*Metaphysics* Z, 3:1029a11-12) the characters from the substratum. (iii) The interpretation of the "nature" that remains as, in and of itself, indeterminate and without internal whole-part structure calls to mind Aristotle's characterizations of matter as ἄμορφον (*Physics* A, 7:191a10), ἀρρύθμιστον καθ᾽ ἑαυτό (*Physics* B, 1:193a11), and ἀόριστον (*Physics* Γ, 2:209b9; *Metaphysics* Γ, 4:1007b28; Z, 11:1037a27; Θ, 7:1049b1; M, 10:1087a16), as well as Aristotle's simile of the "heap" (σωρός, *Metaphysics* Z, 16:1040b8-10). (iv) Indeed, Aristotle's negative characterization of matter as "neither being *one* nor *being* in the manner of the this" (οὐχ οὕτω μία οὖσα οὐδὲ οὕτως ὂν ὡς τὸ τόδε τι, *Physics* A, 7:191a12-13), repeated in a different but related formulation in *Metaphysics* Z, 3 (1029a20-21), could serve as a gloss on Parmenides' formula τὰ μὴ ἕν. (v) As in the account Aristotle offers in *Metaphysics* Z, 3, so with the πλῆθος Parmenides reveals in the reduction: the substratum cannot exist independently. Both hypothesis III and the argument of hypothesis IV as a whole (see section A.3 below) show that, "deprived" of form, τὰ ἄλλα lose their very being. Thus Plato appears to verge on the discovery of two crucial Aristotelian theses: in neither existing independently nor lacking existence altogether, that is, in having existence only as together with and available for structuring by form, πλῆθος is, and is only, *potentially*; and in this being, standing as both "unlike" and yet the "same" as the physical-sensible thing, it must be understood as standing in a *constitutive*, hence *not in a real*, relation to the thing.

(2)(i) In showing, in the reduction, what he first asserts at 157c-d, namely, that the One (the form) makes what by itself would be merely a "many" into a "whole" and a "complete one," Plato's *Parmenides* appears to give the outlines of the account that Aristotle offers in *Metaphysics* Z, 16-17: the form structures and integrates the plurality that matter is, "work[ing it] up" (1040b9) into a "compound of something, in such a way that 'the all of it' (τὸ πᾶν) is one, not like a heap but like a syllable" (1041b11-12). (ii) The terse Platonic account of the fourfold function of πέρας in providing internal arrangement and external delimitation to the thing (158c7-d2) applies to the Aristotelian compound precisely.

(3) What is more, at a number of moments in the course of *Metaphysics* Z Aristotle appears to repeat points in the Platonic account, presented in hypothesis I, of the transcendence that the form must have in order to perform its constitutive role as the immanent basis for the thing. (i) Thus Aristotle establishes that form itself—in distinction from form κατὰ συμβεβηκὸς (1033a30)—prescinds from generation and change (Z 8: 1033a28 ff., b5-11, b16-18). (ii) In a

striking passage (subject, however, to interpretation and possibly to contradiction by other passages, in particular 1071a20-29—see Cherniss, 1944, pp. 506-508, and Albritton, 1957), he seems to suggest as well that form itself, even in its immanence, is not subject to plurality: "When we have the whole," Aristotle writes at 1034a5-8, "such and such a form (εἶδος) in this flesh and these bones, this is Callias or Socrates; and they are different in virtue of their matter (for that is different), but the same in form (for the form is indivisible) (ταὐτὸ δὲ ἐν εἴδει [ἄτομον γὰρ τὸ εἶδος])." (iii) At the close of Z 17, he establishes by regress arguments that form can be neither an "element" in the concrete individual—that is, make up a part of it in the same way its material parts do—nor itself a whole of such parts (1041b20-25).

As before, the full study that these points of convergence require would, I think, complicate and deepen, rather than do away with, our sense for the basic divergence of Aristotle from Plato. On the one hand, it seems clear that Aristotle's own rather wooden characterizations of the Platonic forms and participation, especially, for example, the polemics of *Metaphysics* A, 9, will not do justice to the deep affinities of his thought with Plato's. Above all, their conflict cannot be reduced to an exclusive disjunction between transcendent and immanent form; (3)(i)-(iii) suggest that both recognized transcendence as a precondition for immanence, and (2)(i) shows that neither took form to stand in a real relation to thing. On the other hand, it must also be noted from the start that whereas the points of convergence are picked, on Aristotle's side, out of the *Physics* and *Metaphysics* Z, Aristotle's full account of form, matter, and thing is dialectically structured (see Owen, 1978/9) and stretches beyond Z into H (see Rorty, 1973) and Θ (see Kosman, 1983). Thus, for example, Plato's notion of the material constituent might best be situated between Aristotle's introductory account of matter in *Physics* A, 7 (see Jones, 1974, noting n. 22) and the ultimate account he provides by way of the distinction of motion and ἐνέργεια in Θ 6 (Kosman, 1985, pp. 14-16): like Aristotle's remarks in Z, 3, the Platonic suggestions in hypothesis III undercut the idea that matter is a discrete 'this' but do not go so far as to suggest its identity with form. Likewise, whereas Plato will go on from his disclosure of the constitutive work—one might *almost* say ἐνέργεια—of the form in III to show how the form and the thing stand in contrast as what "truly" is what it is (hypothesis V) and what only "apparently" is what it is (hypothesis VII), respectively,

Aristotle, it seems, goes on from Z, 17, to identify the being of the form with its work, hence with ἐνέργεια, and in this way to clarify, in H and Θ, the identity of essence with individual by way of that of form as ἐνέργεια with matter as potentiality.

17. As soon as the hearer has grasped the shift in the sense of the One from form to thing in passing from hypothesis I to hypothesis II, he is naturally inclined to ask if there is a comparable shift in its sense in passing from III to IV. Parmenides makes clear that that is *not* the case, and therefore that the contradiction between III and IV will have to be penetrated and dissolved on another basis, when he declares, near the beginning of the argument in IV, that the One— more precisely, "the truly One," τὸ ὡς ἀληθῶς ἕν—has no parts. This establishes that the One of IV is, like the One of III, the simple One (the form) considered in I, and it also points ahead (though the hearer will see this only in retrospect) to the contrast between the simple One, or the form, as a "true" one and its participant things, "the others," as merely "apparent" and "seeming" ones (hypothesis VII). See V.C.2.

18. This argument in particular shows that Parmenides intends "the others" to refer to things. At the same time, however, since he studies things as "deprived" of the unity they gain from participation, and since the "*mere* many" is in precisely this condition, it is also possible to read IV as a study of the "mere many." Such a reading will confirm our earlier characterization of the πλῆθος as, in and of itself, nonexistent and utterly indeterminate.

19. Zeno surely alludes to this in praising the young Socrates for "pursu[ing] and pick[ing] up the trail like a Spartan hound" (128c1).

20. There are several significant difficulties with Sayre's summary characterization of hypothesis V as showing that the One "has all characters (apparently)" (1978, p. 140; 1983, p. 44). First, it should *not* be presumed that the conclusion of each hypothesis "either attributes or denies basically the same set of characters either to Unity or to the others" (1983, p. 41). Such an assumption obscures the specificity of the One in V and so conceals, without justification, the place of hypothesis V in the subsurface argument. Note that Parmenides, even while making other positive attributions, does not predicate of the One "having contacts"; on the contrary, at 162d he in effect denies it. Nor does he ascribe shape or place to the One; again, at 162c he asserts the impossibility of these predications. Nor does he ever ascribe likeness or sameness with "the

others" to the One, attributes that would undercut his assertion of difference in kind. Finally, note Parmenides' tacit distinction, effectively covered over by Sayre's summary, between *being* great, small, and equal and *having* or *sharing in* great*ness*, small*ness*, and equa*lity*. The point of all these odd details will be of focal concern in the interpretation I shall offer in this section.

Second, in both 1978 and 1983, Sayre takes Parmenides to make the One of V like "the others" of VII (and, in the mode of negation, of VIII) in having its characters only "apparently." His argument (1978, pp. 135-136) is that "Although no term of appearance enters into the final conclusion of hypothesis V at 163b, the characters attributed to Unity there are consequential upon its having being, which it only *appears* (φαίνεται: 162b) to have, and upon its having, *as it appears* (ὡς ἔοικε(ν): 161d, 162e), equality, greatness, smallness, rest and motion." But is it correct to assimilate the qualifications in V and VII? In VII, as we shall see in V.C.2, Parmenides makes φαίνεται govern all the attributions, and he makes it stand in apposition with variants of δοκεῖ, "it seems" (see 164d2, d3, e1, e4, 165a4, c6, and note 165a2), and in pointed contrast to ὤν, "being . . ." (164d7), and ὄντα . . . ἀληθῶς, "being truly . . ." (164e2-3). In hypothesis V, on the other hand, φαίνεται is introduced only occasionally, at 162b6 in the summary of the ascription of being to the One ("So the One appears to share in being, if it is not") and at 162c3-4 to qualify the ascription to the One, on the basis of its participation in both being and not being, of motion. It is used similarly not with δοκεῖ but with ἔοικε (162c4) and ὡς ἔοικε (161e1-2, 162e3)—expressions that function to give assent but express perplexity or hesitation—and there is no contrast with truth or true being. Close reading of these passages shows that whereas in VII Parmenides implies an ontological contrast between appearance and being, or seeming and truth, in V he means rather to underscore the paradoxicality of the particular attributions qualified and, so, to stress the need to interpret their sense. That is, if in VII he invokes the qualification, "apparently," as a means of substantive doctrine, in V he uses it for rhetorical purposes, to signal a problem and prod the reader to dig beneath the surface. These are very different intentions and ought not be assimilated. My exegesis here and in V.C.2 should make this difference clear.

21. Allen, 1983, p. 286, states, "In [hypothesis V] Unity began as equivalent to Unity conceived apart from its own being, as in [hypothesis II]. . . ." Allen must argue this in order to work out his

thesis that the hypotheses display the implications of the dilemma of participation, but the text does not support him. Parmenides begins, "If the One is not (μὴ ἔστι)" (160b5), and he calls the One "the One which is not" (τὸ μὴ ὂν ἕν, 160e4, 162d3; τὸ ἓν μὴ ὄν, 161e1, 162d4, 163a6, 163b2, b4; τὸ ἓν οὐκ ὄν, 162a2, e2-3; τὸ οὐκ ὂν ἕν, 162c5, 163a4-5); this language refers us to the close of hypothesis I, not to II. Note that when in hypothesis II Parmenides does want to single out Unity as such, conceiving it apart from the being with which it is joined in any "One which is," he does not introduce nonbeing at all; rather, he focuses directly on αὐτὸ τὸ ἕν, asking Aristotle to "conceive it (τῇ διανοίᾳ . . . λάβωμεν) just by itself alone apart from the being which we say it has" (143a7-8).

22. My italics. Parmenides' introduction of this term is conspicuous and pointed. Whereas ἕτερος (and its derivative noun ἑτερότης) refers primarily to difference between terms on par or likes, ἑτεροῖος and ἑτεροιότης introduce, through the -οι- (cf. οἷος), the notion of kind or sort and, so, indicate difference in kind. Thus, whereas ἕτερος was the appropriate term in Parmenides' discussion of the relation of the One *of II* (the thing) to "the others" *qua* other Ones (other things), ἑτεροιότης is the appropriate term here in V, where Parmenides refers to the distinction between the One *of I* (the form) and "the others" (things). See the entries under ἕτερος and ἑτεροιότης in Liddell and Scott's *Greek-English Lexicon*.

23. My italics. Both here and in the translation to come of 142a1-4, I have used prepositions to signify the functions that the Greek original expresses by case endings.

24. Once again, Parmenides puts the burden on Aristotle—and correlatively, Plato puts the burden on us—by asking rather than asserting, then by developing the implications of Aristotle's answers (see, in the cited passage, ἄρα, "consequently"). We shall observe a number of such passages in the discussion to come. Recall Ch. III, n. 22.

25. Recall IV.C.1.

26. Analogously with ἑτεροῖος, so ἀλλοῖος indicates otherness *in kind*. The contrast between ἄλλος and ἀλλοῖος is comparable to that between ἕτερος and ἑτεροῖος. See n. 22 and, again, the entries in Liddell and Scott, *Greek-English Lexicon*.

27. This shift in senses is all the more conspicuous here because, as Allen (1983, p. 282) also observes, Parmenides kept "not equal" clearly distinct from "unequal" in hypothesis I, 140b-d. Allen's at-

tempt to justify Parmenides' arguments is flawed in several notable ways. In taking the One as greater than the others because it contains them and fewer than the others because they are a multitude, he allows the sense of great and small to slide from magnitude (extent) to multitude (number); but Parmenides is very clear in keeping these senses distinct in hypotheses I and II. More fundamentally, in making both of these comparisons in size, Allen lets the One have size in the same ways that the others have size; thus he violates Parmenides' emphatic characterization of the One as having "difference in kind" (160a8, e1, 161a7, a8; see n. 22 above) and "otherness in kind" (161a8; see n. 26 above) with respect to the others.

28. By contrast, Parmenides did use the finite "is" plus the adjective in step (2)(i) of the argument. See 161c3, c6. Thus the shift in phrasing at (2)(ii) and (iii) is conspicuous.

29. This passage is the culmination of a series of passages in the *Parmenides* in which we can see emerging—and more clearly on my reading, I think, than on Sayre's, 1983—that nexus of concepts that he finds central to Plato's "late ontology." Sayre looks in the *Parmenides* for preliminary formulations of the ideas, reported in the *Metaphysics* by Aristotle, that the great and the small are "the underlying matter of which the Forms are predicated in the case of sensible things, and Unity in the case of the Forms" (988a 11-13, as quoted in Sayre, p. 11). Consider, by means of several friendly refinements that my reading allows of Sayre's interpretation, how much that interpretation has brought into view.

(1) Because he does not explore the systematic ambiguity of τὸ ἕν, Sayre does not give himself occasion to see how fully the *Parmenides* articulates the thesis that it is forms that (to borrow Aristotle's language) are predicated of the great and small to compose sensible things. Hypothesis III speaks of τὸ ἕν as providing "limit," and Sayre translates it, as usual, as "Unity" (p. 167); but as we have argued earlier (V.A.1), τὸ ἕν there refers to the (one) form.

(2) If it is the form that, in part, constitutes the sensible, it is the One, according to Aristotle, that in part constitutes the form. Because the *Parmenides* is not about the One in the sense of the form Unity (except for the brief passage at 143a-144e, as noted), it gives no direct evidence on this point. But it does give indirect evidence. If each form is considered as a simple and unique one, then each must instantiate Oneness itself (and—since each is simple and unique—it must do so more purely than the composite singulars

referred to at 143a-144e). But in this case, just as each form is said to be in part constitutive of its instances, so this Oneness must be in part constitutive of each of the forms.

(3) Sayre finds that "Plato seems to be doing in these passages of the *Parmenides* with the Unlimited Multitude and Unity . . . just what Aristotle said he did with Unity and the Great and Small" (p. 67). To overcome the terminological gap between "Unlimited Multitude" ($\mathring{a}\pi\epsilon\iota\rho o\nu$ $\pi\lambda\hat{\eta}\theta o\varsigma$) and "the Great and the Small" ($\tau\grave{o}$ $\mu\acute{\epsilon}\gamma a$ $\kappa a\grave{\iota}$ $\tau\grave{o}$ $\mu\iota\kappa\rho\acute{o}\nu$), he hypothesizes that "maybe Aristotle used different terminology in describing Plato's ontological position from what Plato himself ever used in the dialogues" (p. 67). On our interpretation of the connection of hypotheses II, 149d-151d, with III, 158b-d, however, there is no need to look to Aristotelian inventiveness. In the first passage we are given a proof that without "these forms" (149e9), greatness and smallness, things could not have size; in the second passage we are led by "an exercise in abstraction" (Sayre, p. 64) to see that the element of size in a thing— that is, that in the participant thing that it derives from "the Great and the Small"—just is, considered by itself, an "Unlimited Many." Taken together, the passages thus show the sense in which Aristotle is reporting, not inventing, when he says that *it is the great and the small* that is "the underlying matter" on which the forms are imposed in constituting sensible things.

(4) The present passage, 161c-e, in effect sums up the whole reflection about the constitution of sensible things (that is, points (1) and (3)); in doing so, moreover, it takes us back to an observation we made earlier in commenting on Sayre's discovery of the $\mathring{a}\pi\epsilon\iota$-$\rho o\nu$ $\pi\lambda\hat{\eta}\theta o\varsigma$ in 142d-143a of hypothesis II (recall Ch. IV, n. 15). "The One which is" (that is, the sensible thing) is neither a pure One nor an Unlimited Many; rather, as the participant in (to put it inelegantly for the sake of clarity) the-defining-form-in-communion-with-the-great-and-the-small, it is constituted by *both* and exists as the Unlimited-Many-under-structuring-limitation-by-the-defining-form.

(5) Only one element of Aristotle's report still remains completely obscure. In what sense can it be said that the great and the small are constitutive of the (defining) form itself? Presumably, Plato only just begins to open this up in the *Parmenides* when, at 161e-163b, he introduces a sense of being that allows each form to be analyzed in terms of other forms. This raises questions regarding the notion of simplicity that Plato doesn't make conspicuous

until the *Sophist* (see the Epilogue, B) and questions about an eidetic sense of the great and the small that he doesn't explore until
the *Philebus* (see Sayre's stimulating account, 1983, Ch. 3, section
1).

30. If this interpretation is correct, then Parmenides' attributions of
greatness and smallness to the One would seem to verge on being
deliberate cases of "Pauline predication" (see Vlastos, 1970 and
1972). It is not the One (form) but its participants that are great or
small.

31. The Greek is not precisely translatable, and the approximation is
misleading. Parmenides' ἀληθῆ is a plural adjective used as an indefinite substantive: he says, to put it literally, "we would not be
saying trues. . . ." These "trues" are, *qua* spoken, predicates, and
the latter, in turn, refer to *forms*. Thus the approximate translation,
"we would not be saying true '*things*' . . . ," is misleading. My single quotes are intended to signal that I do not mean "thing" in the
usual sense of spatio-temporally existent participant. The same
point exactly holds for my translation of the adjectival participle
ὄντα in the next lines. (Usually it is possible to render that, in its
plural, as "beings," but in this case, that would be awkward and
opaque.)

32. By interpreting "what-*is*" in terms of "what-is-*true*," Parmenides
introduces what Kahn has named the "veridical" sense of the verb
"to be." (See Kahn, 1966, 1978, and 1981, esp. pp. 115-117. For a
recent alternative analysis, see Matthen, 1983.) As Kahn holds
(and, as well, as Matthen's display of the interchangeability of the
"dyadic" and "monadic" uses of ἔστι may also be taken to imply),
the veridical sense lies deeper than the distinction between existential and predicative uses. The veridical is therefore not a contrary to
the existential, as, e.g., the Meinongian reading Allen disputes
(1983, p. 285) would imply. Nonetheless, the introduction of the
veridical in hypothesis V does accentuate the predicative ἔστι. To
situate the point within the overall context of the subsurface content of the hypotheses: The movement from the denial of being in
the sense of temporally determinate existence to the affirmation of
being in the veridical sense would be misconstrued if we were to
take it to recover—or, rather, if we were to take it *simply* to recover—a nontemporal sense of *existence*. Of course, for Plato,
forms exist. But to focus one's thought or conception of forms on
this is perilous, for it may incline us, like the youthful Socrates, to
think of forms after the model of things. To say of forms that their

existence is not temporally determinate—the insight that Plato's irony at the close of hypothesis I (141e) is aimed to provoke—is only the first step. The second, equally crucial step is to shift one's focus to what forms exist *as*, namely, the *true natures of things*; this is what Plato's introduction of the veridical (which includes the existential but puts its weight, so to speak, on the predicative) in the present hypothesis, combined, as we shall see, with his introduction of the notion of "appearing" in hypothesis VII, is designed to provoke. It is instructive to note a certain substantive irony in this, one that may bear importantly on the question of what "Platonism" really comes to: just by itself the first step lifts thought "beyond" things (to borrow Aristotle's language in *Metaphysics* A 9), but, *taken by itself*, it risks making the forms into a "separate set of things." The second step, since it turns thought to forms as the true natures of . . . , brings it back to things, but in such a way as to ground them and, so, thereby to leave forms as both basic and *not* reduced to thinghood. For an illuminating reflection on this in the context of the *Sophist*, see Lee's remarkable aside in 1972, p. 276, n. 14; although that essay is concerned with the *Sophist*, his comment might profitably be taken as a titling of the project of the *Parmenides* as a whole.

33. For this characterization of the "what" of an entity as its being (in the primary sense of its timelessly present nature), see the *Seventh Letter* 343b-c.

34. Parmenides' language is provocative. By putting ἔστι at the head of the sentence, he stresses the *being* of "the One which is not." Yet this "is" is grammatically predicative, as the next clause, which presents the contrary (εἰ γὰρ μὴ ἔσται μὴ ὄν, . . . , "for if it should not be not being, . . . ," 162a2), makes clear.

35. Thus, to take the examples of the angler, sophist, statesman, and weaver from the *Sophist* and *Statesman*, these are all on the one hand things in time that, on the other hand, are considered and examined with regard to their defining forms.

36. See *Sophist* 256d ff.

37. It is strange to hear Allen, 1983, pp. 285-286, argue that the collapse of being with spatial being (i.e., to be is to be somewhere, 145e and 151a) governs and justifies Parmenides' attributions of motion and rest here. Doesn't the text at 162c7, in asserting that the One is μηδαμοῦ . . . τῶν ὄντων ("nowhere among the things that are"), undermine this interpretive tactic?

38. My italics. See n. 24 above.

39. But see n. 32 above. The point is not that the existential/predicative distinction is basic in Parmenides' presentation; rather, the predicative use of γίγνεσθαι and ἀπόλλυσθαι signals that Parmenides intends them not in their most familiar sense, as referring to origination and passing-away in time, but, rather, in a *nontemporal eidetic sense* somehow correlative with the newly introduced eidetic sense of εἶναι.

40. Recall Socrates' effort in the first part of the dialogue to free the form from reduction to the status of the physical-sensible by asserting its presence ἐν ψυχαῖς ("in souls," 132b5). Note, too, that Parmenides did not deny this presence; rather, he distinguished it, as the form's being in thought (νόημα), from the form's being as the referent of that thought (νοούμενον). Thus he made the form's own being prior to its givenness in thought.

41. Cf. McPherran, 1985. Although I think it is the fifth hypothesis, not 133a-135a, to which *Sophist* 248a-249d responds, and although the sort of change to which the forms are subject needs be understood broadly enough to accommodate their status as the referents of diairesis, McPherran is right to point out that the forms must be "capable of the change involved in gaining and losing the property (-ies) of being 'known (by x)' " and that this is "change of an accidental sort, not one of nature" (p. 11).

42. This includes both the case in which a form is directly under scrutiny and the case in which a thing is being considered and examined with regard to its form(s). See n. 35 above.

43. This initial recognition may be accomplished by a process of "collection," as in the *Sophist* (see the penetrating discussion by Sayre, 1969, Ch. III) or by an inaugurating intuition, as in the *Statesman* (see Miller, 1980, Ch. III). In any case, the goal is to identify the most general but essentially relevant form proper to the form in question.

44. Once the philosophical intuition of the being of the subject has taken hold, however, bifurcation may give way to a structure determined by that being itself. Plato shows us this in the *Statesman*; see Miller, 1980, Ch. IV(a).

45. 'Vision' may be an indispensable simile for this apprehension, inasmuch as it is not discursive. But (as the single quotes are meant to signal) this is only simile—recall Socrates' difficulties at 132a ff., discussed in II.B.2.b.

46. See the Epilogue, B.

47. In hypothesis V, Parmenides argued for "unlikeness toward the

others" in the specific sense of "difference-in-kind" (161a) and for "likeness to itself" (161b).

48. I take it that likeness and difference-in-kind are meant to represent like/unlike and same/different and, so, the whole category of identity, as I named the generic unity of attributions (7) and (8) in hypothesis II, treated in IV.B.2.

49. My italics. See n. 23 above.

50. See n. 39 above.

51. Thus the critical hearer will note that Parmenides' seeming retraction, in hypothesis VI, of the attributions in V is just that, seeming and not real. Since what he denies—coming-to-be/ceasing-to-be, rest, being, etc.—is meant in a different sense in VI than in V, the real effect of VI is to help focus and sharpen the sense in which these characters were asserted in V.

52. Recall the discussion of this in II.B.2.b and IV.C.2. And note: it is not the reciprocity, as such, of the relation which distinguishes this form of difference from difference-in-kind; rather, it is what this reciprocity attests, namely, the equality in status and the general likeness of the terms. Parmenides' formulas, ἕτερον ἑτέρου and ἄλλο ἄλλου, make this equality and likeness conspicuous.

53. The main phases of the argument are clearly marked by Οὐκοῦν καὶ at 165a5 (after which the attribute of limit is introduced) and at 165c6 (after which all the other sorts of character, representing all the categorial types under the notion of spatio-temporal being, are introduced).

54. This appears to support, if not confirm, our earlier interpretive objection to and reconstruction of the argument in hypothesis II that the One (thing) is larger and smaller than itself (150e-151a). Recall IV.C.3.

55. Note that "from far off" (πόρρωθεν, 165b7) and "from up close" (ἐγγύθεν, c1) are both points of view giving specifically visual perspectives. In moving from "far off" to "up close" to a thing, one doesn't move from appearance to reality, only from one appearance to another. This is presumably why Parmenides applies his φαίνεσθαι evenhandedly when, in his summation at 165c4-5, he asserts that "it is necessary that the others each appear (φαίνεσθαι) one and [then] many (καὶ ἓν καὶ πολλὰ). . . ." Note, also, this use of καὶ . . . καὶ . . . to conjoin "one" and "many" in the closing phrase. In all but one case in the attributions that follow he uses the καὶ . . . καὶ . . . construction. Smyth (1963, section 2877) writes that καὶ . . . καὶ . . . "emphasizes each member separately, and forms a less

close combination than τε καί." Parmenides' observation at 165b7-c2, quoted on p. 163 above, suggests that each attribution pertains to a separate experience—indeed, a separate and distinct sense-perception—of each of "the others," and I have tried to express this by my interpolation of "[then]" in the translation just above. There is a purely mechanical explanation, it seems, for the one exception, the use of τε καί at 165c6: Οὐκοῦν καὶ ὅμοιά τε καὶ ἀνόμοια δόξει εἶναι. To use both the articulative οὐκοῦν καί—see n. 53 above—and a καί . . . καί . . . conjunction, Parmenides would have had to repeat καί in an impossibly awkward Οὐκοῦν καὶ καὶ ὅμοια καὶ ἀνόμοια. . . . On the other hand, the less awkward Οὐκοῦν καὶ ὅμοια καὶ ἀνόμοια . . . would have been ambiguous: would the first καί work with Οὐκοῦν, and so *not* form a conjunctive καί . . . καί . . . , or would it form a καί . . . καί . . . , and so *not* work with Οὐκοῦν? By resorting to τε καί in this one case, Parmenides can both preserve the articulative Οὐκοῦν καί and link the contraries (as he also does in every other case.)

56. This, I take it, is the sense of 165e5: ἐν γὰρ πολλοῖς οὖσιν ἐνείη ἂν καὶ ἕν. Parmenides thus reiterates 164d8-e1 and indicates, too, that he is not here entertaining any thought of the "mere many," the sheer πλῆθος, studied focally in IIa and III and indirectly in IV.

Epilogue: Connections and Possibilities

1. Thus the argument of the *Parmenides* appears to rearticulate the *Republic*'s distinction of the more from the less real (cf. μᾶλλον ὄντα, 515d3) as, now, a distinction between kinds. Consider, in this light, Vlastos's closing remarks in "Degrees of Reality in Plato," 1965.

2. When read as clarifying reappropriation of the contraposition of "being purely" with "being and not being" in the *Republic*, hypotheses V and VII imply that the true sense of being intended in the *Republic* is neither the existential alone (see Cross and Woozley, 1964) nor the predicative alone (see Vlastos, 1966) but the veridical (see Teloh, 1981, pp. 125-133). Recall Ch. V, n. 32.

3. Though Patterson's valuable study (1985) of the simile of model and likeness in Plato makes no reference to the hypotheses in the *Parmenides*, in the general position it imputes to Plato it both diverges from and dovetails with my reading in interesting ways. On the one hand, Patterson stresses only the positive value and power of the simile, noting, in his conclusion, its usefulness ". . .

throughout [his own] investigation not only for illustrating points reasonably clear in themselves, but also for avoiding potential misunderstanding of the nature of Forms and their relation to worldly individuals" (p. 159); he does not really acknowledge the danger of the simile, namely, its power to occasion the very "misunderstanding" that, on his own reading of the first half of the *Parmenides*, Plato there sets out to expose and undercut. On the other hand, in his efforts to explicate the conceptual content of the simile Patterson articulates a position strikingly convergent with (my reading of) the subsurface argument of the hypotheses, especially I-III. Note, for instance, his remark that the forms of circle, triangle, and line are ". . . the intelligible and unique natures . . . that sensibles of whatever radius, triangularity, or length only image by virtue of a proper distribution of their spatially scattered parts" (p. 89), and see esp. pp. 84-90, 132, and 160.

4. Just noting this potential similarity brings an actual dissimilarity into sharp focus. The surface of the hypotheses is both forbiddingly and exasperatingly empty of positive substantive meaning; one therefore feels driven to search for subsurface meaning. This effect, I have argued, is deliberately intended by Plato. With the *Republic*, by contrast, the surface is rich and fascinating and compelling, so much so, indeed, that the reader may well feel a certain dismay at the prospect of "destroying" it for the sake of a further content. This allure is also, surely, deliberately intended by Plato; it is part of the rhetorical power of the *Republic* as an invitation to suspend the immediate concerns of political life in order to make a beginning in philosophy. Once we recognize this dissimilarity, however, we can also see that it hardly closes the matter; rather we must ask, does someone who accepts the invitation of the *Republic* *then* find himself faced with the need to go beyond its very terms? In order to bring a bit more focus to this question in its bearing on the relation of the *Parmenides* to the *Republic*, we might note the following: (1) There are many indications that Plato casts the elder Socrates in the role of a dialectical *provocateur*, one who speaks with the aim of eliciting objections that, by compelling him to speak again more radically, function to deepen the common search. See, for instance, 329d7-e1, 336d6-8, 423e with 502d and 503b, and consider how Socrates' words repeatedly drive members of the group to interrupt with objections (331d4-5, 336b1 ff., 357a1 ff., 372c2-3, 419a1 ff., 449a7 ff., 471c4 ff., 475d1 ff., 487b1 ff.). (2) There are, moreover, several key passages in which Socrates indi-

cates explicitly certain failings or limitations in his interlocutors (see, esp., 504b ff. with 435c ff., 506d ff., 527d ff. and 529a ff., 533a ff.). If our account of mimetic irony (see Preface) is correct, that Socrates does this serves to quicken the alert hearer to seek to overcome these failings or limitations in himself. (3) There is a striking tension between the content and the form of Socrates' similes of the sun, the line, and the cave: they express in concrete (and, in the cases of the sun and the cave, richly sensory) imagery the claims that the Good and the forms are ontologically ultimate and that this itself can be fully appreciated only by overcoming our usual "trust" in sense-perception. Thus they appear to require, for their own full intelligibility, that their content be grasped in a higher form. (4) Such an "overcoming," moreover, will involve a rethinking of the earlier distinction of forms (as, in each case, a one which *is*) from things (as a many, each of which "is" and "is not") at 475e-480a. By making a point of beginning his construction of the simile of the sun with an explicit restatement of that distinction (507a-b), Socrates includes it within the content of the simile; insofar, therefore, as the simile needs to be rethought from a higher standpoint, *so must the unity and being of form and thing.* (5) Now, Socrates does not attempt such an "overcoming" in the dialogue. He does, however, make a point of indicating that reliance on sensible models is one of the limitations of mathematical practice that the aspiring philosopher must overcome in his passage beyond mathematics to dialectic (see 510b and d together with 511c). Taken together, these points are striking; they suggest the following heuristic questions: Does Plato have Socrates hold back because he, Plato, does not see how to proceed, or does he have Socrates hold back because the limitations that he, Plato, has given Socrates' interlocutors would prevent them from being able to follow? If the latter, does Plato intend, by this portrayal of limitations, to play for his hearer the role he has Socrates play, on other issues, for his interlocutors, the role, namely, of dialectical *provocateur*? Does the *Republic* aim to provoke its hearer to make the "overcoming" of its similes for himself? (Note: Since completing this study, I have made a beginning with some of these questions in the essay, "Platonic Provocations," 1985.)

5. Seminal for this position are Owen's account (1953, pp. 318-322) of Parmenides' regress arguments as Plato's exposure of the fallaciousness of paradigmatism and Vlastos' view (1954, especially pp. 254-255) that they constitute a "record of honest perplexity" about

the status of forms as both separate and self-predicative. Another starting-point is provided by Runciman (1959), who, as noted in Ch. III, n. 8, interprets the hypotheses as serving to display the impotence of the method of hypothesis itself and thereby clearing the stage for the new method of diairesis. An interesting demonstration of the way Runciman's and Vlastos' views, suitably modified, can be integrated is provided by Weingartner, 1973; he exploits the "parallelism" that Plato asserts in the divided line passage in the *Republic* "between the modes of apprehension and their objects" (p. 139) in order to suggest a correlation between the changes Plato makes in philosophical method with those he makes in his conception of the forms as the objects of that method. Yet another point of departure is provided by those who interpret the first hypothesis as showing that each form must be in some sense many as well as one and must combine with other forms rather than be isolated (recall Ch. IV, n. 4). For an illustration of the natural connection of this position with Runciman's thesis, see Moravcsik, 1973, especially pp. 158-160. Runciman himself gives an indication of this connection (1962, p. 128). There is also Teloh's position (1981, especially ch. 4)—which intersects at various points with all three of the preceding positions—that the *Parmenides* expresses the "crisis" that moves Plato to turn from a visually to a discursively oriented conception of forms. (I shall come back to some of the possibilities opened up by Teloh, Moravcsik, and Weingartner in section B.)

6. For a masterful version of this way of interpreting the Good, see Santas, 1983.

7. What might such limiting specificity consist in? Note, first, that the hypotheses are utterly without simile; that, however, is the elder Socrates' sole means of referring to the Good in the *Republic*. Second, the hypotheses are thoroughly formal in their references to forms; Parmenides' phrase τὸ ἕν refers indifferently to each form alike, without regard, therefore, to the specificity of any particular form. Third, the argument of the hypotheses is transcendental in character; it addresses the forms indirectly, in the sense that it studies them as the necessary conditions for the phenomenal being of things, rather than invoking the direct 'seeing' that the *Republic* posits as an aim of dialectic. Thus we might argue that whereas the mode of argument in the hypotheses enables one to transcend reliance on simile and, so, to move beyond the *actual* insight achieved in the *Republic*, it leaves one short of the *potential* insight—the

noetic 'seeing,' on the one hand, of the Good in particular, on the other—that the *Republic* projects as the ultimate goal of philosophical education.

8. Interestingly, the one passage that appears to bear on the question of the silence of the hypotheses, Parmenides' explanation at 135c8-d1 for Socrates' aporia, may be construed to support either of the two lines of interpretation. Parmenides tells Socrates that he is "trying to define 'beautiful' and 'just' and 'good' and each one of the forms too soon, before you have had a preliminary training (γυμνασθῆναι)." These are the forms that are most stressed in the *Republic*; moreover, they all have the status of ideals. Is Plato here repudiating the *Republic* as a premature search—indeed, as a search that, because it was not first tempered by a general or formal examination of the status of the forms as forms, lost itself in the peculiar contents of these three and, as a result, developed a theory that mistook all forms for ideals (superlative "goods") with, therefore, the Good itself as their basis? Thus read, the passage seems to support the first line of interpretation. On the other hand, Plato may simply be marking the limits and function of the hypotheses in relation to the goal of 'seeing' the Good: as the proper "preliminary training," the hypotheses would not themselves include—but would prepare the way for—such an insight. For formulations of this second position, see Schaerer, 1938, especially pp. 112-116, and 1955, and Brumbaugh, 1961.

9. On the self-predication implied here, see Ch. II, n. 35.

10. For presentation of the opposite—perhaps, indeed, extreme opposite—sides of this issue, see Cross, 1954, and Bluck, 1956. See also Cornford's explication of the revelatory aspect of the metaphor of 'vision' (1932).

11. The quoted phrases are borrowed from Teloh, 1981.

12. For illustrative statements of the way the first half of the *Parmenides* appears to bear out the thesis that the turn to discourse replaces or eclipses the earlier concern with noetic "seeing," see the closing remarks in Ackrill, 1955, and in Hicken, 1957.

13. Since I see no consistent terminological distinction between ἰδέα, εἶδος, and γένος in the *Sophist* and the *Statesman*, I mean to refer to them all alike when I use the word "form" here and further on. In so doing, I intend to hold open the question whether Plato now understands his terms to refer to characters, kinds, classes, concepts, or some combination of these. For incisive discussion of this, see Striker, 1970, Ch. II. See also Richard Ketchum, 1978, and Teloh, 1981, especially pp. 189-199. See also n. 16, below.

14. Gomez-Lobo, 1977, and, still more thoroughly, Waletzki, 1979, have recently provided alternatives to the general position established by Stenzel, 1940, that *Sophist* 253d-e describes the relations of the forms required by the method of diairesis.

15. On *Sophist* 258b1, see Lee, 1972, pp. 283-284.

16. For a diverse range of accounts of the sort of entity a form must be in order to be subject to diairetic analysis into parts, see Stenzel, 1940; Cornford, 1935; Cherniss, 1944, especially Ch. 1; Sayre, 1969; Moravcsik, 1973, together with the commentary by Cohen, 1973; and Miller, 1980, especially Chs. II and IVa. See also Ryle, 1966, ch. IV, and the response by Ackrill, 1970. For interesting efforts to reconstruct mathematical formulations of diairetic analysis, see Lloyd, 1954, and Gaiser, 1963, especially p. 125 ff.

17. To phrase the matter this way is to suggest a developmental account. It should be noted, however, that it is in principle possible to give this first general possibility a unitarian formulation. To do so, we would have to treat the shift from the focus on simplicity to the focus on complexity as primarily pedagogical, that is, not as one that Plato himself undergoes in the course of writing the *Parmenides*, the *Sophist*, and the *Statesman* but rather as one that he anticipates and seeks to occasion for the student of these dialogues.

18. Several passages in the *Philebus* might be construed to support this general line of interpretation. First, at 15b-c, Socrates offers what is at least a partial restatement of the dilemma of participation at *Parmenides* 131a-c. (The debate over how to interpret this passage is complex and quite unresolved. For a canvass, see Hahn, 1978.) Then at 16c-17a, with concrete illustrations at 17b-18d, he describes how the method of collection and division shows the "form" (ἰδέαν, 16d1) to be one, determinately many, and unlimitedly many: as the generic term under which the many particulars are collected, the form is one, but as this generic one it is also the determinately many species forms that together make it up and the unlimitedly many particulars that are its concrete instances. Now, *if* 15b1-8 is about forms, and *if* Plato intends its language of "whole" and "part" to apply to the one-many relations elaborated in 16c-17a, *then* the *Philebus* shows how, by replacing the physical sense of "whole" and "part" still implicit at 15b5-6 and 6-8 with the eidetic sense proper to collection and division, the forms may be understood as wholes and parts and the dilemma of participation rendered harmless. (For an exposition of this new eidetic sense of the whole-part relation in the *Philebus*—and of the way Plato thus anticipates Aristotle's notion of "nicht physische, sondern 'begrif-

fliche' Teile" [p. 29] in the *Categories*, see Frede, 1979, especially pp. 23-24, 25-31. See also Teloh, 1981, p. 181 ff.)

19. If Desjardins is correct in her interpretation of Socrates' refutation of his dream in the closing part of the *Theaetetus*, then there may be a striking connection between that passage and the general interpretive possibility we are here proposing. In the refutation, Socrates argues that the "object of knowledge" can be *neither* "the same as its elements in the sense that it is reducible to the sum of its constituent elements" *nor* "different from its elements in the sense that it is a unity unanalyzable into its elements" (Desjardins, 1981, p. 115). That is, in our terms, it can be neither composite nor simple (see ἀμέριστος, "partless," 205c2). As Desjardins points out, this is tantamount to denying that there can be an "object of knowledge" in the first place. She argues that the very absurdity of this has the function of eliciting—"if not for Theaetetus, then at least for the reader" (p. 119)—the possibility of challenging the "original disjunction" (p. 115) itself. Knowledge, we come to see, presupposes of its object that it be *both* "analyzable into [its] elements" *and* "not . . . reducible to those elements" (p. 116). But this is to say, again in our terms, that the "object of knowledge" must be both composite and simple, both a whole of parts and partless. Of course, two major questions remain before the connection between the *Theaetetus* passage and our possible reading of the *Parmenides* and the *Sophist* and *Statesman* can be secured. First, how is the "object of knowledge" in the *Theaetetus* related to the forms? (In introducing his "dream," Socrates characterizes the elements of the object of knowledge as "perceptible" [αἰσθητὰ, 202b6]. His examples at 204d-e, moreover, are physical-sensible wholes. Is there irony here? In another setting we would want to explore Cornford's thesis [1935]—argued in fresh ways by Sayre, 1969, and Haring, 1982—that by the apparent failure of the *Theaetetus* Plato intends to provoke the hearer to turn to the forms as the proper subject matter for λόγος. For a challenge to Cornford's thesis, see Cooper, 1970.) Second, in just what senses of simplicity and complexity is the "object of knowledge" both simple and composite? (If our recognition of a tension between hypotheses I and V is correct, then the *Parmenides* may provide the key to this question. To see whether this is so, however, requires the examination of the practice of diairesis projected at the close of this Epilogue.)

20. It is a manifold irony that the most explicit discursive characterization of this nondiscursive insight that 'Plato' gives in his later

writings appears in a questionably authentic part of a questionably authentic text, the *Seventh Letter*. Without attempting here to provide the full argument that they require, I would offer these observations: (1) 'Plato' makes a strong connection between λόγος and ἐπιστήμη at 342a. And he expressly includes the "fourth" kind—which he has spelled out as ἐπιστήμη and νοῦς and ἀληθὴς δόξα at 342c4-5—with the other three, name and image and λόγος, as "naturally defective" at 343d-e. Thus, when he describes the "seeing" (ἰδεῖν, 344a1) or "sudden flash" of "understanding and intelligence" (φρόνησις . . . καὶ νοῦς, 344b7) that overcomes this deficiency, he is not only distinguishing insight from speech; more deeply, he is distinguishing a kind of ἐπιστήμη that shares the limitedness of discourse from a kind that does not. (2) This limitedness, 'Plato' twice explains, consists in the capacity to grasp only τὸ ποιόν τι (342e3, 343b8-c1), that is, only "the particular quality," and not τὸ ὄν (343a1, b8) or τὸ τί (343c1), "the being" or "the what," of the subject under examination. The phrase τὸ ποιόν τι appears to mean some feature(s) or aspect(s) of the subject, more specifically, the feature(s) or aspect(s) that set it apart from other things. That it is set into contrast with τὸ ὄν and τὸ τί implies, in turn, that to know such feature(s) or aspect(s) is not yet to know what the subject essentially is. If this is so, it has interesting implications for the method of collection and division: just insofar as the method treats its subject only in terms of its relations, that is, its sameness and difference, it will yield a "defectively" superficial knowledge, not the essential insight that philosophy aims for. (One qualification is urgent here: the distinction between τὸ ποιόν τι and τὸ τί does not imply that there is no connection between a subject's distinguishing features and its essence; it does imply, however, that these features must be—and, indeed, can only be first—understood in light of the essence, not the other way around. Only thus can there be an insightful distinction between merely relative features and essential relations.) (3) 'Plato' offers the whole of the digression at 342a-344c as an account explaining why he finds it inappropriate, if not impossible, to give an account of philosophical insight. *If* the digression is authentic or, equally valuable, a genuinely insightful forgery, it explains why the dialogues—and especially, perhaps, the later ones like the *Sophist* and the *Statesman* that are particularly aimed at those most deeply accomplished in philosophical education—are deliberately and on principle silent about their highest goal. (4) At the same time, this nondiscursive and es-

sential insight would indeed be their highest goal. We should therefore expect to find the *practice* of dialectic in these dialogues oriented toward this goal. In this regard it is striking to discover how
fully, both in its methodological details and in its central moment
of intuitive discovery, the practice of the *Statesman* conforms to the
description of dialectical inquiry that 'Plato' offers at *Seventh Letter*
344b1-c1. (For detailed argument, see Schröder, 1935, and Miller,
1980, especially pp. 79 ff.)

21. Sayre's analysis of *Sophist* 253d in 1969, pp. 178-179, lays the
groundwork for this application.

22. See the stranger's explication at 262b-264b. Young Socrates has
favored mankind by lumping together all other animals as "beasts"
and opposing the two. This is anthropocentric prejudice, analogous on its level with the division of mankind into Greeks and bar-
barians, or into Lydians and everyone else. Such prejudice mistakes
a negative aggregate for an εἶδος. "Cutting down the middle," on
the other hand, avoids this. When the stranger illustrates his point
by citing the division of mankind into male and female, or of number into odd and even, he seems to point to the qualitative principle
that underlies the quantitative notion of cutting into halves—the
principle, namely, that the εἴδη in a bifurcatory division should be
positive contraries. Note that following this rule—as the stranger
does, for the most part, in all the divisions in the *Sophist* and in the
Statesman up to 287b—assures that the "parts" will have their own
intrinsic unity as kinds (or features marking off kinds). What is not
assured, however, is that such divisions will reach "the what" and
"the being" of the form under examination; indeed, the stranger's
jokes in completing the divisions at 266a-d seem to point out that
the distinguishing features through which mankind has been suc-
cessfully set apart serve to conceal, not reveal, what mankind essentially *is*. Recall n. 20 above, esp. (2). For explication, see Miller,
1980, Ch. II.

23. The stranger drops bifurcatory diairesis for the diairetic series at
287b ff. Since statesmanship is, by its very nature, related to the
other arts, any form of diairesis that would conceal these—as bifurcation would (287c)—would conceal statesmanship. See Miller,
1980, Ch. IV, for discussion.

24. Thus it appears that the two possible ways of interpreting the *Parmenides'* relation to the *Sophist* and the *Statesman* on the question of
the simplicity of the form correlate with the two general approaches to the issue of the turn from noetic 'seeing' to discourse.

Insofar as the first possibility focuses exclusively on Plato's new stress on the complexity of the forms as objects for discursive knowledge, it fits easily with the position that Plato gives up the middle period notion of noetic 'seeing.' The second possibility, on the other hand, fits naturally with the interpretation of the new discursive account of knowledge as the complement to, rather than the replacement of, the notion of knowledge as noetic 'seeing.' What is more, these connections may also extend back to the two possible positions on the *Parmenides'* silence on the Good. On the one hand, that Plato drops the Good and, so, the construal of the forms as ideals would seem to fit naturally with the position that because he now concentrates on the forms as referents of λόγος, he sees them ever more steadily as kinds. (See, for instance, the otherwise different positions of Stenzel, 1940, and Moravcsik, 1973.) On the other hand, it is striking that the *Statesman's* closing diairesis opposes statesmanship *both* to the other arts associated with the polis (in this context it emerges as a kind) *and* to ordinary partisan politics (in this context it emerges as the superlative good or perfection of its kind, an ideal). This, together with the natural association between the notions of ideal (the form as a case of goodness) and of model (the form as given to a 'seeing'), seems to invite a weaving together of the positions that Plato retains the doctrines of the Good and of noetic 'seeing' in his later dialectic.

25. This line of analysis presupposes the general point asserted by Weingartner (1973, p. 139) that "nowhere does [Plato] give us reason to think that he abandoned [the sort of] parallelism between the modes of apprehension and their objects" that he has Socrates assert in the divided line passage of the *Republic*. For a very different position, see Cooper, 1970. Note, however, that my distinction between objective correlates is a distinction not between separate realities but between different aspects under which what is itself selfsame may be present to mind.

26. That no such account is ever explicitly given reminds us, again, of 'Plato's' doubts about the real point of an account of philosophical insight, in the *Seventh Letter* at 342a–344c. See n. 20 above, especially (3) and (4).

WORKS CITED

Ackrill, J. L., 1955. "Symplokē Eidōn." *Bulletin for the Institute of Classical Studies, University of London* II. In *Studies in Plato's Metaphysics*, edited by R. E. Allen. London, 1965, pp. 199-206. (From here on, Allen's anthology will be referred to as *SPM.*)

———, 1970. "In Defense of Platonic Division." In *Ryle*, edited by O. P. Wood and G. Pitcher. Garden City, N.Y., pp. 373-392.

Albritton, Rogers, 1957. "Forms of Particular Substances in Aristotle's *Metaphysics.*" *Journl of Philosophy* 54, pp. 699-708.

Allen, R. E., 1960. "Participation and Predication in Plato's Middle Dialogues." *Philosophical Review* 69. In *SPM*, pp. 43-60.

———, 1964. "The Interpretation of Plato's *Parmenides*: Zeno's Paradox and the Theory of Forms." *Journal of the History of Philosophy* 2, pp. 143-155.

———, 1974. "Unity and Infinity: *Parmenides* 142b-145a." *Review of Metaphysics* 27, pp. 697-724.

———, 1983. *Plato's Parmenides, Translation and Analysis.* Minneapolis.

Aubenque, Pierre, 1962. *Le Problème de l'être chez Aristote.* Paris.

Barford, Robert, 1978. "The Context of the Third Man Argument in Plato's *Parmenides.*" *Journal of the History of Philosophy* 16, pp. 1-11.

Bestor, Thomas Wheaton, 1980. "Plato's Semantics and Plato's *Parmenides.*" *Phronesis* 25, pp. 38-75.

Bluck, R. S., 1965. "Logos and Forms in Plato: A Reply to Professor Cross." *Mind* 65. In *SPM*, pp. 33-42.

Brumbaugh, Robert, 1960. "A Latin Translation of Plato's *Parmenides.*" *Review of Metaphysics* 14, pp. 91-109.

———, 1961. *Plato on the One.* New Haven.

———, 1976. "Notes on the History of Plato's Text: With the *Parmenides* as a Case Study." *Paideia* Special Plato Issue, pp. 67-80.

———, 1982. "The History and an Interpretation of the Text of Plato's *Parmenides.*" *Philosophy Research Archives* 8, microfiche.

Chen, C.-H., 1944. "On the *Parmenides* of Plato." *Classical Quarterly* 38, pp. 101-114.

Cherniss, Harold, 1944. *Aristotle's Criticism of Plato and the Academy.* Baltimore.

———, 1945. *The Riddle of the Early Academy.* Berkeley.

———, 1957. "The Relation of the *Timaeus* to Plato's Later Dialogues." *American Journal of Philology* 78. In *SPM*, 339-378.

Cohen, S. Marc, 1973. Commentary to Moravcsik's "Plato's Method of Division." In *Patterns in Plato's Thought*, edited by J.M.E. Moravcsik. Dordrecht, pp. 181-191.

Cooper, John, 1970. "Plato on Sense-Perception and Knowledge (*Theaetetus* 184-186)." *Phronesis* 15, pp. 123-146.

Cornford, Francis M., 1932. "Mathematics and Dialectic in the *Republic* VI-VII." *Mind* 41. In *SPM*, pp. 61-95.

———, 1935. *Plato's Theory of Knowledge: the Theaetetus and the Sophist*. London.

———, 1939. *Plato and Parmenides*. London.

Cross, R. C., 1954. "Logos and Forms in Plato." *Mind* 63. In *SPM*, pp. 13-31.

Cross, R. C., and Woozley, A. D., 1964. *Plato's Republic*. London.

Denniston, J. D., 1959. *The Greek Particles*. Oxford.

Desjardins, Rosemary, 1981. "The Horns of Dilemma: Dreaming and Waking Vision in the *Theaetetus*." *Ancient Philosophy* 1, pp. 109-126.

Diès, Auguste, translator, 1956. *Platon: Oeuvres complètes*, VIII—Ier Partie. Paris.

Festugière, R. P. 1936. *Contemplation et vie contemplative selon Platon*. Paris.

Forrester, James, 1972. "Plato's *Parmenides*: The Structure of the First Hypothesis." *Journal of the History of Philosophy* 10, pp. 1-14.

———, 1974. "Arguments an Able Man Could Refute. *Parmenides* 133b-134e." *Phronesis* 19, pp. 233-237.

Frede, Michael, 1978. "Individuen bei Aristoteles." *Antike und Abendland* 24, pp. 16-39.

Friedländer, Paul, 1958, 1964, 1969. *Plato*. 3 volumes, translated by Hans Meyerhoff. Princeton.

Gaiser, Konrad, 1963. *Platons ungeschriebene Lehre*. Stuttgart.

———, 1980. "Plato's Enigmatic Lecture on the Good." *Phronesis* 25, pp. 5-37.

Geach, P. T., 1956. "The Third Man Again." *Philosophical Review* 55. In *SPM*, pp. 265-277.

Goldschmidt, Victor, 1947. *Les Dialogs de Platon*. Paris.

Gomez-Lobo, Alfonso, 1977. "Plato's Description of Dialectic in the *Sophist* 253d1-e2." *Phronesis* 22, pp. 29-47.

Gosling, J.C.B., 1975. *Plato, Philebus*. Oxford.

Griswold, Charles, 1985. "Irony and Aesthetic Language in Plato's Dialogues." In *Literature as Art: Essays in Honor of Murray Krieger*, edited by D. Bolling. New York.

Gundert, H., 1971. *Dialog und Dialektik, zur Struktur des platonischen Dialogs*. Amsterdam.

Guthrie, W.K.C., 1975, 1978. *The History of Greek Philosophy*. Volumes IV and V. Cambridge University Press.

Hahn, Robert, 1978. "On Plato's *Philebus* 15b1-8." *Phronesis* 23, pp. 158-172.

Hamilton, Edith, and Cairns, Huntington, editors, 1961. *Plato: Collected Dialogues*. New York.

Hardie, W.F.R., 1936. *A Study in Plato*. Oxford.

Haring, E. S., 1982. "The *Theaetetus* Ends Well." *Review of Metaphysics* 35, pp. 509-528.

Hicken, Winifred F., 1957. "Knowledge and Forms in Plato's *Theaetetus*." *Journal of Hellenic Studies* 77. In *SPM*, pp. 185-198.

Holland, A. J., 1973. "An Argument in Plato's *Theaetetus*: 184-186." *Philosophical Quarterly* 23, pp. 97-116.

Jones, Barrington, 1974. "Aristotle's Introduction of Matter." *Philosophical Review* 83, pp. 474-500.

Kahn, Charles, 1966. "The Greek Verb 'To Be' and the Concept of Being." *Foundations of Language* 2, pp. 245-265.

————, 1978. "Linguistic Relativism and the Greek Project of Ontology." In *The Question of Being*, edited by M. Sprung. University Park, Pa., pp. 31-44.

————, 1981. "Some Philosophical Uses of 'to be' in Plato." *Phronesis* 26, pp. 105-134.

Kerferd, G. B., 1969. "Anaxagoras and the Concept of Matter before Aristotle." *Bulletin of the John Rylands Library* 52. In *The Pre-Socratics*, edited by A.P.D. Mourelatos. Garden City, N.Y., 1974, pp. 489-503.

Ketchum, Jonathan, 1980. "The Structure of the Plato Dialogue." Doctoral dissertation, SUNY, Buffalo.

Ketchum, Richard, 1978. "Participation and Predication in the *Sophist* 251-260." *Phronesis* 23, pp. 42-62.

Kierkegaard, Søren, 1971. *The Concept of Irony, with Constant Reference to Socrates*. Translated by Lee Capel, Bloomington.

Kirk, G. S., and Raven, J. E., 1964. *The Presocratic Philosophers*. Cambridge.

Klein, Jacob, 1965. *A Commentary on Plato's Meno*. Chapel Hill.

Klibansky, Raymond, 1943. *Plato's Parmenides in the Middle Ages and Renaissance. Medieval and Renaissance Studies* 1, Pt. II.

Kosman, L. A., 1985. "Substance, Being, and *Energeia*: The Argument of *Metaphysics Theta*." *Oxford Studies in Ancient Philosophy* 2.

Krämer, Hans Joachim, 1959. *Arete bei Platon und Aristoteles: Zum Wesen und Geschichte der platonischen Ontologie.* Heidelberg.

Lee, Edward, 1966. "On the Metaphysics of the Image in Plato's *Timaeus.*" *Monist* 50, pp. 341-368.

―――, 1972. "Plato on Negation and Not-Being in the *Sophist.*" *Philosophical Review* 81, pp. 267-304.

―――, 1973. "The Second 'Third Man': An Interpretation." In *Patterns in Plato's Thought,* edited by J.M.E. Moravcsik. Dordrecht, pp. 101-122.

―――, 1976. "Reason and Rotation: Circular Movement as the Model of Mind (Nous) in the Later Plato." In *Facets of Plato's Philosophy,* edited by W. H. Werkmeister. Amsterdam, pp. 70-102.

Lewis, Frank, 1979. "Parmenides on Separation and the Knowability of the Forms: Plato *Parmenides* 133a ff." *Philosophical Studies* 35, pp. 105-127.

Liebrucks, Bruno, 1949. *Platons Entwicklung zur Dialektik.* Frankfurt am Main.

Lloyd, A. C., 1954. "Plato's Description of Division." *Classical Quarterly* n.s. 4. In *SPM,* 219-230.

Lynch, W. F., 1959. *An Approach to the Metaphysics of Plato through the Parmenides.* Washington.

Matthen, Mohan, 1983. "Greek Ontology and the 'Is' of Truth." *Phronesis* 28, pp. 113-135.

McPherran, Mark, 1985. "Plato's Reply to the 'Worst Difficulty' Argument of the *Parmenides: Sophist* 248a-249d." Paper presented to the meeting of the Society for Ancient Greek Philosophy, Western Division of the American Philosophical Association, April 25, 1985.

Miller, Mitchell H., Jr., 1977. "La Logique implicite de la cosmogonie d'Hésiode." Translated by Louis Pamplume. *Revue de métaphysique et de morale* 82, pp. 433-456. (Republished in the English original in *The Independent Journal of Philosophy* 4 (1980), pp. 131-142.)

―――, 1979. "Parmenides and the Disclosure of Being." *Apeiron* 13, pp. 12-35.

―――, 1980. *The Philosopher in Plato's Statesman.* The Hague.

―――, 1985. "Platonic Provocations: Reflections on the Soul and the Good in the *Republic.*" In *Platonic Investigations,* edited by D. O'Meara. Washington.

Mohr, Richard, 1984. "Plato on Time and Eternity." A paper extracted from chapter two of *The Platonic Cosmology* (Leiden, in press) and presented at the Eastern division meetings of the American Philosophical Association, Winter, 1984.

Moravcsik, J.M.E., 1963. "The 'Third Man' Argument and Plato's Theory of Forms." *Phronesis* 8, pp. 50-62.

———, 1973. "Plato's Method of Division." In *Patterns in Plato's Thought*, edited by J.M.E. Moravcsik. Dordrecht, pp. 158-180.

Mourelatos, A.P.D., 1970. *The Route of Parmenides*. New Haven.

Nehamas, Alexander, 1979. "Self-Predication and Plato's Theory of Forms." *American Philosophical Quarterly* 16, pp. 93-103.

Owen, G.E.L., 1953. "The Place of the *Timaeus* in Plato's Dialogues." *Classical Quarterly* n.s. 3. In *SPM*, pp. 313-338.

———, 1957. "A Proof in the *Peri Ideon*." *Journal of Hellenic Studies* 57, part 1. In *SPM*, pp. 293-312.

———, 1966. "Plato and Parmenides on the Timeless Present." *Monist* 50. In *The Pre-Socratics*, edited by A.P.D. Mourelatos. Garden City, N.Y., 1974, pp. 271-292.

———, 1970. "Notes on Ryle's Plato." In *Ryle*, edited by O. P. Wood and G. Pitcher. Garden City, N.Y., 1970, pp. 341-372.

———, 1978/79. "Particular and General." *Proceedings of the Aristotelian Society*, New Series 79, pp. 1-21.

Patterson, Richard, 1985. *Image and Reality in Plato's Metaphysics*. Indianapolis.

Perelman, Chaim, 1955. "La Méthode dialectique et le rôle de l'interlocutor dans le dialogue." *Revue de métaphysique et de morale* 60, pp. 26-31.

Peterson, Sandra, 1973. "A Reasonable Self-Predication Premise for the Third Man Argument." *Philosophical Review* 82, pp. 451-470.

———, 1975. "A Correction to 'A Reasonable Self-Predication Premise for the Third Man Argument.' " *Philosophical Review* 84, p. 96.

———, 1981. "The Greatest Difficulty for Plato's Theory of Forms." *Archiv für Geschichte der Philosophie* 63, pp. 1-16.

Pickering, F. R., 1981. "Plato's 'Third Man' Arguments." *Mind* 90, pp. 263-269.

Prior, William, 1983. "*Timaeus* 48e-52d and the Third Man Argument." *Canadian Journal of Philosophy*, Supplementary Volume 9, pp. 123-147.

Proclus, 1984. *In Platonis Parmenidem Commentarium*. Edited by V. Cousin. Paris.

Robinson, Richard, 1941. *Plato's Earlier Dialectic*. Ithaca.

Rochol, H., 1971. "The Dialogue 'Parmenides': An Insoluble

Enigma in Platonism?" *International Philosophical Quarterly* 11, pp. 496-520.

Rorty, Richard, 1973. "Genus as Matter: A Reading of *Metaphysics* Z-H." *Exegesis and Argument* (*Phronesis*, supplementary volume I, pp. 393-420.

Rosen, Stanley, 1968. *Plato's Symposium*. New Haven.

————, 1983. *Plato's Sophist, The Drama of Original and Image*. New Haven.

Ross, W. D., 1951. *Plato's Theory of Ideas*. Oxford.

Runciman, W. G., 1959. "Plato's *Parmenides*." *Harvard Studies in Classical Philology* 64. In *SPM*, 149-184.

————, 1962. *Plato's Later Epistemology*. Cambridge.

Ryle, Gilbert, 1939. "Plato's 'Parmenides.' " *Mind* 48. In *SPM*, pp. 97-147.

————, 1966. *Plato's Progress*. London.

————, 1968. "Dialectic in the Academy." In *Aristotle on Dialectic*, edited by G.E.L. Owen. Oxford, pp. 69-79.

Santas, Gerasimos, 1983. "The Form of the Good in Plato's *Republic*." In *Essays in Greek Philosophy* II, edited by J. P. Anton and A. Preus. Albany.

Salman, Charles, 1977. "Eidos and Thing in Plato's *Parmenides*." Senior thesis, Vassar College.

Sayre, Kenneth, 1969. *Plato's Analytic Method*. Chicago.

————, 1978. "Why the Eight Hypotheses in the *Parmenides* Are Not Contradictory." *Phronesis* 23, pp. 133-150.

————, 1983. *Plato's Late Ontology, A Riddle Resolved*. Princeton.

Schaerer, René, 1938. *La Question platonicienne*. Neuchâtel.

————. 1941. "Le Mécanisme de l'ironie dans ses rapports avec la dialectique." *Revue de métaphysique et de morale* 48, pp. 181-209.

————, 1955. "La Structure des dialogues métaphysiques." *Revue internationale de philosophie* 9, pp. 197-220.

Schleiermacher, Friedrich, translator, 1966. *Platon: Sämtliche Werke* 4. Reinbek bei Hamburg.

Schofield, Malcolm, 1977. "The Antinomies of Plato's *Parmenides*." *Classical Quarterly*, New Series 27, pp. 139-158.

Schröder, M., 1935. *Zum Aufbau des platonischen Politikos*. Jena.

Sellars, Wilfrid, 1955. "Vlastos and 'The Third Man.' " *Philosophical Review* 64, pp. 405-437.

Sinaiko, H., 1965. *Love, Knowledge, and Discourse in Plato*. Chicago.

Sinnige, T. H., 1968. *Matter and Infinity in the Presocratic Schools and Plato*. Assen.

Smyth, H. W., 1963. *Greek Grammar*. Cambridge, Mass.

Solmsen, Friedrich, 1971a. "The Tradition about Zeno Re-examined." *Phronesis* 16. In *The Pre-Socratics*, edited by A.P.D. Mourelatos. Garden City, N.Y., 1974, pp. 368-393.

———, 1971b. "Parmenides and the Description of Perfect Beauty in Plato's *Symposium*." *American Journal of Philology* 92, pp. 62-70.

Speiser, Andreas, 1937. *Ein Parmenideskommentar*. Leipzig.

Stenzel, Julius, 1940. *Plato's Method of Dialectic*. Translated by D. J. Allan. Oxford.

Strang, Colin, 1963. "Plato and the Third Man." *Proceedings of the Aristotelian Society*, supplementary volume XXXVII, pp. 147-164.

Striker, Gisela, 1970. *PERAS und APEIRON, das Problem der Formen in Platons Philebos*. Göttingen.

Szlezák, Th. A., 1983. Review of Miller, 1980. *Philosophische Rundschau* Heft 1-2, pp. 135-138.

Taylor, A. E., 1926. *Plato*. New York.

———, 1940. *The Parmenides of Plato*. Oxford.

Teloh, Henry, 1976. "Parmenides and Plato's *Parmenides* 131a-132c." *Journal of the History of Philosophy* 14, pp. 125-130.

———, 1981. *The Development of Plato's Metaphysics*. University Park, Pa.

Turnbull, Robert, 1958. "Aristotle's Debt to the 'Natural Philosophy' of the *Phaedo*." *Philosophical Quarterly* 8, pp. 131-143.

Vlastos, Gregory, 1954. "The Third Man Argument in the *Parmenides*." *Philosophical Review* 63. In *SPM*, pp. 231-263.

———, 1955. "Addenda to the Third Man Argument: A Reply to Professor Sellars." *Philosophical Review* 64, pp. 438-448.

———, 1956. "Postscript to the Third Man: A Reply to Mr. Geach." *Philosophical Review* 65. In *SPM*, pp. 279-291.

———, 1965. "Degrees of Reality in Plato." In *New Essays in Plato and Aristotle*, edited by R. Bambrough. London. Also in *Platonic Studies*. Princeton, 1973, pp. 58-75.

———, 1966. "A Metaphysical Paradox." *Proceedings and Addresses of the American Philosophical Association* 39. Also in *Platonic Studies*. Princeton, 1973, pp. 43-57.

———, 1969a. "Plato's 'Third Man' Argument (*Parm.* 132a1-b2): Text and Logic." *Philosophical Quarterly* 19, pp. 289-301.

———, 1969b. "Self-Predication in Plato's Later Period." *Philosophical Review* 78, pp. 74-78.

———, 1970. "An Ambiguity in the *Sophist*." In *Platonic Studies*. Princeton, 1973, pp. 270-322.

Vlastos, Gregory, 1972. "The Unity of the Virtues in the *Protagoras*." *Review of Metaphysics* 25. In *Platonic Studies*. Princeton, 1973, pp. 221-269.

————, 1981. "On a Proposed Redefinition of 'Self-Predication' in Plato." *Phronesis* 26, pp. 76-79.

Voegelin, Eric, 1957. *Plato and Aristotle*. (Volume 3 of *Order and History*.) Baton Rouge.

Wahl, Jean, 1951. *Étude sur le Parménide de Platon*. Paris.

Waletzki, Wolfgang, 1979. "Platons Ideenlehre und Dialektik im *Sophistes* 253d." *Phronesis* 24, pp. 241-252.

Weingartner, Rudolph, 1973. *The Unity of the Platonic Dialogue*. Indianapolis.

Whittaker, John, 1968. "The Eternity of the Platonic Forms." *Phronesis* 13, pp. 131-144.

Wyller, Egil, 1962. "Plato's *Parmenides*: Another Interpretation." *Review of Metaphysics* 15, pp. 621-646.

INDEX

General Index

(Note: *Dramatis personae* in the dialogues are not indexed.)

Index of Passages Cited

(Note: For passages in the *Parmenides*, see the Table of Contents.)

LIBRARY OF CONGRESS CATALOGING-IN-PUBLICATION DATA

Miller, Mitchell H.
Plato's Parmenides : the conversion of the soul / Mitchell
p.   cm.
Reprint. Originally published: Princeton, N.J. : Princeton
University Press, 1986.
Includes bibliographical references and index.
ISBN 0-271-00803-2 (pbk. : alk. paper)
1. Plato.   Parmenides.   2. Socrates.   3. Zeno, of Elea.
4. Reasoning.   I. Title.
[B378.M55   1991]   184—dc20   91-19087 CIP